IOWA PUBLICATIONS IN PHILOSOPHY

Volume 1: Edwin B. Allaire et al., *Essays in Ontology*

IOWA PUBLICATIONS IN PHILOSOPHY
VOLUME 2

MOORE AND RYLE:
TWO ONTOLOGISTS

LAIRD ADDIS
DOUGLAS LEWIS

UNIVERSITY OF IOWA
IOWA CITY, IOWA
1965

MARTINUS NIJHOFF
THE HAGUE
1965

EDITORS' PREFACE

The Iowa Publications in Philosophy is a series of analytical studies –
essay collections, monographs, books – in ontology, the history of
philosophy, the philosophy of science, and other branches of philosophy. The senior members of the Philosophy Department of the University of Iowa serve as editors of the series. Of the authors of the
two monographs which make up the present volume, Laird Addis is
a member of the Philosophy Department of the University of Iowa;
Douglas Lewis, of the Philosophy Department of the University of
Minnesota.

CONTENTS

RYLE'S ONTOLOGY OF MIND

INTRODUCTION

Commonsense holds that there are two kinds of objects – physical (bodies) and mental (minds). The philosopher's task, or one of his tasks, is to secure dialectically the ontological status of both kinds without, as it were, letting either be "absorbed" by the other. It should not, therefore, be controversial among philosophers whether minds exist. Yet, there is such controversy.

Materialism, the doctrine that there are no mental entities, has a long history, reaching as far back as ancient Greece. Today materialism gains specious support from the so-called Oxford school of philosophy. Gilbert Ryle is perhaps the most influential member of this school. In 1949 he published a book entitled *The Concept of Mind* in which, even though he refused to call himself a materialist, he proudly proclaimed that there are no mental entities.

This essay consists of five chapters. The first three are devoted to Ryle's book. Chapter One has two parts. The first is an exposition of the main doctrine of the book; the second attempts to make explicit what I believe to be the ontology implicit in the doctrine. Chapter Two critically examines this ontology. In Chapter Three, I try to refute Ryle's two crucial arguments against the existence of minds.

In Chapters Four and Five, the task I set myself is to show how Ryle's early thought led eventually to the doctrines of *The Concept of Mind*. Chapter Four is devoted to (1) the early ontology and its connection with that of the book and (2) the early philosophy of mind as expressed mainly in Ryle's attack on representationalism. In Chapter Five I complete my task by exhibiting the two sources of Ryle's materialism: an inadequate ontology and an inability to solve the problems of intentionality.

While close attention will be paid to what Ryle says, it would yet be inaccurate to call this essay a study in intellectual biography. Rather, the emphasis is structural; that is, more on the logical connections among ideas, less on those which are merely historical or biographical.

I. MATERIALISM AND THE ATTACK ON DUALISM

The task of philosophy of mind is to give an account or assay of that part or aspect of the world which is mental. In giving such an account, one will of necessity concern himself with the non-mental part of the world as well. Putting it linguistically, an adequate philosophy of mind must be able to give an account of (the meaning of) any sentence which contains a "mental" word. For example, the sentence 'John suddenly remembered where he was' contains the "mental" word 'remembered' and hence is one of the sentences for which the view must be able to account.

With this I believe Gilbert Ryle would agree. With something else he would not agree; viz., that a crucial problem in the philosophy of mind has to do with the connection between a mind and whatever it thinks or wonders about, imagines or perceives, and so on. This connection is sometimes called the intentional connection. That this is not a problem and hence a fortiori not a crucial problem for Ryle is a consequence of his answers to the problems raised in the opening paragraph.[1]

Ryle's philosophy of mind has both a positive and a negative aspect. He argues throughout *The Concept of Mind* that a certain view as to what "mental" statements are about is false. This is the destructive, negative aspect. He also puts forward a doctrine of his own concerning the kinds of things "mental" statements are about. This is the positive aspect. Ryle's positive view I believe to be largely mistaken. The negative part, although usually misdirected, has an occasional point worth making.

This chapter has four sections. In the first section we shall try to understand what Ryle takes the "official" theory or doctrine concerning the nature of mind to be. This "official" view is the doctrine he wishes to refute. The second section will be devoted to an exposition of his own doctrine, as presented in *The Concept of Mind*. The role of Ryle's philosophy of language and logic in his philosophy of mind

---

1 There is a discussion of intentionality with respect to a materialistic philosophy of mind in Chapter V of this monograph.

will be dealt with in the third section. In the fourth and last section I shall undertake to bring out the ontology upon which his doctrines rest. Let us call this the ontology of *The Concept of Mind*.

The "Official" Theory

Ryle refers to the doctrine that he is trying to refute variously as "the two-worlds view", "the doctrine of the ghost in the machine", and "the official theory". As he sees it, this doctrine makes the following claims:

(1) Minds and bodies exist in the same sense of 'exist'.

(2) Bodies are in both space and time; minds are only in time.

(3) Each mind has direct access only to itself.

(4) One cannot help being directly aware of his mind's workings and contents. Furthermore, one can make no mistakes in what he there discovers.

(5) One should be skeptical of the existence of others' minds and inclined to solipsism.

(6) Minds and bodies *interact*. Intelligent behavior is *caused* by mental events.

(7) "Mental-conduct" words always signify the occurrence of non-physical processes.

(8) Disposition words are really occurrence words.[2]

(1) is the heart of the doctrine. Ryle thinks of Descartes as a typical proponent of this view. There is, however, a blur in his presentation of this "heart of the doctrine". Consider the following passages:

Now the dogma of the Ghost in the Machine does just this. It maintains that there exist both bodies and minds; that there occur physical processes and mental processes ...[3]

It is just an inevitable extension of the myth of the ghost in the machine. It assumes that there are mental states and processes enjoying one sort of existence, and bodily states and processes enjoying another.[4]

Later in the chapter [5] I shall discuss in detail the blur as well as the confusions it involves and produces. Now it will suffice to point out where it lies. In the first of these two passages Ryle alleges that the doctrine he wishes to refute holds both minds and bodies to exist in the

---

[2] These eight sentences are not a quote from Ryle, but they are supported by the quotes that follow.

[3] Gilbert Ryle, *The Concept of Mind*, Barnes and Noble, New York, 1949, p. 22. Hereafter referred to as CM.

[4] CM, p. 63.

[5] See pp. 16–17 of this chapter.

same sense of 'exist'. In the second passage minds and bodies are alleged to have different "sorts of existence". Ryle sometimes uses the phrase 'sorts of existence' to mean 'senses of 'exist''. Indeed his own view is that bodies exist in a different sense from that in which minds exist. We have located a source of confusion. If we were to speak philosophically we might say that the view Ryle wishes to dispute holds that minds and bodies are ontologically "independent" of each other. That may produce more confusion than clarity at this point, however.

One difference in the kinds of things minds and bodies are according to the "official" doctrine is that

It is a necessary feature of what has physical existence that it is in space and time; it is a necessary feature of what has mental existence that it is in time but not in space.[6]

Furthermore, each mind has direct access only to itself:

On the one side, according to the official theory, a person has direct knowledge of the best imaginable kind of the workings of his own mind.[7]

But, alas,

On the other side, one person has no direct access of any sort to the events of the inner life of another.[8]

The direct access is indeed so good that

It is often held therefore (1) that a mind cannot help being constantly aware of all the supposed occupants of its private stage, and (2) that it can also deliberately scrutinise by a species of non-sensuous perception at least some of its own states and operations. Moreover both this constant awareness (generally called 'consciousness'), and this non-sensuous inner perception (generally called 'introspection') have been supposed to be exempt from error.[9]

On the other hand indirect access is so poor that we are to be led to skepticism and solipsism:

According to the theory, external observers could never know how the overt behaviour of others is correlated with their mental powers and processes and so they could never know or even plausibly conjecture whether their applications of mental-conduct concepts to these other people were correct or incorrect.[10]

Contemporary philosophers have exercised themselves with the problem of our knowledge of other minds. Enmeshed in the dogma of the ghost in the machine, they have found it impossible to discover any logically satisfactory

---

[6] CM, p. 13.
[7] CM, p. 13.
[8] CM, p. 14.
[9] CM, p. 154.
[10] CM, p. 21.

evidence warranting one person in believing that there exist minds other than his own. I can witness what your body does, but I cannot witness what your mind does, and my pretensions to infer from what your body does to what your mind does all collapse, since the premisses for such inferences are either inadequate or unknowable.[11]

If the doctrine of the ghost in the machine were true, not only would people be absolute mysteries to one another, they would also be absolutely intractable. In fact they are relatively tractable and relatively easy to understand.[12]

I note for later comment that Ryle systematically ignores the doctrine of psycho-physical parallelism as a possible solution to many of the alleged difficulties in the two-worlds doctrine.[13] Rather, he attributes to the two-worlds view the doctrine of interactionism, together with the two corollaries that, first, intelligent behavior is *caused* by mental events and, second, "mental-conduct" words *always* signify the occurrence of non-physical processes:

According to the theory, the workings of the body are motions of matter in space. The causes of these motions must then be *either* other motions of matter in space *or*, in the privileged case of human beings, thrusts of another kind. In some way which must forever remain a mystery, mental thrusts, which are not movements of matter in space, can cause muscles to contract.[14]

Transactions between minds and bodies involve links where no links can be. That there should be any causal transactions between minds and matter conflicts with one part, that there should be none conflicts with another part of the theory.[15]

Since mental-conduct words are not to be construed as signifying the occurrence of mechanical processes, they must be construed as signifying the occurrence of non-mechanical processes . . .

. . . .

The difference between the human behaviours which we describe as intelligent and those which we describe as unintelligent must be a difference in their causation . . .[16]

. . . the vogue of the para-mechanical legend has led many people to ignore the ways in which these concepts actually behave and to construe them instead as items in the descriptions of occult causes and effects.[17]

Since many disposition words are "mental" words, they must, as Ryle construes the "official" theory, record mental occurrences:

[11] CM, p. 60.
[12] CM, p. 114.
[13] See Chapter III.
[14] CM, pp. 63–64.
[15] CM, p. 66.
[16] CM, p. 19.
[17] CM, p. 117.

The temptation to construe dispositional words as episodic words and this other temptation to postulate that any verb that has a dispositional use must also have a corresponding episodic use are two sources of one and the same myth.[18]

The last pages are a summary of the doctrine Ryle rejects. In the next two chapters I shall argue that he has set up some straw men, i.e., that (1), which I earlier called the "heart of the doctrine" – that both minds and bodies exist in the same sense of 'exist' – can be consistently maintained without having to hold some other views, e.g., and most importantly, those numbered (5) through (8). Ryle, though, wishes to make them part and parcel of (1). His main criticisms are in fact directed at (5) through (8). Some criticism is also directed at (3) and (4). But he mistakes all these criticisms, (3) through (8), for attacks on (1).

Ryle's Doctrine

What view as to the nature of mind does Ryle propose as an alternative to the "official" theory? Traditional philosophers, if asked what a mind is, might reply either that it consists of mental acts, or of sense data (or something like them), or of a non-material self, or of some combination of these. No such things exist according to Ryle:

The radical objection to the theory that minds must know what they are about, because mental happenings are by definition conscious, or metaphorically self-luminous, is that there are no such happenings; there are no occurrences taking place in a second-status world, since there is no such status and no such world . . .[19]

On the view for which I am arguing consciousness and introspection cannot be what they are officially described as being, since their supposed objects are myths . . .[20]

What then are "mental" statements about? What is the mind?

To talk of a person's mind is not to talk of a repository which is permitted to house objects that something called 'the physical world' is forbidden to house; it is to talk of the person's abilities, liabilities and inclinations to do and undergo certain sorts of things, and of the doing and undergoing of these things in the ordinary world.[21]

The mind then is some combination of at least two kinds of things: (1) behavior and (2) dispositions. There is possibly a third ingredient, however. Consider the following case: one man babbles; another minds what he is saying. Suppose that what comes out of their mouths,

18 CM, p. 119.
19 CM, p. 161.
20 CM, p. 155.
21 CM, p. 199.

i.e., their behavior, is identical. What is the difference between them? The difference lies, according to Ryle, in their "frames of mind".

To restate the problem, it is possible, if not very common, for two or more overt actions done in quite dissimilar frames of mind to be photographically and gramophonically as similar as you please.[22]

The question is, of course, exactly what is a "frame of mind". *Prima facie* one would suspect that for Ryle it would be a kind of disposition. In effect he often backslides into saying just that, yet his intention is to deny it. How does he backslide? On several occasions he speaks of a "frame of mind" as a mood or something like a mood. For example:

Moods or frames of mind are, unlike motives, but like maladies and states of the weather, temporary conditions which in a certain way *collect* occurrences, but they are not themselves extra occurrences.[23]

And again in explaining what we really say in applying a "heed" concept:

He was in the mood or frame of mind to do, if required, lots of things which may not have been actually required; and he was, *ipso facto*, in the mood or frame of mind to do at least this one thing which was actually required.[24]

Furthermore:

Mood words are short-term tendency words . . .[25]

But in spite of this Ryle specifically denies that "frames of mind" are dispositions. His reason is that "frames of mind", like items of behavior, are clockable. This pushes them toward the category of behavior since he wishes to deny that the having of a disposition is, like a bit of behavior, an occurrence. So he is puzzled. His puzzlement shows in passages such as the following, where a "frame of mind" is referred to as a "special character".

But if this special character is unwitnessable, we seem forced to say either that it is some hidden concomitant of the operation to which it is ascribed, or that it is some merely dispositional property of the agent ... To accept the former suggestion would be to relapse into the two-worlds legend.

. . . .

On the other hand, to accept the dispositional account would apparently involve us in saying that though a person may properly be described as whistling now, he cannot be properly described as concentrating or taking care now; and we know quite well that such descriptions are legitimate.[26]

---

[22] CM, p. 140.
[23] CM, p. 83.
[24] CM, p. 141.
[25] CM, p. 100.
[26] CM, p. 139.

"Frames of mind" then at least *seem* to be a third ingredient of minds. That is, they are neither dispositions nor pieces of behavior nor, as far as Ryle is concerned, non-physical events. Sometimes he speaks of them as if they were some kind of property of the pieces of behavior involved:

When I do something intelligently, i.e. thinking what I am doing, I am doing one thing and not two. My performance has a special procedure or manner, not special antecedents.[27]

Sometimes Ryle "analyzes" statements which include a reference to a "frame of mind" as "would" statements:

Being in that frame of mind, he *would* do the thing he did, as well as, if required, lots of other things none of which is he stated to have done.[28]

I shall call statements like 'You *would* do the thing you did' 'semi-hypothetical' or 'mongrel categorical statements'. Most of the examples ordinarily adduced of categorical statements are mongrel categoricals.[29]

There are then "semi-hypotheticals" as well as full "hypotheticals". The latter kind of statement simply reports that something or someone has a certain disposition.

Instead of pursuing the notion of "frame of mind" further at this point, I shall try to make Ryle's general position clearer by contrasting it with the "official" theory. Let us take three sentences each of which contains a "mental" word and ask ourselves what each of them "really" says, once according to Ryle, once according to the "official" theory.

(A) John knows that $2 + 2 = 4$.

(B) John suddenly remembered the name of his boyhood friend.

(C) John typed the letter carefully in order to make no mistakes.

On Ryle's view (A) says simply that John has a disposition to act in certain ways, e.g., to say Yes if asked whether he knows the sum of 2 and 2, to write 4 when given the problem what the sum of 2 and 2 is, and so on. The statement records John's having a certain disposition. It is, therefore, a full "hypothetical". *According to Ryle*, the "official" theory construes the mental verb in (A) either nondispositionally or dispositionally. In the former case, (A) simply records the occurring of a mental act of knowing. In the latter case, (A) states that an act of this sort has occurred and will under certain conditions occur again. In either case, therefore, according to Ryle, the "official" theory

---

[27] CM, p. 32.
[28] CM, p. 141.
[29] CM, p. 141.

takes (A) to be a statement about alleged occurrences of the kind it calls the mental act of knowing that $2 + 2 = 4$.

Concerning (B) Ryle is less clear. The "official" theory would say that there is a mental (or non-physical) act of remembering which has as its object the name of John's boyhood friend.[30] Ryle, too, holds that (B) reports an occurrence.[31] Nor is it memory in particular that is at issue here. Yet Ryle is not clear as to what the occurrence is since the obvious answer, which is of course that of the "official" theory, is not available to him. Probably his answer is something like this: the occurrence involved is *saying* something like "I just remembered the name of my boyhood friend. It was George", and that this occurrence is an exercise of the disposition of remembering something. One will of course object that *this* disposition is not the same as the disposition to *say* what one is remembering. In other words, one can and does re- member things without reporting them. Ryle would have to hold that in such cases one speaks to himself. I believe that he does in fact hold this view. For that I have two reasons; one is what he says about remembering in particular:

Being good at recalling is not being good at investigating, but being good at presenting. It is a narrative skill, if 'narrative' be allowed to cover non-prosaic as well as prosaic representations.[32]

The other reason is the frequent references he makes throughout to something he calls "internal monologue" or "silent soliloquy". For instance:

Much of our ordinary thinking is conducted in internal monologue or silent soliloquy, usually accompanied by an internal cinematograph-show of visual imagery.[33]

This *is* Ryle speaking for himself, not his presenting the "official" theory. Yet, though he hates what he calls mystery-mongering theories, he leaves it a deep secret what an "internal monologue" or a "silent soliloquy" is, not to mention "visual imagery"!

There is still another possibility as to what the occurrence in a remembering might be. It may be the *acquiring* of a disposition to act in certain ways. That is, while Ryle denies that having a dispo- sition is an occurrence, he might possibly want to say that the ac- quiring (and losing) of dispositions are occurrences. But I mention

[30] Or if awareness is, as one says, propositional, "*that* his boyhood friend's name was ..."
[31] CM, p. 273.
[32] CM, p. 279.
[33] CM, p. 27.

that merely as a possible way out for him. There is no text to support the claim that he takes it.

Note that for Ryle both (A) and (B) are either wholly or in part dispositional; i.e., whatever else they may or may not say, they both say that John has a certain disposition. To that extent they are both "hypothetical".

(C), everyone would surely agree, reports (whatever else it may say) a piece of overt behavior; namely, the typing of a letter. The "mental" word is 'carefully'. According to Ryle, we saw the difference between, say, carefully typing a letter and doing the same thing without heeding what one is doing (and where the overt behavior is by hypothesis identical) lies in something he calls "frame of mind". And we have already wondered what in his framework this could be. The "official" theory, *according to Ryle*, would have it that there is a mental (non-physical) act of a certain kind which accompanies the overt behavior in the one case, that of careful typing, but not in the other.

No "mental" statements, Ryle claims, are straightforward categoricals. Rather, they are always "open", i.e., they have a certain "hypothetical" part to them:

For, roughly, the mind is not the topic of sets of untestable categorical propositions, but the topic of sets of testable hypothetical and semi-hypothetical propositions. [34]

I take my next cue from the two words 'testable' and 'untestable'. On the "official" theory, so Ryle thinks, one explains a piece of intelligent behavior by "positing" it to be an effect of a mental act. All intelligent behavior is caused by mental events. Or perhaps one should say that what makes it intelligent behavior is the mental event. But since on this view mental events are not public, physical events, sentences saying that such and such a piece of intelligent behavior occurred are on the "official" view untestable categoricals.

On Ryle's view intelligent behaviors are not effects of but rather exercises of mind – more particularly, of dispositions. Moreover, a sentence which says that someone acted intelligently on a certain occasion is testable. For it says (on the "analysis") that that piece of behavior was an exercise of a certain disposition; and we can find out whether the person has that disposition by applying other stimuli. For to say that a person has a certain disposition is to say that he (habitually) does or would act in certain ways on certain occasions.

[34] CM, p. 46.

Thus our everyday "explanations" of intelligent behavior do not consist in giving causes but, rather, in subsuming that piece of behavior under a disposition to act in certain ways.

It is being maintained throughout this book that when we characterise people by mental predicates, we are not making untestable inferences to any ghostly processes occurring in streams of consciousness which we are debarred from visiting; we are describing the ways in which those people conduct parts of their predominantly public behaviour. True, we go beyond what we see them do and hear them say, but this going beyond is not a going behind, in the sense of making inferences to occult causes; it is going beyond in the sense of considering, in the first instance, the powers and propensities of which their actions are exercises.[35]

The sense in which we 'explain' his actions is not that we infer to occult causes, but that we subsume under hypothetical and semi-hypothetical propositions. The explanation is not of the type 'the glass broke because a stone hit it', but more nearly of the different type 'the glass broke when the stone hit it, because it was brittle'.[36]

We can now see why Ryle *claims* that he is not a materialist. The materialist says either (1) Minds don't exist, or (2) Any mental word is definable in terms of behavioral or physiological predicates or both. It is clear that Ryle doesn't want to be held to (1). Since on his view the analysis of any mental sentence always includes a reference to either a disposition or a frame of mind, and since such things are not bodies nor parts of bodies nor behavior, he wants to deny (2) as well.

Philosophy of Language and Logic

So far we have managed to stay away from Ryle's philosophy of language and his notion of "category-mistake". Though language as such ostensibly plays a large part in Ryle's philosophical thinking, there is satisfyingly little talk about language in *The Concept of Mind*. This is as it should be, for *structurally* language plays a smaller role in Ryle's thought than he himself believes. It is also structurally of less importance in him than in the thought of most of those in the movement to which he belongs. The main purpose of this section is therefore to call attention to his conventionalism as well as to remind ourselves of the role that he himself believes language to play in his thought.

The "official" theory of mind rests upon a series of "category-mis-takes". This is Ryle's *claim*. A category-mistake consists roughly in treating a set of "concepts" as if they belonged to one "category"

---

[35] CM, p. 51.
[36] CM, p. 50.

when they actually belong to another. The category or "logical type" to which a concept belongs is

the set of ways in which it is logically legitimate to operate with it.[37]

One shows that concepts have been misplaced by (1) showing that their having been put where they are leads to absurdities, and (2) locating them elsewhere, a place which doesn't lead to absurdities. This indicates the kind of *argument* by which Ryle must be, and is, prepared to support his claims.

For example, and still very roughly, the "official" theory locates the "mental" concepts as if they were "thing" concepts rather than "event-disposition" concepts. Furthermore, category-mistakes are "breaches of logical rules".

The key arguments employed in this book are therefore intended to show why certain sorts of operations with the concepts of mental powers and processes are breaches of logical rules.[38]

To use concepts wrongly is thus not simply to say something false about the world but to misuse language. And to misuse language is to break logical rules. How then does Ryle conceive logical rules? Though he doesn't say so in *The Concept of Mind*, he believes them to be *conventional*. Consider a slightly earlier paper:

Rules of inference, like the rules of grammar, chess, etiquette and military funerals are performance-rules.[39]

Hence, while there can and do occur breaches of logical rules, there cannot and do not occur breaches of laws of nature.[40]

but:

Moreover some performance-rules, like rules of inference and rules of skill, are not results of convention or legislation as rules of games and rules of the road are. There is no M.C.C. which can amend the rules of inference or the canons of style.[41]

Rules of logic are not amendable just as the rules of style are not. (We are never told just *why* they are not amendable.) But, presumably, insofar as the rules of style are conventional (they certainly are not like laws of nature!), to just that extent the rules of logic are con-

[37] CM, p. 8.
[38] CM, p. 8.
[39] Ryle, "Why Are the Calculuses of Logic and Arithmetic Applicable to Reality?", *Logic and Reality*, Aristotelian Society, Supplementary Volume XX, Harrison and Sons, Ltd., 1946, p. 22.
[40] *Ibid.*, p. 24.
[41] *Ibid.*, p. 23.

ventional. They allow us to make certain linguistic "moves" and leave us liable to censure if we make others. To the extent then that the rules of logic are conventional, to that extent the categories to which various "concepts" belong are conventional. To this extent whether "mental" words refer to non-physical things or to physical events must be construed as conventional. There is one particularly revealing passage in *The Concept of Mind* where this conventionalism of Ryle's which rests on his philosophy of language shows through:

We do not, that is, want tidings or hypotheses about any other things which the listener may have privily done or undergone. Even if there had taken place three, or seventeen, such *entr'actes*, news about them would not explain how detecting a mosquito differs from having a shrill singing in the ears. What we want to know is how the logical behaviour of 'he detected a mosquito' differs from that of 'there was a singing in his ears', from that of 'he tried in vain to make out what was making the noise', and from that of 'he mistook it for the noise of the wind in the telephone wires'.[42]

So to tell the difference between, say, listening and detecting we appeal not to the world but to language. In spite of this preoccupation with language, though it can't be ignored at all points, we shall construe Ryle as telling us something about the world and not just about language. And when a philosopher *qua* philosopher talks about the world, he does ontology – whether he likes it or not.

The Ontology of The Concept of Mind

On one conception of philosophy, the heart of the matter is ontology. This is not to put oneself outside the tradition of the last three centuries or so, in which ostensibly the main concern has often been epistemology. But ontology is never far from the philosophers' pursuits.

In the last several years there has arisen a movement which *claims* to do philosophy without ontology. I reject this claim and hold to the belief that no one can do serious philosophy without at least an *implicit* ontology. That makes it necessary and (hopefully) fruitful to ascribe an ontology to any philosopher who thinks he does philosophy without ontology.

What is one doing when ascribing an ontology to a philosopher who has none that is explicit? Consider the case of Ryle. He has what can reasonably be called a philosophy of mind. This philosophy of mind "presupposes" a certain ontology. This is one way of stating my claim. There are certain ontological considerations "behind" what is explicitly said. This is another way of stating my claim. As yet I am

[42] CM, p. 225.

stating it grossly, neither affirming nor denying a strict logical connection between the implicit ontology ascribed to a philosopher on
the one hand and the views he explicitly holds on the other. In the case
of Ryle, let the connection be displayed by what will now be said in
the sequel.

Fundamentally, Ryle is an Aristotelian.[43] That is my thesis. Others
have pointed to the similarities between Aristotelian philosophy and
the Oxford movement, of course. By calling Ryle an Aristotelian I
mean several things. First and foremost, I mean that his ontology is a
substance ontology with its corollary notions of *nature* and *activity*.
Secondly, I mean that he thinks of mind as Aristotle thought of it, on
one plausible interpretation of the latter's thought. I mean, third,
that he makes a lot of a kind of "scientific" explanation which for
good reasons is usually called Aristotelian. I mean, fourth and finally,
that he is a nominalist. These four claims need explanation and sub-
stantiation. The first will occupy us for most of the rest of the chapter.

After a few introductory comments about *substance*, we will return
to Ryle's notion of "category-mistake". This will lead us naturally
back to substance. Then the notions of *disposition* and *activity* will be
explored.

In the tradition a substance is first and foremost an *individual*.[44]
What, then, is an individual? An individual is something which is in
space or in time or in both. This will suffice for the time being. It also
permits a distinction between two *kinds* of substances. A *physical*
substance is one which is in both space and time; a *mental* or *non-
physical* substance is one which is only in time.[45] For most purposes
we may say that substance philosophers identified physical substances
with bodies, non-physical substances with minds. (Some philosophers
held that only one of these two kinds of substances exist.)

Substances are said to have *natures*.[46] The two kinds of substances
distinguished above were said to have spatial extension and thinking
as their respective natures or "essences". But this is broad use of
'kinds of substances'. The explication of 'nature' is very difficult. We

---

[43] This monograph is not about Aristotle, nor am I particularly concerned as to whether
what I call Aristotelian is truly Aristotle.

[44] An individual without a nature is of course a bare particular.

[45] It may be held that only the activities or properties of substance are in space and/or
time and not the substances themselves. In this case the explications offered here would
obviously be inadequate as they stand.

[46] We are not interested in what some philosophers, including Aristotle, called secondary
substances.

need pick out only certain features for our purposes.[47] Think of "kinds of substance" in a way that makes men, lions, and elm trees all different kinds of substances. One important feature of *nature* is that it is or "contains" the "defining" properties of a substance-kind. For example, the nature of man (so we are told) is his rationality and his animality. The other important feature of *nature* which will be useful to mention now is this: A substance is said to *act* or *create* or *do* by its nature. The nature is, or is the seat of, certain dispositions to act or behave in certain ways. The explications ignore many subtleties, but they will do for the moment.

Let us turn to Ryle's notion of "category-mistake". He explains what it means by a well-known example.[48] A foreigner is shown the buildings of a university campus. At the end of the tour he asks where the university is. This foreigner doesn't realize that the university *is* (in one sense) the collection of buildings he has just seen. In supposing the university to be another building he made a category-mistake. Was he simply supposing the university to have a property which it doesn't have? No, and this is the point. Rather, he was supposing the university to have a property (being a building) which its "nature" in fact excludes (i.e., it is by nature a collection of buildings). A category-mistake then is to ascribe to something a property which is "incompatible" with its "nature". Ryle of course expresses this idea differently:

The theoretically interesting category-mistakes are those made by people who are perfectly competent to apply concepts, at least in the situations with which they are familiar, but are still liable in their abstract thinking *to allocate those concepts to logical types to which they do not belong.*[49]

If we were to express the italicized phrase ontologically, we would say that making a category-mistake is supposing that something which in fact has a "nature" of a certain kind has a "nature" of a certain other kind. Ryle believes that the view that minds are something which exist over and against bodies arises from certain important category-mistakes. This is indeed the main import of the passage I just quoted.

Making a category-mistake is not (except *per accidens*) doing or trying to do ontology, of course. If, on the other hand, a philosopher

---

[47] For a more detailed analysis see Gustav Bergmann's "Russell's Examination of Leibniz Examined", appearing originally in *Philosophy of Science* (the journal) 23, 1956, and reprinted in Bergmann's *Meaning and Existence*, University of Wisconsin Press, 1960.

[48] CM, p. 16.

[49] CM, p. 17, my emphasis.

has an explicit ontology of different *kinds* of things (substances, universals, particulars, relations or what-have-you) he might make a "category-mistake" by supposing some *member* of one of the kinds to be a member of another kind. In this minimal sense, no ontologist may escape this sort of mistake. In a more interesting sense, a category-mistake consists in imagining that an instance of an ontological kind has some property which is excluded by the *nature* of this (ontological) kind.

We have come upon one reason (though not yet the main reason) we have for supposing Ryle to have an implicit substance ontology in *The Concept of Mind*. The notion of a category-mistake if it is to have any philosophical interest requires the notion of nature. The notion of nature is in turn historically and structurally tied to substance ontologies. Now for two comments.

First. Ryle believes that "a family of radical category-mistakes is the source of the double-life theory".[50] According to Ryle, the view that there are minds and there are bodies as, say, Descartes understood it, is false. The kind of category-mistake it involves according to Ryle (though he himself naturally doesn't use these words) is mistaking something of one *ontological kind* for something of another ontological kind. Specifically, the mistake consists in mistaking doings (*qua* exercises of certain dispositions) of a physical substance for a non-physical substance. Hence the problem is philosophical, i.e. ontological.

Second. That Ryle does think of bodies and minds as belonging to different ontological kinds is substantiated by the text. Consider the following passages from *The Concept of Mind*:

I am not, for example, denying that there occur mental processes. Doing long division is a mental process and so is making a joke. But I am saying that the phrase 'there occur mental processes' does not mean the same sort of thing as 'there occur physical processes', and, therefore, that it makes no sense to conjoin or disjoin the two.[51]

It is perfectly proper to say, in one logical tone of voice, that there exist minds and to say, in another logical tone of voice, that there exist bodies. But these expressions do not indicate two different species of existence, for 'existence' is not a generic word like 'coloured' or 'sexed'. They indicate two different senses of 'exist'. . .

. . . .

It would be just as good or bad a joke to say that there exist prime numbers and Wednesdays and public opinions and navies; or that there exist both minds and bodies.[52]

[50] CM, p. 18.
[51] CM, p. 22.
[52] CM, p. 23.

Let us look at 'exist'. The ordinary use of this word allows its replacement by 'there are'. In this use, 'exist' is univocal and indefinable. Prime numbers, Wednesdays, *et al.* are all there. They all exist. It is not because of different senses of 'exist' that it is a good or bad joke to say in one breath that both Wednesdays and numbers exist. It is one, if at all, because numbers and Wednesdays are quite different sorts of things. To put it another way, numbers and Wednesdays go into classes in which, say, mermaids and the perfect society do not.[53]

That supports my suggestion that Rule wishes to put minds and bodies into two different ontological categories. Bodies are substances; minds, loosely, properties of substances. I say "loosely" because many qualifications will be required. Substance ontologies are traditionally nominalistic or nominalistically-inclined. Substances somehow have "more reality" than their properties. Part of what that means is that while substances *could* presumably exist without their properties, these properties *couldn't* exist without their substances. This is also, if I am not mistaken, what Ryle means when he says that minds and bodies exist in different senses of 'exist'. Again, this is quite consistent with his lifelong nominalism of which I shall make much later. Thus one may come to understand his confused talk about the several "senses" of 'exist'.

So far we have come upon substances in Ryle's ontology. It has at least two further ontological kinds. There are *dispositions* and there are *events* (doings, occurrences, processes). Dispositions, we shall shortly see, are not really first-class existents. On occasion Ryle even sees fit to deny that they exist. An event is the doing of some substance. Jones' running, the horse's kicking, the stone's rolling are all events. Let it be understood that such a doing does not include the substance, although it is a substance which does it. According to Ryle, since there are only physical substances, all events are *a fortiori* physical events.

Let me next try to substantiate the claim that implicitly, at least, events are for Ryle a distinct ontological category. I quote first from *The Concept of Mind:*

... there are just things and events, people witnessing some of these things and events, and people fancying themselves witnessing things and events that they are not witnessing.[54]

---

[53] This of course does not commit me to saying that 'existence' is a predicate in the sense in which philosophers have wished to deny that it is one.

[54] CM, p. 249.

That makes it even more revealing that it lists among what is there (and not merely fancied) things *and* events and nothing else. Permit me also to adduce two passages from a very early paper.

But if I say "the defeat of the Labour Party occurred in 1931," my "the"-phrase is referentially used to describe an event and not as a condensed record of a fact. For events have dates, but facts do not.[55]

For "Jones hates the thought of going to hospital" only means what is meant by "Jones feels distressed when he thinks of what he will undergo if he goes to hospital." The phrase "the thought of ..." is transmuted into "whenever he thinks of ...," which does not even seem to contain a reference to any other entity than Jones and, perhaps, the hospital. For it to be true, the world must contain a Jones who is sometimes thinking and sometimes, say, sleeping; but it need no more contain both Jones and "the thought or idea of so and so" than it need contain both someone called "Jones" and something called "Sleep."[56]

Thinking is being thought of as a doing as early as 1932. In the second passage events (Jones' thinking and Jones' sleeping) are taken not to be anything other than Jones. Do then events have no distinct onto-logical status? Their status is indeed greatly depressed – almost to nothing in this passage. This is of course Ryle's nominalism. The mind is thought of as a series of events. Thus it has not only a causal dependence on the body, but an ontological one as well. To this extent Ryle's nominalism and his crypto-materialism are intimately connected. This will be argued in detail later. Notice in the meantime the connection between time and events in the first of the two passages. Events are clockable. That, we shall see, tends to enhance their ontological status.

In a paper written shortly before *The Concept of Mind* we find:

It also helps to upset the assumed type-difference between thinking and doing, since only subjects belonging to the same type can share predicates. But thinking and doing do share lots of predicates, such as "clever," "stupid," ... [57]

Thinking is (at least) a process of a body, a doing of that body. Doings are a distinct "logical type". In more traditional terms, events are the activities of substances. Substances were said to be active, to create, to do by their natures. This leads us to dispositions.

Some doings are intelligent; some are non-intelligent. We know already that what makes a piece of behavior intelligent is, according to Ryle, not some non-physical event which is its cause (as the "official"

[55] Ryle, "Systematically Misleading Expressions", *Proceedings of the Aristotelian Society*, Vol. XXXII, Harrison and Sons, Ltd., 1932, p. 164.

[56] *Ibid.*, p. 161.

[57] Ryle, "Knowing How and Knowing That", *Proceedings of the Aristotelian Society*, Vol. XLVI, Harrison and Sons, Ltd., 1946, p. 2.

theory is alleged to hold). Rather, the piece of behavior is an *exercise* of some particular kind of disposition. Thus dispositions are necessary to distinguish kinds of events. That is, a doing is classified as intelligent or not according to the kind of disposition of which it is an exercise. Reciting a poem, for example, is a piece of intelligent behavior and hence an exercise of one kind of disposition. A stone's rolling down a hill is non-intelligent behavior and hence is an exercise of another kind of disposition. Eventually, therefore, we shall have to be told what distinguishes "intelligent" from "non-intelligent" *dispositions*. But we need not pursue this question at this moment.

At least some dispositions of a substance form, we may suppose, at least part of its nature. In particular, the more or less permanent dispositions are part of the nature. This connection between dispositions and nature is built into our very language. One speaks of acquired dispositions as "second nature". Also, the notion that dispositions constitute part of the nature fits with one of the traditional notions of nature, as that by or through which the substance acts. Ryle accepts this notion of a "creative" nature. That accounts for a fairly obvious connection in his thought between "creative" natures on the one hand and the "explanation" of behavior on the other. To this connection I shall attend presently.

In spite of the seemingly important role dispositions play in Ryle's account of mind and the nature of things, he also seems to deny that they really exist. That is, of course, his nominalism, at least in part. At this point the dialectics get quite complex. So I shall not try to unravel it until the next chapter. But even this first, rough sketch of Ryle's ontology requires a few more comments supported by a few more passages from the texts.

According to Ryle, dispositions, if only because they are not occurrences, are not causes. It is indeed not clear whether Ryle believes that dispositions really exist.

The temptation to construe dispositional words as episodic words and this other temptation to postulate that any verb that has a dispositional use must also have a corresponding episodic use are two sources of one and the same myth.[58]

Dispositional statements are neither reports of observed or observable states of affairs, nor yet reports of unobserved or unobservable states of affairs. They narrate no incidents. But their jobs are intimately connected with narratives of incidents, for, if they are true, they are satisfied by narrated incidents.[59]

[58] CM, p. 119.
[59] CM, p. 125.

Clearly, these passages support the claim that events do have *some* ontological status, are in a category of their own. For the rest, we are told that just as events are not substances, so dispositions are not events. I do believe that Ryle wants to tell us that dispositions literally do not exist. "There are" only substances and events. This fits with the traditional pattern by which the nature of a substance is nothing more than the substance itself.

The core of Ryle's ontology is already beyond doubt: There are substances and there are doings. Probably we may add that substances have a higher ontological status ("more reality") than doings, i.e. substances are "independent"; doings, "dependent". The idea is that substances can exist without doing anything (unless existing be a kind of doing) whereas there are no doings without substances. The onto-logical status, if any, of dispositions is even less than that of doings (events). But this is not yet the complete ontology. For example, the status, if any, of properties in general has not yet been considered. Ulti-mately more important, the ontology of time has not been considered.

Time enters the picture in two ways. There is first the question what ontology, if any, of time a substance metaphysics commits one to. Secondly, it may be asked what in Ryle's view is in time. Do substances or their doings or both stand in temporal relations, or are they, all or some, "at" a time. I shall raise all these questions in the next chapter. I shall try to find out what, if anything, Ryle has to say about them. And I shall, of course, point out the difficulties which his answers, such as they are, create for his ontology. I shall indeed argue that the weaknesses of his ontology reveal themselves most strikingly if it is probed on the issues of time.

As to mind, Ryle's view is by now clear. A mind is some dispositions and some doings of a body. Since a substance's dispositions and doings are ontologically "dependent" on it, we may say that a mind is onto-logically "dependent" on its body. This fits quite well with what we are told:

It is being maintained throughout this book that when we characterise people by mental predicates, we are not making untestable inferences to any ghostly processes occurring in streams of consciousness which we are debarred from visiting; we are describing the ways in which those people conduct parts of their predominantly public behaviour. True, we go beyond what we see them do and hear them say, but this going beyond is not a going behind, in the sense of making inferences to occult causes; it is going beyond in the sense of considering, in the first instance, the powers and propensities of which their actions are exercises.[60]

60 CM, p. 51.

It has been argued from a number of directions that when we speak of a person's mind, we are not speaking of a second theatre of special-status incidents, but of certain ways in which some of the incidents of his one life are ordered.[61]

To talk of a person's mind is not to talk of a repository which is permitted to house objects that something called 'the physical world' is forbidden to house; it is to talk of the person's abilities, liabilities and inclinations to do and undergo certain sorts of things, and of the doing and undergoing of these things in the ordinary world.[62]

Moreover, if I am not mistaken, this view is very similar to Aristotle's:

But since it is also a *body* of such and such a kind, viz. having life, the *body* cannot be soul; the body is the subject or matter, not what is attributed to it. Hence the soul must be a substance in the sense of the form of a natural body having life potentially within it.

. . . .

That is why the soul is the first grade of actuality of a natural body having life potentially in it. The body so described is a body which is organized.

. . . .

That is why we can wholly dismiss as unnecessary the question whether the soul and body are one: it is as meaningless as to ask whether the wax and the shape given to it by the stamp are one . . .[63]

On one plausible interpretation (which I believe is Ross') of this passage, the soul (mind) is the "organization", i.e. the doings, *qua* exercises of dispositions or potentialities, of the body. A conscious human being is one which acts or would act in certain ways. Both Aristotle and Ryle accept this behavioristic account as a philosophy of mind.

Ryle's metaphysics may tempt one and has in fact tempted him, into a very odd sort of alleged "explanation" of human as well as non-human behavior. Not by chance, this kind of "explanation" is usually associated with Aristotelian "science" and the metaphysics that went with it. To put it in the traditional terms, Ryle thinks that we usually "explain" a piece of behavior in terms of formal rather than efficient causes. At least, this is one plausible way of rendering Ryle's claim that for the most part we "explain" a piece of behavior by subsuming it under a disposition (which he denies is a cause).

[61] CM, p. 167.
[62] CM, p. 199.
[63] Aristotle, *On the Soul*, from *The Basic Works of Aristotle*, edited by Richard McKeon, Random House, 1941, p. 555.

The sense in which we 'explain' his actions is not that we infer to occult causes, but that we subsume under hypothetical and semi-hypothetical propositions. The explanation is not of the type 'the glass broke because a stone hit it', but more nearly of the different type 'the glass broke when the stone hit it, because it was brittle'.[64]

In the third chapter it will be argued that Ryle's "unofficial" yet most deeply ingrained notion of a *cause* is that of a creative substance. Effects, that is, are always the behavior (and the properties?) of substances. Causes are always substances creating or acting through or by their natures. This fits well with the notion of "explanation" to which attention has just been called. It also helps us to make sense of some puzzling passages about the science of psychology in the last chapter of *The Concept of Mind*. Furthermore, Ryle's ontology and its "unofficial" attendant notion of cause constitute what one might call a metaphysics of "freedom" or at least of libertarianism. The idea is that the cause of (normal) behavior lies "within" a "creative" substance. What "causes" this substance to "create" this, that substance to "create" that? One who asks makes a "category-mistake". Whether Ryle is moved by a desire to "save" freedom is not clear. But it is safe to say that this spurious motive has moved quite a few philosophers to hold an otherwise inadequate metaphysics.

Something more can now be said about those mysterious entities Ryle calls frames of mind. His problem, it will be recalled, is to distinguish between, say, driving carefully and driving without care when, by hypothesis, the two events are "photographically identical", i.e. when the overt physical behavior is the same. Since he is so obviously puzzled, we can only state the correct solution and then show why he could not accept it. Or to say the same thing differently, rather than showing what Ryle's answer is, we shall show why he has no answer.

A frame of mind may be a disposition to have certain mental events as well as to have the disposition to act in certain ways. Such a frame of mind may have connected with it certain actual mental events. In the case at hand driving carefully involves, say, not merely looking at the road signs but actually reading them. Or a frame of mind may be a second-order disposition, i.e. a disposition to have a disposition. For example, someone may be in such a frame of mind that he would become depressed over some slight incident.

[64] CM, p. 50. This point has been discussed very effectively by May Brodbeck, "Explanation, Prediction, and 'Imperfect' Knowledge", *Minnesota Studies in the Philosophy of Science*, Vol. III: *Scientific Explanation, Space, and Time*, edited by H. Feigl and G. Maxwell, University of Minnesota Press, 1962.

Ryle cannot accept such an account because he insists that (1) there are no mental events (in the traditional sense) and, more importantly for the argument, (2) to have a disposition is not to be in a certain state, i.e., dispositions are nothing. Yet frames of mind are, as Ryle claims, "clockable". This would seem to make them states of affairs. So he is puzzled that they cannot ever be identified with observable physical events or properties. Consider what he has to say about the frame of mind called *paying attention:*

Perhaps knitted brows, taciturnity and fixity of gaze may be evidence of intentness; but these can be simulated, or they can be purely habitual. In any case, in describing him as applying his mind to his task, we do not mean that this is how he looks and sounds while engaged in it . . .[65]

The puzzlement is so great that in the next passage, from the same page, he is even willing to see some merit in what, for me, amounts to the suggestion that properties may have properties.

We commonly speak of reading attentively, driving carefully and conning studiously, and this usage has the merit of suggesting that what is being described is one operation with a special character and not two operations executed in different 'places', with a peculiar cable between them.

. . . .

What then is this special character? The question is perplexing . . . [66]

There is first the claim that frames of mind are clockable.[67] That puts them in the category of occurrences. By this line of thought, they are events. This also makes them "existents". But by hypothesis they are unobservable.[68] Now by one line of thought to be exhibited in the next chapter, that is exactly what a mental event in the traditional sense is – an unobservable "existent" occurrence. But mental events in the traditional sense are not supposed to exist. This is one clash or predicament.

Secondly, a property is for Ryle not an occurrence. Nor is having a property. Given the nominalism, therefore, insofar as frames of mind are properties, they are non-existent non-occurrences.[69] Yet, once

---

[65] CM, p. 138.
[66] CM, p. 138.
[67] CM, p. 139.
[68] 'Unobservable' here means 'unobservable in principle' as one says.
[69] If one holds, as I believe one should, that doings are properties, then frames of mind if they are properties of doings are properties of properties. On Ryle's view, this would make frames of mind doubly "non-existent" – once for being properties (nominalism) and once for being properties of properties (elementarism). Of course Ryle doesn't hold that doings are properties. For further discussion of Ryle's nominalism-cum-elementarism, see Chapter IV.

more, being clockable, they are existent occurrences. This is the second clash or predicament. Frames of mind, that is, mark the point where the strict distinction between occurrences or doings on the one hand, and having properties, in particular dispositional properties, on the other begins to look doubtful to Ryle himself. Hence his preoccupations.

By nominalism I mean the doctrine that properties do not "exist"; by Aristotelianism, the doctrine that they are not universals. Historically, the two doctrines have not been always distinguished. Ryle holds them both, and they both enter at certain points into the dialectic of his philosophy of mind.

There is no direct textual evidence for Ryle's nominalism in *The Concept of Mind*, though there is, of course, most substantial indirect evidence, some of which I have already cited. Besides, there is also, as we shall see, most explicit evidence from other texts, written when he was not yet embarrassed by explicitly expressing his ontological views.

A general dissatisfaction with Ryle's philosophy of mind and its underlying ontology has not only been stated once or twice, it has been freely exhibited by the tone of both exposition and comment throughout this chapter. Yet I have not engaged in detailed analysis. This is the next task. It requires another chapter.

II. THE ONTOLOGY OF *THE CONCEPT OF MIND*

Ontology asks what exists. Some ontologists, operating with a certain meaning of 'exist', deny the "existence" of certain kinds of objects of which commonsense affirms the existence. That makes it fruitful to distinguish the ordinary from the various philosophical uses of 'exist'. Ryle is not so subtle; he sometimes speaks as an ontologist, sometimes commonsensically without either being clear or making it clear in which way he is speaking.

Speaking commonsensically, Ryle would say that there are, at least, physical objects, their properties, their dispositions, and their behaviors. On one level this *is* Ryle's ontology – substances, properties (including dispositions), and doings. But when he speaks from his philosophical depths, then only substances and doings "exist". Properties, that is, including dispositions, don't really "exist". When his nominalism and this confused notion of existence combine, problems ensue. This I shall show.

The four sections of this chapter contain a discussion of (1) the ontological status of doings and an analysis of Ryle's "reasons" for the status he assigns them, (2) dispositions and the beginning of an analysis of his views on them, (3) the notions of existence and occurrence and the conclusion of the analysis of Ryle's views on dispositions, and (4) the way in which time enters into and reveals the weaknesses of his ontology. Finally, there will be a summary of what has been secured.

Doings

Suppose that there are natured substances; dispositions, at least some of which are parts of the natures; and doings. Doings are the behaviors of bodies (substances). Some behavior is "normal", some isn't. When it is, then it is the exercise of a certain disposition to act. "Normal" behavior is also "natural"; it flows from the nature of a certain substance to act in a certain way under certain circumstances. Hence, "normal" behavior needs for its explanation no further appeal than to the nature of the thing (and to the circumstances), whereas in the case of "unnatural" behavior one must look elsewhere for the explanation. This is the picture we get from Ryle.[1]

But what *are* doings? On one ontological analysis of doings or behaviors, one would say that a piece of behavior is a succession of properties in a substance, or, perhaps, a succession of properties in a succession of momentary individuals. That is, doings do not constitute a further ontological kind in addition to individuals, be they substances or bare particulars, momentary or continuants, and properties, be they accidents (perfect particulars) or universals. This, though, is not Ryle's opinion.

In the twenties and thirties of this century there was considerable discussion as to whether events constitute an ontological category of its own. Can a stroke of lightning be "reduced" to or analyzed as a substance having properties? The question illustrates the form the debate often took. For two reasons, the "problem" presents itself most forcefully in a substance ontology, as opposed to one where all individuals are momentary. (1) Strokes of lightning are momentary; substances persist. (2) The substantialist's account of time and change seems to preclude the coming to be and passing away of substances. Ryle stands at the tail-end of this earlier, inconclusive debate. Doings remain in a kind of ontological limbo. I shall next show in what regards doings are like substances, in what others they are like properties. Then

---

[1] See in particular the last chapter of *The Concept of Mind* with its attack on modern psychology.

we shall be able to understand why Ryle didn't want to make doings either substances or properties or, for that matter, a combination of both.

In what respect is a doing like a substance, as substances have often been conceived by philosophers? For one, doings are in time. But so are properties on the substance-accident schema. So we must cut it finer. Doings "take" time; their being by their "nature" spreads through time. Accidents, too, are in time, yet they may be momentary. Let us say then that doings, like substances, are continuants; their "natures" require them to persist.[2]

The idea that doings "take" time is close to another, concerning a further similarity between substances and doings. This is the idea that doings, while "complex", are not analyzable without residue. That is, as soon as one tries to speak of the constituents of doings, something is lost. As with doings, so with substances. Substances are "complex"; but they don't, in the relevant sense, have parts. Or, if you like, substances and doings are both more than the sums of their respective parts.

Finally, and structurally the most important, doings are like substances in that they have properties. One reads carefully, yells loudly, runs slowly. Why does this make doings like substances? The answer is that "second-order" properties, i.e., properties of properties, are foreign to a substance-accident ontology. This, we shall see, is particularly clear in Ryle's case. To grant "second-order" properties would be to grant too much status to "first-order" properties, for they (the latter) would then be "subjects of attributes". Hence, anything which has properties is a substance or a substance-like entity.

Yet doings are, in some regards, like properties. They are, in particular, like Aristotelian accidents in that they "belong to" a substance. *This* substance and not that one "exhibits" *this* behavior. On the view under consideration some behaviors "flow" from the nature of the substance to act in that way. A certain kind of behavior is something which is "appropriate" to one substance or one kind of substance much as some properties are "appropriate" to a substance or kind of substance due to the nature of that substance. "Properties must inhere in a substance." Beside that formula we might put "Doings require doers." Both properties and doings require substances for their "existence". They are both "dependent" entities.

Furthermore, a behavior is a "repeatable". I put 'repeatable'

---

[2] But see the last section of this chapter in which the possibility that substances are not in time (and so are not continuants) is explored.

between double quotes because in the scheme there are no universals. So nothing is literally repeated. But the idea is clear. Just as two substances may both be blue, so two substances may exhibit like behavior.

Having seen that a doing is neither a substance nor a property nor a combination of them while yet, on Ryle's view, sharing certain features with both categories, we must ask why he would wish to keep them in this kind of ontological limbo. In asking this, we really ask two questions. What reasons might he himself give if questioned? What features of his thought can we identify as likely structural reasons for this wish?

One way to enter in the dialectic of doings is to analyze a piece of behavior into a number of properties successively exemplified by the substance or the individuals which make up the physical object. If this is, as it seems, the most natural move, why does Ryle reject it? Why does he push doings in the direction of individuals? One traditional motive is, I believe, the idea that an individual-property view commits one to a static universe, or, at best, to one that "jumps" from state to state, which view is felt to ignore the "flow" of nature. Whether this motive also moves Ryle, either psychologically or structurally, is not clear.

Structurally, his main reason for pushing doings toward individuals is, I submit, his nominalism. This, I believe, is clear. But it needs showing. Ryle would never say that there are no minds. Of course there are. He rightly feels the need to give mind relatively firm ontological status. But if he is to locate the mind in dispositions and behavior, then it becomes necessary to show that at least one of these two is something more than properties, as in effect the "usual" analysis of doings would have it. For properties, for a nominalist, don't "exist". Dispositions, we know, if they are anything, are properties. That leaves only behavior. That is why it is so important to Ryle to make of doings something that has more ontological status than properties. If so, what else can he do but make them crypto-individuals?

This, if I am right, is the way in which Ryle's materialism and his nominalism both feed his "eventism". His materialism keeps him from saying that minds are individuals; his nominalism, from saying that they are properties. Yet he doesn't want to say that minds are nothing. He locates them in an ontological category of their own by making them "doings".

I just called Ryle a materialist. He says and believes that his theory of dispositions saves him from materialism. Yet dispositions don't "exist". This spots another unresolved tension in his thought. Let us look in detail at his view of dispositions.

Dispositions

One might say that Ryle sees himself in relation to the "materialists" as Aristotle saw himself in relation to the Megarics. Take the following passage from Ross:

> The Megaric school had denied the existence of potentiality. A thing, they said, either is or is not in a certain state, and that is all that there is to be said about it. What Aristotle does is to insist that that is *not* all that there is to be said about it.[3]

What Ryle insists on is that to say of a man that he made certain sounds or bodily movements is *not*, as the "materialists" hold, all that can be said about his *action*, his behavior. That behavior also either is or is not the exercise of some disposition or other. Or, to put it more nearly in his own terms: When we say of someone, for example, that he recited his multiplication tables we say something not only about some actual behavior that has occurred or is occurring but about possible future behavior, i.e., a disposition or potentiality to act in certain ways either in the future or now.

About two other matters, however, Aristotle and Ryle seem to disagree; Ross goes on to say:

> ... and no doubt if we answer the question "why did A become B actually" by saying "because it already was B potentially," we are giving an answer which is no answer. The conception of potentiality has often been used to cover mere barrenness of thought. Yet there is a real point in Aristotle's insistence on the conception. The point is that change is not catastrophic. It is not the case that A which is sheerly not-B suddenly becomes B. Consider A more carefully and you will find some of the conditions of B-ness already present ...[4]

The two points of disagreement are: (1) Whereas Aristotle, according to Ross, holds that appeal to potentiality is not explanation, Ryle seems to think otherwise. (2) Aristotle holds that potentialities *are* something whereas Ryle at least *seems* to deny it. What concerns us here is (2). But I want to present what I believe to be the correct view of dispositions first. That will also provide an opportunity for making, incidentally, as it were, some other points that will be useful.

Are there dispositions? Of course there are. Jones has the disposition to blow his nose whenever he is nervous; my chair has the disposition to creak whenever I sit on it, and so on. All of us constantly use words

---

[3] W. D. Ross, *Aristotle*, Meridian Book, World Publishing Co., 1961, p. 173.
[4] *Ibid.*

which are "dispositional", either obviously so or less obviously so. Some things have certain dispositions throughout their existence, e.g. the brittleness of the window in my office; other dispositions are short-term, e.g. the former disposition of my recently oiled chair to creak when sat upon. According to their length and strength and other features, we refer to dispositions variously as traits, states, inclinations, tendencies, conditions, capabilities, abilities, limitations, liabilities, powers, propensities, and so on. We also talk about dispositions to have dispositions. If Jones' knowing French is a disposition, then if he doesn't know French but wants to and has the ability to learn it, we might speak of his disposition to acquire a disposition.

Philosophers quite rightly have raised problems about dispositions. If 'This window is brittle' *means* 'This window *would* break if it *were* struck', does saying the window is brittle say anything about the window's *"present"* properties or only about possible *"future"* properties? If the window is never struck, is it *true* that this window is brittle? If brittleness is a "present" property, what kind of property is it? The second of these questions is *part* of the familiar problem of counterfactuals. Let me say that this is one problem I wish to stay away from as much as possible in this essay. Or, rather, let me say that I shall stick with commonsense to the extent of assuming that of the following two propositions the first is true and the second false, although they both have false antecedents (and consequents):

(1) If I jump out the window in the next minute, I shall be injured (in the next minute).

(2) If I jump out the window in the next minute, the earth will break in half (in the next minute).

Take three propositions:

(P_1) John is now irritated.
(P_2) John is now irritable.
(P_3) John is an irritable person.

Assume for the moment that being irritated is to be in a certain mental state (in the traditional sense). Call that mental state f_1. Call its parallel neurological state f_2. Let a stimulus which brings about these two states (f_1 and f_2) be f_4. Call the (overt) behavior which we associate with irritated persons f_3. Finally, call a stimulus which elicits this overt behavior f_5. My schematic "transcriptions" of (P_1), (P_2) and (P_3) are respectively as follows (where 'a' names John, 't_0' stands for "now", and 't' is a time variable):

(P4) $f_1 (a, t_0)$
(P5) $f_4 (t_0) \supset f_1 (a, t_0)$
(P6) $(t)[f_4 (t) \supset f_1 (a, t)]$

Now for several comments:

(1) Notice that f_3 and f_5 do not appear in (P4), (P5), and (P6). It might be suggested that (P1) should have been "transcribed" as

(P7) $[f_1 (a, t_0)] \cdot [f_5 (t) \supset f_3 (a, t_0)]$

because

(P8) $[f_1 (, t_0)] \equiv [f_5 (t) \supset f_3 (a, t_0)]$

is true. Generalizing (P8), one obtains:

(P9) $(x)(t) [[f_1 (x, t)] \equiv [f_5 \supset f_3 (x, t)]]$

This, if true, is a law of nature. There is a meaning of 'meaning' with which the Oxford people toy according to which the discovery of laws adds to the meaning of terms. That there is such a meaning of 'meaning' no one would wish to dispute. To hold that it is philosophically useful is another matter; indeed, one may hold that fascination with it leads to philosophical disaster. For example, one may be tempted, since (P9) is true, either (1) to make (P7) the transcription of (P1), or, (2) what in some circumstances is even worse, to identify f_1 with $f_5 \supset f_3$. In the case at hand, the mistake need not be as disastrous as in some others, for one may reasonably claim that being irritable doesn't involve a mental occurrence, and is indeed nothing more than having a certain disposition and (perhaps) acting in certain ways. But if the analogous claim is made for any mental *occurrence* (a remembering, a wondering, etc.), then the likely result will be materialism.

(2)   One can with a semblance of reason say that being irritable in the mental occurrence sense f_1 "is" a dispositional property, not because it *is* $f_5 \supset f_3$, but because (P9) is true. But then, that makes the 'is' in 'Being irritable is a dispositional property' merely a misleading expression for the equivalence in the law (P9).

(3) A behavior scientist might well say that in his special usage 'f_1' *means* (stands as an abbreviation for) '$f_5 \supset f_3$', since it is his program to "replace" all "mental" expressions (e.g., f_1) by "physical" ones (e.g., $f_5 \supset f_3$) such that the former are connected with the latter by laws such as (P9). This kind of thing should not surprise anyone.

Nor should it be taken as a point in the philosophy of mind. Behavior scientists are not philosophers, though some philosophers may think so. Behavior scientists merely want to explain such events as, say, the instances of f_3. Is not, then, it may be asked, on my view f_3 explained by a joint appeal to f_1 and f_4 ($[[f_1 (a) \equiv f_4 \supset f_5 (a)]$ $\supset [(f_1 (a) \cdot f_4(a)) \supset f_5 (a)]$)? And isn't f_1 "inaccessible" to the scientist? Let this be the cue for the next comment.

(4) f_1 and f_2 are two things and not one. Yet if the commonsense doctrine of parallelism is true, then $f_1 \equiv f_2$ expresses that truth. Perhaps it would be safer to express it by $f_1 \equiv (f_2 \text{ v } f_2' \text{ v } f_2'' \dots)$. This, though, is scientific detail that needn't concern us. The point is that since (or if) $f_1 \equiv f_2$ is true, our behaviorist need not in any case apprise himself of f_1 in order to explain f_5; he need only go to f_2. So f_1 is not needed for explanation.

(5) At this point, Ryle may think he has won his case. For, we may imagine him to ask us, if things like f_1 are not needed for explanation, what point is there in introducing them. Yet, he merely gives himself away by demonstrating his belief that the only reason for embracing dualism is its alleged capacity of explaining (in a causal way) certain facts about behavior. In this he is obviously, terribly, and thoroughly mistaken. The dualist insists that minds are there for the simple reason that they are.

(6) Just as f_1 and $f_5 \supset f_3$ are two entities, so f_2 is not the same entity as $f_5 \supset f_3$. It is rather, as one may want to say, the physiological "ground" of the disposition, somewhat as the physical "ground" of being brittle is a certain molecular structure.

Notice finally that I have throughout this discussion treated dispositions as properties. A disposition, while complex in its if-then way, is indeed just as much a property as any other.

Ryle's discussion of dispositions is both confused and confusing. He, too, speaks of dispositions as properties; but then oddities are introduced in the same breath:

A statement ascribing a dispositional property to a thing has much, though not everything, in common with a statement subsuming the thing under a law. To possess a dispositional property is not to be in a particular state, or to undergo a particular change; it is to be bound or liable to be in a particular state, or to undergo a particular change, when a particular condition is realised.[5]

Three points are made: (1) Dispositions are a kind of property. (2) Disposition statements are in some important sense like law statements.

[5] CM, p. 43.

(3) To have a disposition is not to be in a particular state. (2) is, I believe, part of Ryle's reason for saying (3). The point he wishes to make in (3) is expressed in other ways on other occasions – that dispositions are not occurrences, that they are not actualities, and so on.

Dispositional statements are neither reports of observed or observable states of affairs, nor yet reports of unobserved or unobservable states of affairs. They narrate no incidents.[6]

Potentialities, it is truistically said, are nothing actual. The world does not contain, over and above what exists and happens, some other things which are mere would-be things and could-be happenings.[7]

The last quotation tends to confirm my view that for Ryle all that really "exists" are substances and doings (events, happenings). If this is not so, then what else, I ask, is he trying to tell us when he denies that the having of dispositions are occurrences or that disposition statements are categorical statements? Why, furthermore, would he think it to be so important to distinguish between dispositions, or the having of them, and occurrences?

These questions have answers on several levels of the dialectic. We saw already that for whatever reasons, Ryle does not want to analyze behavior as a series of properties of a thing. Behaviors, being doings, go into an ontological category all their own. Insofar then as dispositions are properties and insofar as properties and doings (occurrences) are two ontological categories, an item of behavior and (the having of) a disposition are two things and not one. Having a disposition, that is, is not behaving. Two comments are relevant.

(1) If dispositions are properties, then they do not, in Ryle's world, "really" "exist". Even so, the claim that dispositions fall into a category different from doings does not as such establish that disposition statements are not categoricals. Nor do I think Ryle believes it does. Accordingly I hope to show that Ryle may at this point plausibly be credited with ideas much more interesting than the simple claim that dispositions are not behaviors.

(2) The earlier suggestion that Ryle may have had Bergsonian reasons for making doings a distinct category becomes relevant here. When one "merely" has a disposition, he doesn't *do* anything. More generally, just having a property is not yet *doing* anything. If one insists too vehemently in the distinction he may end up with an onto-

---

6 CM, p. 125.
7 CM, p. 119.

logy such as Ryle's. Every philosopher must, of course, make his peace with the world as it is. The commonsensical active/passive distinction must be accounted for, *even if eventually discarded at the basic ontological level.* Some philosophers do believe that the *ordinary* distinctions between properties and doings, things and events, doing things and having them done to one's self, can be accounted for without making them "ontological", i.e., without building them into one's basic ontological categories. Some others, like Bergson and Ryle, do not see how that can be done. But I am getting ahead of myself.

"There are only things [substances] and events [doings]". If this is, as I supposed, an ontological proposition, then it follows that properties don't "exist". Indeed one need hardly argue for the claim that Ryle is a nominalist in the sense that he denies or depresses the ontological status of properties, whether they be "universals" or "perfect particulars". If properties don't "exist" and if dispositions are properties, then dispositions don't "exist". This is *one* claim. Dispositions are not occurrences. This is a *second* claim. In Ryle's ontology the second claim follows from the first. This is *one* thing. Ryle, though, has confused the two claims with each other. That is quite *another* thing. We have come to the heart of the matter.

Existence, Occurrence, and Dispositions

Naturally, the addicts of the superstition that all true indicative sentences either describe existents or report occurrences will demand that sentences such as 'this wire conducts electricity', or 'John Doe knows French', shall be construed as conveying factual information of the same type as that conveyed by 'this wire is conducting electricity' and 'John Doe is speaking French'. How could the statements be true unless there were something now going on, even though going on, unfortunately, behind the scenes?[8]

It needs no argument to show that interrogative, imperative and optative sentences are used for other ends than that of notifying their recipients of the existence or occurrence of things.[9]

The world does not contain, over and above what exists and happens ...[10]

From the first of these paragraphs we may gather Ryle's belief that if one grants that disposition statements report occurrences, he is committed to mental events. This *is* his reason for denying that the having of a disposition is an occurrence. We will come back to this shortly.

I argued that Ryle's basic ontology is one of substances and oc-

---

[8] CM, p. 124.
[9] CM, p. 120.
[10] CM, p. 119.

currences. Only substances and occurrences "exist". Verbally, that doesn't quite jibe with what he says above. There are, indeed, three "possible" views to be found in *The Concept of Mind*.

(1) There are two modes of being – existing and occurring.

(2) What exists are substances and occurrences.

(3) Only occurrences exist. The existence of a substance is an occurrence.

The texts above may seem to support (1). The burden of this essay as a whole is that Ryle's "real" view is (2). The point I am trying to establish right now is that an implicit acceptance of (3) or, rather, a confusion of (1), (2) and (3) is at the root of Ryle's rejection of dispositions. (1) and (2), however, say in effect the same thing. Upon (1), a "being" is either an existent or an occurrence, and all existents are substances. Upon (2), what exists (or has "being") is either a substance or an occurrence and all substances are existents. So the interesting distinction is between, let us say, (2) and (3).

The linguistic counterpart of the ontological confusions is a confusion as to what a "fact-stating" sentence is. Ryle talks as if the only truly "fact-stating" sentences report either existence (of substances) or occurrences. In a grotesque sort of way, this fits with his ontology. For, it commits him to holding that 'The chair is red' does not state a fact – at least none beyond the chair's existence. Absurd as this kind of thought is, it is nevertheless a partial motive of Ryle's denial that disposition statements state "facts". To see how it works, consider that, grammatically at least, disposition-ascribing sentences are subject-predicate sentences. That is why Ryle fears that, if he grants that property-ascribing statements are statments of fact, he may also be forced to grant that disposition-ascribing statements state facts, which, we know, would embarrass him. So he makes sure he won't be embarrassed by denying that such property-ascribing statements as 'This chair is red' state any fact over and above, perhaps, the chair's existence. Presently we shall also see that Ryle wouldn't have needed to take this precaution. He, though, from where he stands, could not have seen that.

What then, according to Ryle, are disposition statements? He compares them to law statements. So we must first look at his analysis of law statements.[11] In its essentials it is only too well-known. Law statements are not statements of fact; they do not "really" enter as premises in explanatory arguments. Rather, they are like rules of

[11] CM, pp. 119–123.

inference, allowing us to move from one "particular" fact to another. (A "particular fact", we now understand, is a substance's existing or a substance's doing something.) One major theory of explanation would have it that to explain, say, g(a), one must, schematically speaking, present a valid deductive argument of the following kind:

$$\frac{(x) [f (x) \supset g (x)]}{g (a)}$$

where $(x)[f (x) \supset g (x)]$ is a law statement and the rule of inference (or its "instantiation") involved obviously that '$[f (x) \supset g (x)]$' and '$f(a)$' deductively imply '$g(a)$'.[12] Ryle thinks otherwise. On his view, the explanation of g(a) is of the following form:

$$\frac{f (a)}{g (a)}$$

with the law statement involved not being a premise but, rather, itself *an inferential rule of a non-formal kind*. For example, to explain or predict the fact that Jones dies, one points out that Jones is a man. The "informal" rule of inference involved is, of course, that all men are mortal.

A law statement for Ryle, then, is an "inference-ticket" and not a statement of "fact". The ontological ground for denying that law statements when in their original form, e.g. 'All men are mortal', are fact-stating is the view that there are no "general" facts, but only "particular" facts. Presently we shall see that if the law statement is taken hypothetically, e.g., 'If anything is a man, then it is mortal', then it may, in Ryle's ontology, commit us to something which, for him, is even worse than a "general" fact. But let me first state his view in another way.

The view I hold and presented first, the so-called deductive model of explanation, makes the premises of an explanation consist of both law statements and statements of "particular" fact (existence or occurrence statements). According to Ryle, it thus joins together sentences of different "logical types". Its proponents, therefore, or so we may suppose, commit a kind of category error. But obviously

---

[12] For further discussion of this issue see Ryle, ""If," "So," and "Because" ", *Philosophical Analysis*, edited by Max Black, Cornell University Press, 1950. Also see N. H. Colburn, "Logic and Professor Ryle", *Philosophy of Science*, 21, 1954, for a detailed analysis of Ryle's logic.

law statements have to enter into explanation somehow. So Ryle proposes the "inference-ticket" view.

As to the distinction I just made between law statements and disposition statements in the "original" form on the one hand, and their "if-then" form on the other, Ryle himself never verbally makes it. Yet, we shall see, he has different things to say about them in their different forms. Let us turn to disposition statements.

The paradigm of a disposition statement is, for Ryle, 'This piece of sugar is soluble'. Such law statements as 'Sugar is soluble' are obviously relegated to a much more complex "type". If one keeps that in mind, then one understands that for him [13] disposition statements, being about particular things, are not law statements. Yet, they are like law statements in that they are "inference-tickets" which allow us to move from one "particular" fact to another. Ryle claims and I of course agree that (in one meaning of 'meaning') 'This piece of sugar is soluble' means 'If this piece of sugar is put into water, then it dissolves'. Thus *two* "particular" facts (occurrences) are involved, the sugar's being in water and the sugar's dissolving. Neither is individually asserted, nor are they jointly asserted. Is then no fact asserted? According to Ryle, because the only "real" facts are "particular" facts, no fact is asserted. Nor is that all. He also seems to believe that one who holds that an "if-then" statement states a fact is committed to grant ontological status to either a causal tie or, perhaps even worse, to the logical tie of material implication. This is a second reason why disposition statements, at least in their "if-then" aspect, cannot, according to Ryle, state facts. But let me return to some matters less subtle and, accordingly, more central in Ryle's own thought.

As we saw, he believes and says that unless one avoids at all costs the doctrine that disposition statements state facts, one will be committed to *mental events*. When he says such things, he is using 'mental event' in its traditional sense, in which, we know, mental events are non-physical occurrences. He is also thinking of the disposition statement in what I called its "original" form, i.e., ascribing a property that cannot be exhaustively analyzed in the customary "if-then" way. Here we stand at the root of another confusion. One may deny (rightly, I believe) that dispositions exist in the sense of being properties not completely analyzable in an "if-then" way. E.g., to be soluble is more than to dissolve if put into water. Or one

13 CM, p. 123.

may deny (wrongly, I believe) that dispositions exist because they are properties and because he is a nominalist for whom no properties exist. Ryle, I submit, does not grasp this distinction. So he is confused.

We know already why Ryle wants to deny that the having of a disposition is an occurrence. The next step is to understand how this denial may engender the further claim that dispositions are nothing, i.e., that they do not exist. The crucial link in Ryle's thought is, I believe, his implicitly equating existence and occurrence. If every existent is an occurrence and if my having a disposition is not an occurrence, then it does not exist. Of course it doesn't.

That Ryle does in fact, at least implicitly, equate existence with occurrence is shown by his belief that one who says that dispositions are something is thereby committed to mental *events*, in the traditional sense, rather than to, say, mental *properties* or, even, to *substances*. One need not, we see, be a self-conscious ontologist, as Ryle indeed is not, in order to be confused as to what one's own ontology is. At this point, the substantialism in its nominalistic aspect, if I may so put it, fuses confusedly with the "eventism". Insofar, then, as eventism is adduced as a reason for denying that dispositions exist, the argument collapses.

Why should granting ontological status to dispositions as such commit one to something *mental* (in the traditional sense)? Think of dispositions as powers again, not as occurrences. Then we can see that to say they *are* something is, for Ryle, to fall back into the old Faculty theories of the Medievals:

This [construing dispositional statements as fact-stating] was indeed the mistake of the old Faculty theories which construed dispositional words as denoting occult agencies or causes, i.e. things existing, or processes taking place, in a sort of limbo world.[14]

Yet, Ryle's own view of the nature of mind is not so different from these Faculty theories. That must by now be obvious. Why then shouldn't we fall back on the old Faculty theories? The answer is that the (traditional) faculties, being "parts" of the mind, are something mental (in the traditional sense). That Ryle cannot accept. We have, I believe, come upon the ultimate reason why he cannot grant ontological status to dispositions, and admit that they are "something". Dispositions are unobservable, and he identifies the unobservable with the mental (in the traditional sense which he rejects). Thus he naturally identifies the unobservable *that is there*

[14] CM, pp. 119-120.

with the mental in the traditional sense.[15] Stones, as it happens, do have dispositions. Fortunately, though, their dispositions, like everything else's, are nothing; otherwise Ryle, if he were consistent, would have to suppose that stones have minds.

In the light of what we already know of Ryle's ontological thinking, one of the three passages I last quoted very naturally permits the following interpretation. *Since* only substances and processes exist, dispositions, if they existed, would be either substances or processes. With 'Since', which I therefore italicized, the proposition merely prejudges the ontological status of dispositions. If we replace 'Since' by 'If' the proposition becomes a truism. If we consider it as it stands, with the 'Since', it will help us to understand how Ryle came to identify the unobservable with the mental (in the traditional sense). Dispositions are of course not observable in the same sense in which *physical substances* or *physical processes* are observable. Hence, if they "exist" and therefore are either substances or processes, they must be *non-physical*. But the non-physical is the *mental*! The argument collapses, of course, if we admit that properties exist and that dispositions are properties. Thus we see once more how Ryle is continuously victimized by his nominalism.

One may of course (1) analyze dispositions as properties and (2) grant ontological status to properties without *thereby* being committed to (3) granting such status to mental entities. That I take to be obvious. Ryle believes that (1) and (2) commit one to (3). Thus he is simply mistaken. Take 'John knows French'. 'Know', to be sure, has mental uses. But then Ryle knows and we know that the behaviorist can and for his purposes must so "construe" it that nothing but the disposition to make certain noises on certain occasions is involved in what the sentence asserts. To say that (a) the disposition in question is a property is one thing. To say that (b) it is a mental property, i.e., a property of a non-physical substance or individual is quite another thing. One may consistently hold (a) and reject (b). As the behaviorist construes (a), the disposition in question is indeed a property of John's body. The distinction seems obvious. Yet, strangely, it escapes the "behaviorist" Ryle. The price a philosopher must pay for an ontology *implicitly* held is high indeed!

On reason I spent so much time on dispositions is the opportunity they provided for exploring the intrinsically more interesting and more fundamental issue of *existence* versus *occurrence*. One reason why

[15] See the first quote on page 33 of this chapter.

the latter issue is so fundamental is its connection with that of time. That brings us to the last topic I promised to touch upon in this chapter.

Time

An adequate ontology must of course present an assay of or an account for time. While Ryle is even less explicit on this topic than he is on others, he has, nevertheless, an implicit ontology of time. More precisely, I shall try to show first that the less implicit aspects of his ontology presuppose a certain ontology of time, and second, that this implicit account of time is unacceptable.

There is, of course, a connection between the issues of time and substance. Thus I shall try to establish the following points. (1) Since Ryle is a substantialist, he is committed to "absolute" time. (2) It is difficult to hold that substances are in time, even though they are conceived to be continuants. This is especially true in Ryle's case, since for him doings are in time. (3) There is the possibility that Ryle thinks of existing as a kind of doing. If he does, he could, verbally at least, have a way out of certain difficulties. (4) Whether or not he takes this way, he is committed to "absolute" time, which is unacceptable.

Suppose Ryle's substances to be continuants, i.e., entities which are "at" more than one time (moment). This contrasts them on the one hand with entities which are, as one says, momentary, and, on the other hand, with entities that aren't "in" time at all such as, say, numbers. I put 'at' and 'in' between double quotes because, although I used them in perfectly good English locutions, these locutions nevertheless suggest the notion of "absolute" time which is built into our language. The double quotes avoid the suggestion by pointing to it.

The immediate task is twofold: First I must show what is meant by "absolute" time. Then I shall endeavor to show that one who holds that there are continuants is thereby committed to "absolute" time.

Absolutism is usually contrasted with relativism. For our purposes it will be safe to say that for the relativist time consists simply of relations. These relations are held to obtain between entities which are not themselves temporal except, of course, insofar as they exemplify these relations. The absolutist holds that, either in addition to or instead of these relations, time consists of *moments*. Moments in turn he holds to be a very special kind of individual to which other individuals stand in the "at-ness" relation.

A substance, being a continuant, may have a property at one moment and not have it at another.[16] Let 'a' name the substance, 'f' the property. Then '$f(a)$' and '$\sim f(a)$' are both true. But this is a contradiction. The only way out is to add time in a way that makes f a relation between a and a moment. That yields '$f(a,t_1)$' and '$\sim f(a, t_2)$' which of course do not contradict each other. But this also shows that the price is absolute time.

This result is familiar just as the familiar notion of a substance is that of a continuant. Yet one may wonder whether Ryle or indeed any substantialist should not hold that substances are not in time at all. At first blush this seems an odd thing to suggest, for the tradition, as we just saw, thinks of substances as continuants. Yet some philosophers, e.g., Spinoza and Kant,[17] wondered for good dialectical reasons whether substance(s) is (are) in time at all. If they aren't, then, of course, they are neither continuants nor momentary. In Ryle's case, this possibility, if it be one, appears even more attractive since he has another kind of entity which he obviously takes to be a continuant, viz., a doing. So one may wonder whether he really is committed to absolute time even if his substances are not or perhaps even could not themselves be in time.

Those who, like Kant and Spinoza, carried the substance philosophy to its logical conclusion saw that unless it remains unchanging a substance cannot do one of the many jobs traditionally assigned to it. That is, in the end one must hold that there is but one, eternal, unchanging substance. The job that otherwise remains undone is that of initiator and "ground" of all change, i.e., of the entity which, while producing changes, remains one and the same throughout them. In such a world, one may hope to account for change in terms of the coming and ceasing to be of accidents of the one substance. If, on the other hand, substances can come and cease to be, that is, *if they are in time*, then the system has a gap. For there is then change that remains unaccounted for by either a "ground" or an initiator. At least, this is where the dialectics seem to lead. Whether this conclusion can be staved off we needn't here inquire.

There is no doubt that Ryle thinks of events or doings as in time. Whether a doing is a substance plus its behavior or this behavior alone

---

[16] The next several paragraphs are based on Bergmann's "Some Reflections on Time", which appeared originally in *Il Tempo*, Archivio di Filosofia, Padova: Cedam, 1958, and is reprinted in his *Meaning and Existence*.

[17] For a fuller exploration of the dialectics of this issue with respect to Kant, see my "Kant's First Analogy", *Kant-Studien*, January, 1963.

makes no difference for the point I am about to make. That point is that Ryle remains committed to absolute time even if, under dialectical pressure, he were prepared to admit that his substances themselves are not in time.

Doings, it may be claimed, though they are continuants, never have a property at one moment and not at another. If that claim can be upheld, then the familiar classical argument won't work against doings, and Ryle may indeed not be committed to absolute time. Hence, if he is to escape the classical objection, he must hold that doings, even though they have duration, undergo no change. This, clearly, isn't his notion of a doing. (If it were, all doings might as well be instantaneous!) So he remains committed to absolute time.

It may be of some use if, in conclusion, I point at certain weaknesses of the doctrines to which, as I believe to have shown, Ryle is committed. If one dismisses the possibility of substances being sequences of changeless (instantaneous) doings, then there are in this world *three kinds of individuals:* substances, doings, and moments. A doing is "of" a substance and "at" a time. That requires a minimum of two ties, "of-ness" and "at-ness". To see that they are different ties one need only reflect that a doing is of only one substance but may be at many moments. Made articulate, the ontology which at first looked poverty-stricken, begins to look rather bloated.

To the extent that *properties* are taken to exist other complications arise. To begin with, we need at least one and perhaps two more ties, between a substance and its properties and between a doing and its properties. More importantly, a property such as, say, being green, becomes, as we have seen, a relation between a substance and a moment. Furthermore, properties are on this view probably themselves "at" a time. Otherwise, how is the change of properties in a substance to be accounted for? To this extent, properties and doings become alike. That produces a picture that reminds us of Kant. Time and substance are the unchanging, the permanent; properties and activities are the changing, the temporal.

In Chapter IV I shall call attention to a certain specific claim Ryle once made the most plausible interpretation of which, as I shall show, is that what is in time is not substances but events.[18] On the other hand, we shall see that he believed, at one time at least, like Kant, that absolute space and time produce antinomies. Thus he rejected

[18] See Ryle, "Systematically Misleading Expressions", *Proceedings of the Aristotelian Society*, Vol. XXXII, Harrison and Sons, Ltd., 1932, p. 164.

absolutism as an illusion produced by "systematically misleading expressions". Nor have I any doubt that he still rejects absolutism as either false or meaningless. I quite agree. But, then, I don't have a substance metaphysics to defend.

The dialectic has one final turn. Return to the idea that to "exist" is to occur. Then substances, not being occurrences, don't exist. Neither of course would time or properties. One might think then that since time doesn't "exist", Ryle wouldn't need to be bothered by a commitment to absolute time. There is, finally, the possibility (3) mentioned on page 34. Upon this view only occurrences exist and the existence of a substance at a certain moment is an occurrence. Nor is it difficult to see how one may arrive at this structural possibility as the most satisfactory basic gambit available to him if he is moved by the following three ideas:

(1) Only substances "exist".
(2) Only what is in time "exists".
(3) Only events are in time.

There is no doubt that Ryle was moved by these three ideas. That is why I have begun to explore them here. I shall return to them in Chapter IV.

Materialists hold that there are no non-physical individuals. Ryle clearly wants to be a materialist in this sense. Yet he uses 'materialism' in a way that, he thinks, permits him to deny that he is a materialist. A "materialist" for him is one who identifies thinking with saying. He, Ryle, identifies thinking with saying plus a disposition. This, he believes, saves him from materialism. But dispositions do not, on his own view, really exist. That makes thinking, on his own view, really identical with saying. That sayings enter into laws is quite irrelevant to the ontological issue. Ryle is a materialist on his own grounds.

Ryle's "intention" is to give doings an ontological status which, if not lesser, is certainly not higher than, that of substances. Yet if doings are given the status of a category, then the dialectics tends to enhance their status in many ways. This tendency comes to a head in that phase of Ryle's thought in which he equates, or comes near equating, occurrence and existence. The lesson to be learned is, I think, that ontology is fundamentally the search for "simples", and that, therefore, to treat doings, which are essentially "complex" as if they were simples,[19] is inevitably to court confusion. For, in a sense

---

[19] 'Simple' is of course used philosophically. Two explications suggest themselves: (1) having no constituents, and (2) being unanalyzable without residue or distortion.

one has given up philosophical *analysis*. Perhaps analysis cannot solve all the problems one may reasonably call philosophical. Perhaps it cannot even solve all the ontological problems. I, however, am not ready to give up yet.

In this chapter I have examined in detail what I believe to be Ryle's ontology. In the next I shall examine what I take to be his two major arguments against dualism.

III. INTERACTIONISM AND INFINITE REGRESS ARGUMENTS

Two main arguments which run through *The Concept of Mind* are designed to show that dualism is either false or incoherent.[1] I shall call them (1) the argument from interaction, and (2) the infinite regress of awarenesses argument. In the two main parts of this chapter these arguments will be taken up successively. One reason for the first part's being considerably longer than the second is that Ryle's views on interaction tend to support my claims about his implicit ontology. This I shall try to show.

Part One, then, will be concerned with issues surrounding inter-action. Specifically, this part has four sections. In the first I shall explain what I believe to be the only clear notions of interaction and parallelism, independently of the mind/body issue. Secondly, the results of the first section will be applied to mind, in an attempt to determine the several logical possibilities of the "causal" connection between minds and bodies. In the third section I shall turn to Ryle, showing that he believes the dualist to be committed to one among these "possibilities". In this, I shall argue, he is mistaken. His mistake, I shall show, arises from his ontology. In the fourth and last section of Part One, I shall use Passmore's objections to parallelism as a cue for making clearer and securing further the respectability of parallelism – the doctrine I believe to be true.

In Part Two I shall take up briefly three variants of an argument Ryle makes against minds. The "three" arguments share a feature. They all purport to show that a vicious infinite regress of awarenesses is involved in certain dualistic assumptions. Then these assumptions are alleged to be among those every dualist must make. Thus dualism stands "refuted". One of the forms of this argument may be called the causal variant; another, the direct awareness variant; the third, the introspection variant. Eventually I shall take them up in this

---

[1] There are other arguments, of course, but I believe these two to be the most important.

order, trying to show that each fails of its purpose. First, though, let us turn to Part One.

PART ONE

Interaction and Parallelism

Consider a universe of three individuals, three properties, space and time. (Whether space and time are "absolute" or "relative" is here irrelevant.) Suppose that the three properties are mass, position, and velocity. Allow me to speak quantitatively about each property of each individual so that I may speak of, say, the *value m* of the mass of an individual *a*. Now consider the following *two* situations:

(1) At time t_1 the values of the three properties m, p and v for the three individuals *a*, *b* and *c* are as follows:

$$m_2 (a), \quad p_3 (a), \quad v_6 (a),$$
$$m_3 (b), \quad p_2 (b), \quad v_0 (b),$$
$$m_2 (c), \quad p_1 (c), \quad v_4 (c).$$

This is the first situation.

(2) In the second situation the values of *a*, *b* and *c* at t_1 are as follows:

$$m_2 (a), \quad p_3 (a), \quad v_3 (a),$$
$$m_3 (b), \quad p_2 (b), \quad v_5 (b),$$
$$m_2 (c), \quad p_1 (c), \quad v_0 (c).$$

Call each description a *state description*. Suppose that our universe contains no other properties (variables), i.e., that m, p and v are a complete set of relevant variables.[2] Notice that in the two situations the values of m and p are the same for each individual while those of v are not. Now suppose there is a law (sometimes called a *process law*) which allows one to compute the values of each property for each individual for some later time t_2 from their values at time t_1. If in the two situations at t_2 our computations show a difference in the values of either m or p *or* of m and p for any individual, then we say that v *interacts* with m or p or m and p. Conversely, if there are no such differences for *any* set of initial values, then it does not interact with the other two variables. This is the only clear notion of 'interaction' I know of.[3]

[2] 'Complete set of relevant variables' doesn't mean all the variables, but rather, all that are relevant to explanation and prediction in a certain situation. If one includes all the variables, then *a fortiori* one has a complete set of relevant variables, although some irrelevant ones may be included, too.

[3] That is, this is the only clear notion of interaction I know of which is relevant to the modern notion of cause.

Now suppose a universe like that just described except that there is in it one additional property, color. Suppose further that we can talk about color quantitatively, i.e., that we can assign a different numerical value to each shade of color. Now imagine that whenever an individual's velocity has the value 1, then its color has the value 1; whenever its velocity has the value, 2, then its color has the value 2, and so on. In this case velocity and color are *parallel* properties. The statement which expresses this parallelism will be called the *law of the parallelism*.

We have provided ourselves with the relevant notions of interaction and of parallelism. At this point two comments are in order.

(1) Though color is, as one might say, "merely" a parallel property it does, of course, make a difference to the subsequent values of m and p if v interacts; for if the law of the parallelism is true, then a difference in the value of color will be parallelled by a difference in the value of v. (In classical mechanics, m, determining the "system" rather than any of its "states", does not interact.) Which property, then, "really" interacts, "really" makes the difference? The question makes no sense. The variables m, v and p constitute a *causally closed system*, i.e., a complete set of relevant variables such that only their values at a time t_1 need be known in order to compute their future (or past) values at time t_2 by means of the process law. But, then, m, p and color also constitute such a system. That follows from the hypothesis that v and color are parallel properties.

(2) Though velocity and color by hypothesis have the connection described by the law of the parallelism, they are still two things and not one. Since they do have this peculiar connection, a philosopher or a scientist might be tempted to say they are really one thing. This temptation may stem from the "axiom" of extensionality, for by this axiom the names of a color and of the corresponding velocity would be "identical", i.e., substitutable for each other *salva veritate* in all contexts. But, then, properly understood, the "axiom" lends no support to the view that two "identical" entities are numerically one and the same.

We are ready to turn to mind and its "causal" connection with the body.

Mind and Body

Ryle states the mind/body problem in terms of mental states on the one hand and overt behavior on the other. I prefer to state it in terms of mental and physiological states. My preference is due to the fact that physiological states are momentary while behaviors are "continuants", i.e., behavior takes time. Furthermore, I take it, there is no special problem as to the causal connections between physiological states and overt behaviors. In any case, I can make all the points I want to make just as easily if I consider only physiological and mental states, both of which I shall take to be momentary.

Ryle's argument is that the connection between mind and body to which the dualist is committed also commits him to skepticism and solipsism. (By skepticism I mean here the doctrine that one can't know what is "going on" in other minds; by solipsism, the even stronger view that one cannot know nor have any good reasons for believing that other minds exist.) Skepticism and solipsism are absurd. So therefore is any view that commits one to either of them. Hence dualism is absurd. This is Ryle's argument. I agree with him that skepticism and solipsism are absurd; but I shall of course argue that the dualist is not committed to either of these two absurd doctrines.

In order to make this argument, I shall state what I take to be the seven "possibilities" as to the connection between mental states and physiological states, and in each case draw out the consequences regarding skepticism and solipsism. In doing this I shall assume without argument that we are or can be "acquainted" with our own mental states, with our own physiological states as well as with the physiological states of others but not, in the same sense, with the mental states of others.

Before stating the "possibilities", one final comment is required. On the views under consideration, mental individuals are not physical individuals. That means that any parallelism involved will be between, say, two properties in *two* individuals and not, as in the case of our model universe of three individuals, between two properties of the *same* individual. Thus to make the analogy more nearly accurate we might change our simple universe such that whenever a, b or c has a velocity of a certain value, there arises beside it an individual with the "same" value. Even so, the analogy is not yet perfect; for mental individuals are not "beside" physical ones, i.e., there are no spatial relations between the mental and the physical. That spots a problem which will be discussed presently.[4] I am now ready to state the seven "possibilities".[5]

---

[4] See p. 55
[5] The "possibilities" are not entirely mutually incompatible. (5), as stated, is compatible

(1) There is a perfect parallelism, that is, as one says, a one/one parallelism, between mental states on the one hand and certain, though of course not all, physiological states on the other. In this case there is, with one slight qualification, no ground whatsoever for either skepticism or solipsism. We could know from our own Self which states of the two kinds "go together". Thus if someone else's body (mind) is in a certain state, we could infer the state his mind (body) is in. The qualification is that if we had never been in a certain physiological state, we might not know what mental state, if any, parallels it.

(2) The parallelism is many/one in the direction from physiological to mental states. This corresponds to the following schema: The physiological state at time t is P_1 or P_2 or ... or P_n if and only if the mental state at t is M. Again, there is no ground for either solipsism or skepticism. For again, with the same qualification as in (1), we could always infer what is going on in another's mind from his physiological state.

(3) The parallelism is many/one in the direction from mental to physiological states. This corresponds to the schema: The physiological state at t is P if and only if the mental state at t is M_1 or M_2 or ... or M_n. Again, solipsism would not be a justified inference. As to how "skeptical" we would have to be as to what goes on in someone's mind, that depends clearly on the variable that is allowed by M_1, M_2 ... M_n. If it were in a certain case limited to, say, the intensity of an imagining, then less "skepticism" would be in order than in a case where, say, the species of a mental act (imagining, doubting, wondering, and so on) is left undetermined by the disjunction of the M's.

(4) The parallelism is many/many. This corresponds to the schema: The mental state is M_1 or M_2 or ... or M_n if and only if the physiological state, at the same time, is either P_1 or P_2 or ... or P_n. Solipsism is still unreasonable. And, again, the amount of "skepticism" called for depends on the case.

(5) The physical universe, including the physiological variables, is causally closed and forms a process. The connection between the physiological and the mental variables is of the kind that has been called historical; i.e., there are laws that "determine" the present mental state not, as in the case of parallelism, as a function of the present physiological state alone but rather, of one or several to-be-

with all but (7). It depends on whether the kind of laws referred to in (5) are taken to be the *only* lawful connections between mental and physiological states. If so, then (5) is compatible only with (6), and not with the strong "parallelistic" views of (1)–(4).

specified past physiological states as well.[6] Clearly, this sort of "historical" connection is a generalization of the idea of parallelism. Equally clearly, it can be shown that in this case, too, we could know both that there are other minds as well as what goes on in them. Indeed we often do guess what is presently going on in someone's mind from what he now says or does in conjunction with what we know of his past behavior (physiological state).

(6) Mind interacts with body; i.e., two bodies could be in exactly the same physiological state, yet the minds which, as one says, inhabit them, could be and in some cases are different, *and* this difference makes a difference for the future states of both minds and both bodies. In this case all depends on whether or not in observing my own mental and physiological states I discover that jointly they form a complete set of relevant variables for the system I am.[7] If they do, then it will at least not be unreasonable to suppose that other people, too, have minds. But I could not know what is going on in them. Thus skepticism would be justified. If one thinks that in this case we could still go by what people "say", let him remember first, that "saying" is behavior, and second, that for purposes of the argument references to behavior on the one hand and to physiological states on the other are interchangeable.

(7) Minds and bodies are neither parallel nor historically connected ("possibility" 5); nor do they interact ("possibility" 6). In this case even solipsism might not be wholly unreasonable and skepticism would surely be justified.

These are the seven "possibilities". Before turning to Ryle, three comments will help.

First. Upon one clear notion of determinism, both interactionism and parallelism are compatible with determinism. Determinism, however roughly, is the thesis that any state of the universe is wholly "computable" from any other state by means of process laws. Clearly, such "computability" does not depend on whether or not minds interact with their bodies. Thus those who wished to save "freedom" (non-determinism) by insisting on interactionism were misled. Or,

---

[6] This possibility and its consequences were specifically suggested to me by Professor Bergmann. Many of the notions in this section such as *interaction* and *process* are discussed in more detail in Bergmann's *Philosophy of Science*, University of Wisconsin Press, 1957. See also his "The Contribution of John B. Watson", *Psychological Review*, 63, 1956.

[7] Notice that as we defined the term, the use of 'interaction' presupposes that there is process. That makes the use of the word in the first sentence of (6) inaccurate, but the inaccuracy does no harm.

rather, they must have had different, albeit confused, notions of interaction and causation.

Second. It has been argued that if parallelism is true we are not "free". The idea seems to be that a mind which is "merely" parallel "makes no difference". This idea is mistaken. For, if a given mental state were other than it is, then on the very thesis of (strict) parallelism, its corresponding physiological state would be other than it is. In this sense my behavior *does* depend on my mental states and would be other than what it is if they were other than what they are.

Third. All the "possibilities" but (6) "save" physics. Let me explain. Physics is "saved" or, as I put it earlier, causally closed if, supposing it possible to find process, the properties which it *must* take into account to predict or postdict states of the physical universe are all physical, i.e., properties of physical things. (A physical thing, in this context, is anything from a star to an atom or an entity of quantum mechanics.) "Possibilities" (1) through (4) all suppose a parallelism such that although mind "makes a difference" in the sense explained and just recalled, we *needn't* take it into account in a way that makes physics causally incomplete (unclosed). On "possibility" (5) physics is causally closed. As (7) has been stated, it may or may not be. We simply did not need to commit ourselves. That leaves (6) as the only "possibility" upon which physics cannot be "saved".

We are ready to turn to Ryle.

Ryle on Mind and Body

Ryle believes that the dualist is committed to (6) above. Or perhaps I should say that (6) is the only one of the "possibilities" which fits with what Ryle has to say about dualism. That is, only (6) supposes interaction and has skepticism and possibly solipsism as its consequences. This we saw already. I have in effect conducted my argument by simply spelling out the "possibilities" which permit one consistently to hold, first, that there are both minds and bodies and, second, to deny that they interact. I should add that one who consistently holds those doctrines can account for everything which needs to be accounted for. But I shall not argue that right now. Rather, I want to inquire why Ryle believes that any dualist either is committed to (6) or at any rate would want to hold (6) as a complement to his dualism. There are two reasons. One is rather uninteresting; the other is more revealing. Let me dispose of the uninteresting one first.

Ryle throughout his philosophical career has had a propensity to oversimplify the motives, structural as well as historical, which have led philosophers to make certain claims. Apparently he believes that the only reason philosophers have said there are minds is to find or "posit" a *cause* of intelligent behavior. He also believes seemingly, that once that motive is removed one will no longer be tempted to believe in minds (in the traditional sense). Hence it seems to him that inter-actionism is an intrinsic part of the view which is dualism. Here are two texts to support these assertions about Ryle.

Transactions between minds and bodies involve links where no links can be. That there should be any causal transactions between minds and matter conflicts with one part, that there should be none conflicts with another part of the theory. Minds, as the whole legend describes them, are what must exist if there is to be a causal explanation of the intelligent behaviour of human bodies; and minds, as the legend describes them, live on a floor of existence defined as being outside the causal system to which bodies belong.[8]

He [Descartes] had mistaken the logic of his problem. Instead of asking by what criteria intelligent behaviour is actually distinguished from non-intelligent behaviour, he asked 'Given that the principle of mechanical causation does not tell us the difference, what other causal principle will tell it us?'[9]

Insofar as the theory holds minds to be radically unlike bodies, it is committed to holding there are no causal connections between them. Yet that some mental events are causes of some physical events is the whole *raison d'être* of the theory. So thinks Ryle. Some of the confusions lurking here have already been discussed.

Parallelism, we saw, allows one to hold that the physical world is causally closed and yet avoid skepticism and solipsism. However, if one wishes, one could give a "causal" account of a piece of intelligent behavior by attending to the mental state parallel to the physical state immediately preceding it. Had this mental state not been there, the physical state would not have been what it was; hence, by the law of the parallelism, the piece of behavior to be accounted for would or may well have been different. Hence, if some dualist does want to account for intelligent behavior in terms of mental events, he still need not be an interactionist. It follows that Ryle is wrong in believing that only (6) can satisfy what he takes to be the very *raison d'être* of dualism. The claim that there *can* be no causal links between mind and body – including, we may suppose, the "causal" link of parallelism – I shall consider later.[10] Let us move on to what I called to more reveal-ing reason for Ryle's belief that the dualist is committed to (6).

[8] CM, p. 66.
[9] CM, p. 21.
[10] See p. 54.

Ryle has two notions of cause, one explicit, one implicit. The explicit notion is connected with his invention of the "inference-ticket". The implicit one is embedded in the ontology which I have ascribed to him. My argument will proceed as follows: Ryle's explicit notion of cause is, roughly, Humean. His implicit notion is Aristotelian. When criticizing dualism on the basis of its alleged interactionism and subsequent skepticism, he falls back on the Aristotelian notion. This accounts for his inability to see the alternatives to (6) proposed above. If I am right, what will be said further supports the claim that Ryle's implicit ontology is what it was said to be in the first two chapters.

His *explicit* philosophy of causation, if I may so express myself, is Humean to this extent: he doesn't suppose that the word 'cause' refers to anything above and beyond the two or several events said to be causally connected. Indeed he believes that it is a category-mistake to suppose otherwise:

> But to speak as if the discovery of a law were the finding of a third, unobservable existence is simply to fall back into the old habit of construing open hypothetical statements as singular categorical statements.[11]

Ryle, we know, thinks of a law as an "inference-ticket", a rule which allows one to "move" from one particular state of affairs to another. For example, if I know that John has leukemia, my "inference-ticket" that all who have leukemia die shortly warrants me in believing that John will die shortly. I am not here interested in either endorsing or criticizing this notion of law-statements; rather, I am anxious to show, and believe to have shown, that in his explicit notion of cause Ryle has no use for any such entities as "powers" or "necessary connections". In what follows, then, it is *not* being argued that Ryle does not explicitly hold this "Humean" view.

Substances, the tradition held, have natures and accidents. The substance is thought of as *producing* its accidents. Substances are active, have a force or thrust. The activities of substances, their doings, *create* their accidents. A kind of doing or activity (or the disposition to it) is part of the nature of a substance. A substance generating its own accidents is a case of what was known as *immanent causality*.

Some philosophers have held that substances can produce effects in others. Starting from the ordinary fact that, for example, when John hits Dick in the eye, it is John and not Dick who is (causally) responsible for Dick's subsequent discoloration, it was supposed that immanent causality is not sufficient to explain the facts. Hence

[11] CM, p. 122.

transeunt causality, the thrust of one substance producing accidents in another, was introduced by some philosophers into the substance metaphysics. Leibniz, among others, held that a substance ontology cannot countenance transeunt causality.

Why have substance philosophers always felt uneasy about transeunt causality? The reasons are several, some deeper than others. The deepest is probably this: the very model of explanation on such a scheme is an appeal to the nature of the thing undergoing change. Within this kind of metaphysics it is therefore "counterstructural" or *ad hoc* to explain a change in one substance by appealing to another substance or to its nature.

Furthermore, transeunt causality seemed to involve action at a distance. A substance and its accidents were thought to be somehow (spatially) contiguous in a way in which no two substances are; that is why it seemed the thrust of a substance can produce only its own accidents. The problem becomes especially acute when it is claimed that substances which are not even in space, i.e., minds, can "affect" substances in space, i.e., bodies. Even if transeunt causality between or among substances, all of which are in space, can be made plausible, it would seem that such causality between or among substances, some of which are and some of which are not in space, is too much to ask. Hence transeunt causality, particularly between mental and physical substances, is dialectically suspect within a substance ontology.

Consider now the following criticism of mind/body dualism as made by Ryle:

According to the theory, the workings of the body are motions of matter in space. The causes of these motions must then be *either* other motions of matter in space *or*, in the privileged case of human beings, thrusts of another kind. In some way which must forever remain a mystery, mental thrusts, which are not movements of matter in space, can cause muscles to contract.[12]

Remember his ontology along with his notion of "explanation" of human behavior. There are substances with dispositions to act. To "explain" a piece of (normal) human behavior one appeals to the nature of the substance, i.e., to some disposition or other to act in that way. Here overt behavior is treated as the tradition treated accidents. Ryle, to be sure, explicitly denies that this is a causal explanation. Of course it isn't, at least not on the most important contemporary notion of cause. Yet he is by his ontology and by his notion of the

12 CM, pp. 63-64.

proper "explanation" of at least human behavior implicitly committed to this historically important notion of cause.

My point can now be made quickly. Unconsciously, but consistently with his ontology, Ryle in his rejection of dualism as implying interactionism falls back on the Aristotelian notion of cause. His "real" argument proceeds as follows: (a) If there are minds, then they are the causes of behavior. (b) Transeunt causality ("interaction") is ontologically impossible between (if not any two substances) two substances one of which is and one of which is not in space. (c) If *per impossibile* there were such causality between spatial and non-spatial substances, physics would be impossible and skepticism and solipsism reign triumphant.[13] Now we can see why Ryle imagines the dualist to be committed to (6). For the "possibilities" (1) through (5) all require some kind of parallelism in order to avoid skepticism, and the idea of parallelism is indeed structurally alien to a substance ontology.

I say "structurally alien" because, strictly, there is no contradiction. Even in a world of substances there could be pairs of substances whose properties are parallel without cross-thrusting in either direction. But, then, the very idea of such "mere correlation" is the very essence of Humean "causation". Structurally that is the point. As to Ryle, we see that his implicit commitment to Aristotle is, at this point at least, much deeper than his explicit Humean orthodoxy. Otherwise why would he have "overlooked" the five "Humean" possibilities?

The lesson to draw from all this is that as long as one works with an anthropomorphic (voluntaristic) notion of cause, the mind/body problem will remain a mystery. Hence we have the odd doctrines of Descartes (pituitary glandism), Malbranche (occasionalism), and Leibniz (pre-established harmony). The solution of the problem requires the rejection of that notion of cause which traditionally goes with substance ontologies. Ryle, blinded by the insuperable difficulties of the substance ontology, attributes some of them to dualism. Thus he remains committed to an ontology which cannot adequately account for mind and its place in nature. Thus he is faced with a dilemma. He must either give up his implicit ontology or give up mind. As we know, he gave up mind.

---

[13] Again if someone wishes to maintain that in no case are substances in either space or time, the arguments can be applied *mutatis mutandis* to their activities.

Passmore's Objections to Parallelism

Since I have committed myself to parallelism, I should probably spell it out in more detail. Also I must take up a matter which was left dangling earlier in this chapter. Passmore's objections to parallelism provide a handy way of doing both these things. Here is what he says:

> Notwithstanding appearances, the parallelist argues, there is in fact no inter-action between the mental and the non-mental, for such an interaction is ontologically impossible. Mental events and non-mental events belong to two distinct series, even although the series run parallel to one another. But what does 'parallel' mean here? Not that certain events in the one series are *like* events in the other; this has been ruled out in advance. Nor that they occur in the same place, for the same reason. The only possible parallelism is a temporal one; certain events in the mental series occur at the same time as, or prior to, or subsequent to, certain events in the non-mental series. But this relation is not close enough to do justice to the admitted facts. Events in my mind are related temporally to all sorts of events, inside and outside my body; what 'parallelism' fails to explain is the *special* relation between what goes on in my brain and what goes on in my mind.[14]

Several points are made in this passage. The two I wish to discuss are (1) that interaction is *ontologically impossible* and (2) that the parallelistic connection is *not intimate enough* to account for the facts.

As to (1): *I* have not argued that interaction is ontologically impossible. Some dualists have indeed argued that. They were also substantialists. Whether parallelism is true or not is not an *a priori* question. Nor is parallelism quite a scientific theory. It is, rather, as one says, the frame of reference of modern science, in particular, of modern psychology. As far as I am concerned one's ontology should therefore be able to accommodate the possibility of either parallelism or interactionism. Passmore thinks the parallelist must hold that inter-action is ontologically impossible, because (a) like Ryle, he thinks of everybody as at least an implicit substantialist and because (b) the only good reason a substantialist can give for rejecting interaction is the "ontological impossibility" of transeunt causation.

Nor have I argued that mind and body are ontologically unlike each other. Both consist of individuals exemplifying properties. In this sense they are ontologically similar. How, then, it may be asked, do mind and body differ? Are "mental" and "bodily" individuals really two kinds of things? Yes, they are two kinds, but not, as I speak, two *ontological* kinds. Rather, they are distinguished by the fact that "mental" individuals exemplify certain properties not exemplified

[14] John Passmore, *Philosophical Reasoning*, Charles Scribner's Sons, 1961, pp. 55–56.

by "bodily" ones and vice versa. The most important of these properties have to do with space, time, and intentionality.

As to (2): In order to understand why Passmore makes his point
the way he does, it is necessary to call attention to a characteristic
difference between the modern and the Aristotelian notions of cause.
Unlike the Aristotelian notion, the modern one is closely linked with
that of lawfulness. The source of this difference is not hard to find.
On the Aristotelian notion, a cause is an entity (whether it is being
given explicit ontological status is beside the point) which appears in
a particular situation. Thus no appeal to law, either implicit or explicit, is required when, thinking in this fashion, one says *this* caused
that. The modern notion of cause is completely bound up with that of
law. For to say that A *caused* B rather than merely preceded it is to say
that things of *kind* A always precede things of *kind* B. A cause, that is,
is not another entity in addition to the things succeeding each other.
Nor need the temporal connection be one of succession, of course; it
may as well be one of co-existence. That enables us to handle
Passmore's objection.

Of course mental states are temporally parallel to all kinds of events.
What the parallelist says is that mental states are *lawfully* parallel
only to certain physiological states. This not very subtle point escapes
Passmore altogether. The only way I can account for his failure is to
suppose that, falling back on the Aristotelian notion of cause, he is
struck by the fact that the parallelist has no further *entities*, in addition to the parallel mental and physiological states. In this respect
my mind and my body are no more intimately connected than the
former and, say, the Gulf of Mexico.[15] That intimacy, what Passmore
calls "the *special* relation between what goes on in my brain and what
goes on in my mind", which he feels the parallelist has ignored, then,
is, we see, the *lawful* connection. Nor need I repeat that the parallelist
has not only not ignored it, but that it is the very heart of his position.[16]

Consider two identical mental states M_1 and M_2 and their parallel
physiological states P_1 and P_2 respectively, all occurring at the same
moment. Since there are no spatial relations between the M's and the
P's, on what grounds should we say that M_1 "attaches" to P_1 and M_2
to P_2 rather than the other way around? This is the problem to which
I referred twice. The cue to the answer is in the paragraph above, that

---

[15] Like Ryle, Passmore is arguing from a substantialist metaphysics to materialist con-
clusions. I have not supported this with quotes from the text, but the relevant passages can
be found in the chapter from *Philosophical Reasoning* entitled "The Two-Worlds Argument".

[16] I am not speaking historically, of course.

is, in the notion of lawfulness. M_1 "attaches" to P_1 rather than to P_2 since of the following two statements (1) is *as a matter of fact* true and (2) is *as a matter of fact* false:

(1) If P_1 were different, M_1 would be different.

(2) If P_2 were different (but P_1 the same), then M_1 would be different. The point is again that the notion of a "causal" connection makes no sense without the notion of law. (I put 'causal' between double quotes because some may wish to reserve the word for the connection between successive rather than coexistent events.) I conclude, not that parallelism is true (although I believe it to be) but, rather, that there are no philosophical or phenomenological reasons why it cannot be true, Ryle and Passmore to the contrary notwithstanding.

Ryle and Passmore suffer from the same delusion. Arguing *from* a substance ontology, they shortly discover its limitations, in particular, the insuperable difficulties the dualistic thesis encounters within it. At this point, rather than rejecting the ontology, they erroneously reject dualism. This error I believe to have exposed.

PART TWO

The other main argument Ryle offers in order to show that there are no mental entities in the traditional sense [17] makes use of an alleged infinite regress of awarenesses. There are actually three arguments, but they are sufficiently similar to justify grouping them together as three variants of one. Yet it will be helpful to give them separate names. So I shall speak of (1) the causal variant, (2) the direct awareness variant, and (3) the introspection variant, taking them up in this order and trying to show that, severally as well as jointly, they are incapable of supporting the conclusion Ryle draws from them.

The Causal Variant

Let us first look at the text:

The crucial objection to the intellectualist legend is this. The consideration of propositions is itself an operation the execution of which can be more or less intelligent, less or more stupid. But if, for any operation to be intelligently executed, a prior theoretical operation had first to be performed and performed intelligently, it would be a logical impossibility for anyone ever to break into the circle.[18]

---

[17] It isn't clear that the conclusion is always supposed to be that radical. At the least, though, the arguments are supposed to "tell" against mental entities.

[18] CM, p. 30.

The dualist (intellectualist), we see, is alleged to hold that any overt intelligent operation must be either preceded or accompanied by some "theoretical" operation such as, say, the consideration of a proposition. But any such "theoretical" operation may be carried out intelligently or unintelligently; and only in the former case can it give rise to an intelligent overt operation. The first-order "theoretical" operation must therefore in turn be either preceded or accompanied by a second-order "theoretical" operation, and so on *ad infinitum*. Hence, if the "intellectualist legend" were true, it would be impossible for any intelligent operation ever to occur.

Ryle's placing so much stock in this argument [19] is due to an error we encountered already. He believes erroneously that the only motive the dualist has for adopting his position is the desire to give a causal account of intelligent human behavior. Clearly, neither the parallelist nor, for that matter, any other dualist needs to hold that every item of overt behavior, intelligent or otherwise, is "caused" by a mental act. Nor need he hold that *every* mental act, intelligent or otherwise, is caused by another such act. But he can consistently hold that *some* items of overt behavior are, in a certain sense, "caused" by mental acts. This sense I have just explained in Part One. So I shall not rehearse it while explicitly refuting Ryle's argument.

His argument stands or falls with the assumption that the "intelligence" of every mental act must be accounted for in the same way the "intelligence" of some pieces of behavior are accounted for. The "intelligence" of the latter is, on the view under consideration, accounted for by their being caused by acts. As for items of overt behavior so for acts. Not every intelligent act need be caused by another. Or, still more strongly, even if, as the dualist need not hold, *every* item of intelligent overt behavior were caused by an act of a certain kind, it would not follow that acts need in turn by caused by further mental acts.[20] For, to suppose that 'intelligent' as applied to pieces of behavior and to mental acts must "mean" the same thing is to suppose in part that pieces of behavior and mental acts are the same kind of thing or, rather, as in Ryle's case, that the latter are a species of the former. But this is exactly what is at issue. We do, as we ordinarily speak, call certain items of behavior "intelligent" even

<hr />

[19] He devotes a whole chapter of *The Concept of Mind* to the argument. That chapter is based heavily on an earlier paper of his, "Knowing How and Knowing That", *Proceedings of the Aristotelian Society*, Vol. XLVI, Harrison and Sons, Ltd., 1946.

[20] Passmore considers this reply in *Philosophical Reasoning*, pp. 25–28. He neither accepts nor rejects the argument.

if they are not either caused or accompanied by acts. This is, of course, the sense in which we speak of the intelligence which "resides" in the fingers of a skilled mechanic even on occasions where he performs rather automatically. Now if Ryle insists on making the dualist use 'intelligent' so that this sort of behavior could not be "intelligent", then all he does is quibble about words.

The Direct Awareness Form of the Argument

Finally, even though the self-intimation supposed to be inherent in any mental state or process is not described as requiring a separate act of attention, or as constituting a separate cognitive operation, still what I am conscious of in a process of inferring, say, is different from what the inferring is an apprehension of. My consciousness is of a process of inferring, but my inferring is, perhaps, of a geometrical conclusion from geometrical premisses. The verbal expression of my inference might be, 'because this is an equilateral triangle, therefore each angle is 60 degrees', but the verbal expression of what I am conscious of might be 'Here I am deducing such and such from so and so'. But, if so, then it would seem to make sense to ask whether, according to the doctrine, I am not also conscious of being conscious of inferring, that is, in a position to say 'Here I am spotting the fact that here I am deducing such and such from so and so'. And then there would be no stopping-place; there would have to be an infinite number of onion-skins of consciousness embedding any mental state or process whatsoever. If this conclusion is rejected, then it will have to be allowed that some elements in mental processes are not themselves things we can be conscious of, namely those elements which constitute the supposed outermost self-intimations of mental processes; and then 'conscious' could no longer be retained as part of the definition of 'mental'.[21]

The hesitation with which Ryle puts this argument shows his doubts about its sufficiency. He first argues that claiming one can be aware of mental acts (in the traditional sense) commits one to holding that there are an infinite number of awarenesses [22] in any given mental state. This conclusion, he suggests, may reasonably be rejected. But then he goes on to argue that a dualist who does reject it is still in trouble. For there is, according to Ryle, something problematic even in the weaker claim that a mental state contains a *finite* number of awarenesses. This alleged difficulty has something to do with the notion of "mental", so we had better look into it.

I want to insist on two things: (1) There is *direct awareness* of mental acts. (2) Every mental state contains only a finite and never an infinite number of awarenesses. So I shall not take issue with the starting point of Ryle's argument. Sometimes we are aware of trees, of people, and so on. Sometimes we are also aware of our awarenesses of trees,

[21] CM, pp. 162–163.
[22] I use 'awareness' to mean any mental act, e.g., a perceiving, a wondering, a direct awareness, and so on.

of people, and so on. Ryle's argument collapses at the next step, though. He asks whether it makes sense to say of an awareness that it is the object of another. The answer is that it *makes sense* to say of any awareness that it is or can be the object of another awareness. This, though, is *one* thing. It is quite *another* thing to say that for an awareness to be an awareness, i.e., for my "having" it, I must also, in the same sense, "have" a further one. Ryle's argument would be valid if this second proposition were true. Since it isn't, the argument is in trouble. This, as I suggested, Ryle seems to sense. For his next step is to argue that there is something absurd in supposing that there are a *finite* number of awarenesses in a mental state. This absurdity is supposed to stem from the fact that "in" any given mental state there will be some awareness of which one is not aware.

Let us look at the alleged absurdity. The "outermost" awareness of the state in question is not itself the intention of an awareness of that state. But then, this is absurd only if for an awareness to be "had" it must be the intention of a further awareness which is also "had". Or, still more strongly, assume that for an awareness to be "had", i.e., for there to be a mental state or a consciousness, there must be another awareness whose intention it is but which need not be and indeed often is not itself "had" at the same time. Even in this case there would be nothing absurd about the "outermost" awareness being "had".

The Introspection Form of the Argument

Ryle properly distinguishes introspection from direct awareness, although he doesn't draw the distinction the way I shall draw it. Begin again with a text:

Now supposing . . . that there did exist events of the postulated ghostly status, there would still be objections to the initially plausible assumption that there also exists a species of perception capable of having any of these events for its proprietary objects. For one thing, the occurrence of such an act of inner perception would require that the observer could attend to two things at the same time.[23]

However, even if it is claimed that in introspecting we are attending twice at once, it will be allowed that there is some limit to the number of possible synchronous acts of attention, and from this it follows that there must be some mental processes which are unintrospectible, namely those introspections which incorporate the maximum possible number of synchronous acts of attention. The question would then arise for the holders of the theory how these acts would be found occurring, since if this knowledge was not introspectively got, it would follow that a person's knowledge of his own mental processes could not always

[23] CM, p. 164.

be based on introspection. But if this knowledge does not always rest on introspection, it is open to question whether it ever does.[24]

Since Ryle distinguishes introspection so-called from direct awareness, I presume he is talking about what psychologists used to call
introspection or "introspective analysis". Classical psychology saw its
task as discovering the "atoms" or "elements" of the mind, or,
rather, of conscious states. This task was to be achieved, if at all, by
what they called introspection. The idea was that one was to hold
before the mind, as it were, a conscious state and say what he there
discovered. That one can literally do this presupposes that he can
"hold on" to a conscious state while calmly and dispassionately
"analyzing" it. Ryle claims that no such events ever occur. I agree.

The classical psychologists' notion of introspection is muddled
indeed. This is one thing. If one wishes, one can so state it that the
muddle disappears.[25] Modern psychologists are not very much interested in introspection, nor therefore in clarifying the notion. Some
psychologists, i.e., the Watsonians, even were materialists. One can
consistently hold (1) that there are mental acts and (2) that the classical
psychologists' notion of introspection was muddled. Conversely, it is
an obvious factual and logical error to hold that the classical introspective psychology "failed" because there are no minds to introspect.
I am not sure whether or not Ryle is prepared to argue this way. The
text quoted suggests that he is. If he is, then he is mistaken. For one
may agree with him, as I do, that "analytical introspection" as conceived by the classical psychologist does not exist and yet consistently
hold, as I also do, that we are directly aware of our acts. When I
remember, I am aware of my remembering; when I imagine, I know
that I imagine, and so on.

I conclude, then, that Ryle has not only failed to establish his
"positive" view; he has also failed to show that dualism is false. At
best he has shown that certain forms of dualism, in particular those
found in substance ontologies, are, if not false, at least irremediably
confused. It is now time for us to find those features of his early thought
which eventually led him to adopt the doctrines of *The Concept of
Mind*. That is the task of the next two chapters.

[24] CM, p. 165.
[25] For more details, see Bergmann's "The Problem of Relations in Classical Psychology",
The Philosophical Quarterly, 7, April, 1952, and reprinted in his *The Metaphysics of Logical
Positivism*, Longmans, Green and Co., 1954. See also his "The Contribution of John B.
Watson" referred to in footnote 6 above.

IV. THE EARLY ONTOLOGY AND THE ATTACK
ON REPRESENTATIONALISM

In this chapter and the next I shall show how Ryle's early thought may have led him to the materialism of the book. More specifically, I propose to show that his early ontology and conception of mind contain the seeds of the eventual rejection of mind. In order to clarify the nature of the task I am setting myself, two comments will be helpful.

First. I am not concerned with Ryle's intellectual biography. Our attention, rather, will be directed to the actual and apparent connections of ideas. Nor am I engaged in mere history of ideas, for I shall try to separate the actual from the merely apparent connections.

Second. It may be objected that Ryle is quite clear why he is a materialist; after all, that is the main *raison d'être* of *The Concept of Mind*. Furthermore, as we shall see, the "reasons" I shall produce for his materialism are quite unrelated to those given in the book. To this I have two answers: one logical, one historical. (1) The reasons or arguments Ryle actually adduces in his book will convince only those already committed to materialism. Nor are they arguments that could have moved Ryle himself to change his position so radically from what it once was. (2) His drift toward materialism is apparent long before the appearance of the book (1949), in particular in the behavioristic analyses to be found in "Conscience and Moral Convictions" (1940)[1] and "Knowing How and Knowing That" (1945).[2] Thus the "explanation" of Ryle's materialism cannot be found in the book itself. It is of course assumed that his thought hangs to gether in an intelligible manner, that there is such an "explanation" to be found. For this assumption I need not and shall not argue. Our task then may be described as an attempt to find what it was in his early thought that allowed, tempted, or even forced Ryle eventually to deny the existence of minds.

There are two features of the world which it is not the proper task of philosophy to question, but rather to account for. They are (1) that there are (exist) objects, call them non-minds, which in no way depend for their existence or nature on minds or their activities; and (2) that there are objects of another kind, minds, which have knowledge

---

[1] Ryle "Conscience and Moral Convictions", *Analysis*, Vol. 7, No. 2, 1940. Some of Ryle's articles were public lectures read at a date earlier than that of publication. In these cases the date given in my text is that of the lecture.

[2] Ryle, "Knowing How and Knowing That", *Proceedings of the Aristotelian Society*, Vol. XLVI, Harrison and Sons, Ltd., 1946.

of non-minds. Whoever denies (1) is an idealist; whoever denies (2) is a materialist. Since idealism maintains that there are two kinds of objects, minds and non-minds, it is, I should want to claim, less absurd than materialism. It is more plausible to say that the objects of knowledge – chairs, people, electrons – in some way have their being in our awareness of them than to say that there is no awareness. And the reason for that is, I suppose, that the existence of something is ordinarily more obvious than its ontological (or logical or causal) status. Idealism is a view about the *status* of certain kinds of objects which, in agreement with commonsense, the idealist asserts to be there; materialism falsely denies the very *existence* of a certain kind of object which commonsense asserts (and phenomenology affirms) to be there.[3]

To (1) Ryle has always been committed. Though he once believed (2), he does no longer, as we know. Indeed, to show the falsehood of (2) is the task of *The Concept of Mind*. Ironically enough, it was partly his belief in (1) that led to a weakening of his belief in (2). How this could happen we shall see later. That he *once* believed in (2) I have not yet substantiated; that will also be shown later. That he never denied (1) I have not and shall not substantiate except to quote from his earliest work:

... I cannot allow that an investigation of the purposes and technique of our intellectual operations can ever afford an answer to questions about the formal or categorial properties of facts.[4]

In short, idealism was never a viable alternative to Ryle's mind. The importance of that statement for my strategy will shortly emerge.

A philosopher who (correctly) accepts both (1) and (2) is a realist. But there are realists and realists. Call such things as chairs, trees, people, electrons, and stars the "objects of knowledge". Take a situation in which Jones sees a tree. There are two relevant analyses of this situation: (1) It may be held that Jones' seeing the tree *consists entirely* of Jones' having an awareness of some object which *represents* the tree. The representing objects may or may not be "in" the mind, depending on the philosopher in question. If it is, the tradition calls it (following Locke and Descartes) an *idea*. If the representing object is *not* "in" the mind, it has been variously called an Idea, a proposition, an objective truth. I shall call all such views *representative realism*. If the view is that the representing object is "in" the mind, I shall

---

[3] Of course Ryle would never *say* that there are no minds. When I say there are minds, I mean in part that there are non-physical objects.

[4] Ryle, "Negation", *Knowledge, Experience and Realism*, Aristotelian Society, Supplementary Volume IX, Harrison and Sons, Ltd., 1929, p. 82.

call it *internal* representative realism; if not "in" the mind, *external* representative realism.

(2) It may be held that Jones' seeing the tree has as a constituent an act the intention of which is the tree. This act may be said to be the only constituent of the state of affairs described as Jones' seeing the tree. Or it may be held that the situation consists of an awareness of some object other than the tree (e.g., a constituent of the tree, or sense data, or a tree percept) *and* of some act the intention of which is the tree. I shall call all such views *direct realism*. The direct realist thus *need not* hold that the "objects of knowledge" are objects of *direct awareness*. He *may* hold there to be such awareness only of some object which might reasonably be said to *represent* the "object of knowledge". What distinguishes the direct from the representative realist is that the former does not hold awareness to consist entirely of awareness of representing objects; rather he insists that there are some acts which have trees, chairs, and so on as their intentions, immediately, so to speak.

Put this way, representative realism is seen to be the nonsense it is; not just because of the familiar epistemological difficulties nor those of making sense of representation; but because it simply fails to explain what it means to explain; because it denies that there are acts which have the "objects of knowledge" as their intentions. One also sees how at least internal representative realism cannot but eventually lead to explicit idealism, since its analysis of the act is implicitly idealistic to begin with.

Ryle's early view is, on the whole, a kind of direct realism. I shall document that only in the next chapter, where that view is at issue. That doctrine, or at least so Ryle came to believe, contains fundamental and insoluble difficulties. The only way he could retain both (1) and (2), then, was to accept some form of *representative* realism. Indeed he seemed to believe that representative realism would solve those difficulties of direct realism which he thought, correctly or otherwise, to be insoluble. Yet he could not accept representative realism. To understand why he could not accept it is the *second* of the two main tasks of this chapter.

We know already that Ryle was never drawn toward idealism. It is outside his tradition in a sense in which neither materialism nor realism are outside of it. This claim I shall not argue for; I take it to be a well-known historical fact. I shall take it, then, that if we understand why Ryle could not accept either direct or representative realism, we shall *ipso facto* understand why he fell into materialism, provided only that materialism does not contain the same difficulties which he believed the realisms to contain. In other words, I need not and shall not also show why under these conditions Ryle did not embrace idealism rather than materialism. As it happens, *some* of the structural (ontological) considerations which tell against representative realism, particularly against internal representative realism, also tell against idealism.

The *first* main task of this chapter is to uncover, to state clearly, and finally to dissect the *early ontology*. By "the early ontology" I mean the more or less explicit ontology of the period 1929–1939. The first date is that of Ryle's first published work; the other that of the last piece in which he does explicit ontology, "Plato's 'Parmenides'". In 1940 Ryle began the behavioristic analysis of mind in "Conscience and Moral Convictions"; he has never since done ontology explicitly.

My purpose in investigating the early ontology is threefold. (1) It is intrinsically interesting and will enable me to make some dialectical points, in particular against nominalism. (2) It will help us to understand why, structurally (ontologically), Ryle could not accept representative realism. (3) It will connect certain of his early ideas with those of *The Concept of Mind*. Thus I shall first examine the ontology as such; secondly, I shall discuss what we may call Ryle's epistemological reasons for rejecting representative realism; thirdly, I shall show how the early ontology could be thought to conflict with representative realism; finally, I shall exhibit some direct connections between the early ontology and that of *The Concept of Mind*.

Ryle's Early Ontology

If I were asked to characterize Ryle's early ontology in one sentence, I would say that it is a world of substances, which do "exist", and of attributes, which do not "exist". 'Exist' I put between double quotes because the use is philosophical. 'Substance' and 'attribute', too, are philosophical terms. On 'exist' I commented before. The view I hold is that 'exist' is univocal in that it has only one commonsensical meaning. This one meaning is also fundamental, cannot be further "explained". To exist, in this sense, is to be there (where 'there' must not be taken spatially). In this sense, there are (exist) properties, numbers, armies, facts, individuals, and so on. The classical ontologist often limits (and occasionally perhaps extends) the realm of what commonsense asserts to exist. Philosophers thus work with special "meanings" of 'exist', thereby creating the several ontological patterns. Ryle does not see the crucial distinction between the ordinary and the philosophical uses of words. That is why he is at times forced to say curious things. This we shall see presently.

In "Are There Propositions?" (1930) there is a minor ontological pattern which may seem to support nominalism. It is the localization pattern (only what is in space and time "exists"). Speaking of "objective truths", Ryle says:

Certainly they do not *exist;* for they are not things in time.[5]

A second, more crucial, pattern emerges in "Systematically Misleading Expressions" (1932):

To put it roughly, *"x* exists" and *"x* does not exist" do not assert or deny that a given subject of attributes *x* has the attribute of existing, but assert or deny the attribute of being *x*-ish or being an *x* of something not named in the statement.[6]

This theme, which we may call the *subject* pattern (only what has properties "exists"), becomes clearer in later papers. In "Imaginary Objects" (1933) we are told:

Rather, though this is again misleading, a thing's being real or being an entity or being an object just consists in the fact that it has attributes.[7]

It is misleading since "really":

To say of something that it is an object or that it exists is to say nothing at all; we are *showing* that it is an object or that it exists when we say of it that it is green or a grandfather or irritated.[8]

From "Phenomenology" (1932) we discover that only *substances* fulfill the qualifications, that to "exist" is to be a subject of attributes and that only substances have attributes. Speaking of Husserl, Ryle says:

... it becomes very hard to see in what sense he holds that "intentional objects" really are genuine objects or subjects of attributes at all.[9]

[5] Ryle, "Are There Propositions?", *Proceedings of the Aristotelian Society*, Vol. XXX, Harrison and Sons, Ltd., 1930, p. 97. Hereafter referred to as ATP.

[6] Ryle, "Systematically Misleading Expressions", *Proceedings of the Aristotelian Society*, Vol. XXXII, Harrison and Sons, Ltd., 1932, p. 145. Hereafter referred to as SME.

[7] Ryle, "Imaginary Objects", *Creativity, Politics and the A Priori*, Aristotelian Society, Supplementary Volume XII, Harrison and Sons, Ltd., 1933, p. 20.

[8] *Ibid.*, p. 20.

[9] Ryle, "Phenomenology", *Phenomenology, Goodness and Beauty*, Aristotelian Society, Supplementary Volume XI, Harrison and Sons, Ltd., 1932, p. 79. Hereafter referred to as Phen.

Furthermore, properties are not themselves subjects of attributes:

I do not myself believe that phrases such as "being a so and so," "being such and such" and "that so and so is such and such" do denote objects or subjects of attributes. For I don't think that they are denoting expressions at all.[10]

Another ontological notion, intimately connected with the subject pattern, is that of elementarism. According to this notion, only substances and their properties "exist", but not properties of properties. Properties are never themselves subjects of attributes. Thus in a narrower and for Ryle more important sense of "exist", only substances "exist". To treat something as a *substance*, then, is to treat it as if it had properties, i.e., as if it "existed". Such a treatment of relations (and thus of space and time) would, he believed, lead to antinomies.

... and just as Kant shows in a similar way that antinomies arise from treating, *e.g.*, Space and Time, as substances; and just as Bradley shows that antinomies arise from treating relations as substances, so, I imagine, it could be shown that antinomies arise from treating propositions as substances.[11]

Ryle tries to show us how we may have been misled into thinking that properties have properties. With a few ill-chosen examples he makes his case seem plausible. For instance:

Nor when we say "unpunctuality is reprehensible" do we really suppose that unpunctuality ought to be ashamed of itself.

. . . .

What we do mean is what is also meant but better expressed by "Whoever is unpunctual deserves that other people should reprove him for being unpunctual." [12]

He then concludes:

It is my own view that all statements which seem to be "about universals" are analysable in the same way, and consequently that general terms are never really the names of subjects of attributes. So "universals" are not objects in the way in which Mt. Everest is one, and therefore the age-old question what *sort* of objects they are is a bogus question.[13]

I would agree, negatively, that universals are not the sort of objects Mt. Everest is. But, then, that only makes it imperative for the ontologist to say, positively, what sort of objects they are. Only the aberrations of nominalism could make a philosopher insensitive to this imperative and, therefore, prone to say what Ryle says.

Notice also that, albeit with some embarrassment, he uses the word

[10] *Ibid.*, p. 73.
[11] ATP, pp. 110–111.
[12] SME, p. 150.
[13] *Ibid.*, p. 151.

'universals' rather than 'properties'. I shall argue that he always confused the ordinary properties of things (attributes) with Platonic universals. Another passage will also show that confusion.

There are several sorts of entities in this [third] realm.
(a) There are universals.
(b) There are relations.
(c) There are numbers.
(d) There are objective truths and objective falsehoods or there are propositions.[14]

The third realm does not exist (or rather, none of its members do) for Ryle. The other two realms mentioned in this essay, both of which have existent members, are the physical and the mental. This shows that universals (and relations) are here treated as Platonic entities. This confusion between Platonic entities and the ordinary properties of things is, I shall shortly argue, the deepest source of Ryle's nominalism. The elementarism, which seems to support his nominalism is, as I shall show, in his case a result of the same confusion. First, though, it is important to establish firmly his distaste for, and distrust of, anything that sounds "abstract" or Platonic. There simply are no such entities, according to Ryle. In "Plato's 'Parmenides'" (1939) we read:

To enquire after the qualities, states, positions, sizes or relations of circularity or unity or civility is to ask a nonsensical question. Abstract nouns are not the names of entities ...[15]

(The passage also shows again the confusion of Platonic universals with the ordinary properties of things.) We recognize yet another, slightly different, ontological pattern, the *concreteness* pattern (only what is concrete "exists"). The following passage reveals how the anti-Platonism, the elementarism and the confusion of properties with "abstract" entities (I use 'entity' neutrally) are all fused together.

The most tempting reading of the position is that Plato realised or nearly realised that antinomies necessarily arise from the attempt to make any concept whatsoever (from the most specific to the most categorial) a subject of attributes. To assert or to deny that a concept does or does not exemplify itself or another concept is to assert something illegitimate, no matter what that concept may be. A quality or a relation neither has nor lacks any quality or relation. The name of a quality or relation cannot significantly occur as the subject of an attributive or relational sentence. Abstract nouns cannot assume the rôles of proper names or demonstratives.[16]

[14] ATP, p. 104.
[15] Ryle, "Plato's 'Parmenides'", published in two parts in *Mind*, Vol. 48, 1939, p. 139. Hereafter referred to as PP.
[16] *Ibid.*, p. 148.

It is worth noting Ryle's use of that most unfortunate word 'concept'. I shall argue later in this chapter that his ambiguous use of this word may have helped ease him into materialism. His nominalism is indubitable. There are in his world only substances. It will be worth our while, both in itself and for what comes later, to unravel the confused sources of this nominalism.

Attention has been called several times to the important distinction between the commonsense and the philosophical uses of 'exist'. It parallels another, viz., that between the commonsense notion of *property* and the philosophical one of *universal*. That things have properties is a commonsense truth. That properties are or "partake in" universals is a philosophical proposition. In the ordinary sense of 'property' and 'exist', there are of course properties, i.e., properties exist. Ryle's early ontology, I claimed earlier, was one of substances which do and of properties which do not "exist". How, then, did he come to think of properties as not "existing"? One cannot answer without first examining the two traditional notions of *universal*. Upon one of these notions, to say that there are universals is to say that, for example, the red in *this* apple and the red in *that* apple is (are) literally one and the same thing. Or, more accurately, this is what some philosophers meant by 'universal' even if they went on to deny that such entities "exist" (or exist). Call such an entity a universal$_1$.

On the other notion of *universal* to say that, for instance, red is a universal is not to say that the red in *this* and the red in *that* apple are literally one and not two, but rather, that these two entities (*this* red and *that* red) stand in some relation to or have some connection with yet a third entity, which relation or connection is the ontological ground of our calling them both red. This third entitiy we may call Red itself. Call such an entity a universal$_2$. Entities such as Red itself were conceived to be "outside" space and time and thus knowable only through a special act of the mind.[17] Furthermore, they were conceived to be "independent". That means that, for instance, Red itself can exist without anything's being red. The last three sentences constitute a partial explication of what was meant by calling universals so conceived "abstract". (Notice that a universal$_1$ is not abstract in the sense of being "independent". Whether or not it is in space and time does not matter for the purpose at hand.)

---

[17] There is a commonly accepted view that only what is in space and time is given to the senses. For a discussion of this view and its consequences, see Reinhardt Grossmann, "Sensory Intuition and the Dogma of Localization", *Inquiry*, Vol. 5, No. 3, Autumn 1962.

Failure to distinguish between these two notions of *universal* yields the following pattern of a fallacious argument for the doctrine that properties do not "exist": (1) To suppose that properties "exist" is to suppose that universals exist. (2) Universals are "abstract" entities. (3) "Abstract" entities don't exist. (4) Hence, properties don't "exist".[18] The argument is fallacious because universal is used ambiguously. The "universals" of (1) are universals$_1$, those of (2), universals$_2$. This error is facilitated by the fact that the properties of ordinary things on the one hand and the abstract entities on the other would have the same name. For example, 'red' would name *this* red and *that* red as well as Red itself.[19] Ryle, I suggested, was swayed by this pattern. If I am right, then his nominalism is at least in part a result of his rejection of "abstract" entities.

(1) Only substances "exist". (2) "Abstract" entities do not exist. It is important to see that (1) and (2) are not equivalent. For one may claim that properties are not in any sense abstract entities. Indeed the attributes of the classical substance-accident pattern are *not*, as I have explicated 'abstract', for they are in space and time as well as "dependent". To hold that there are universals$_2$ is to be a Platonist or an "exaggerated realist" or to hold the doctrine of separated universals. Clearly, one may reject both nominalism and Platonism. Ryle, I believe, conceives Platonism to be the only alternative to his nominalism. I expressed this belief in the last chapter. What has just been said shows my reason for believing it.

Let us look at the matter in another way. Consider the following four ontological "positions":

(1) Only substances exist.

(2) Substances and their properties exist. These properties are Aristotelian accidents.

(3) Substances and their properties exist. These properties are universals$_1$.

(4) At least substances and universals$_2$ exist.

Ryle starts with (2). This, however, or so he comes to believe, commits him to (4). So he ends up with (1). (3), I am convinced, never struck

---

[18] Note the use of 'exist' and '"exist"' in the last several sentences.

[19] Historically, nominalism is often connected with the doctrine of common names. Yet Ryle can be seen to reject this doctrine in the following way: Every name names one thing. Since *this* red and *that* red are two things, 'red' can't name either or both. Hence if 'red' is a name at all, it names a Platonic universal. But there are no Platonic entities. Hence 'red' is not a name. Ryle never seriously considers the possibility that *this* red and *that* red are one thing. This is probably in part because of what Grossmann calls the dogma of localization. See footnote 17.

him as a viable alternative to (2). Also, if one fails to distinguish between universals$_1$ and universals$_2$, then he will indeed feel that (2) commits him to (4), by way of (3), as it were. This is the best I can do by way of accounting for Ryle's obvious confusion, even to the point of apparent identification, of Platonic universals (universals$_2$) with the ordinary properties of things. Perhaps the reason he never seriously considered (3) is what Grossmann calls the "dogma of localization".[20] There is no doubt that this dogma influenced many other Aristotelians.

Ryle's elementarism provides another pattern by which one may arrive at his conclusion that only substances "exist". (1) Only substances have properties; properties themselves never have properties. (2) To "exist" is to be a subject of attributes. (3) Hence, only substances "exist". (We recall that in "Are There Propositions?" Ryle accuses some philosophers of making propositions into substances, by assigning qualities and relations to them.[21]) One may, of course, question whether (2) is an adequate "criterion" of existence. One may also wonder about (1). Why shouldn't properties have properties? The conviction that they can't is, to say the least, facilitated by failure to distinguish between the two kinds of universals.

To suppose that Platonic universals (universals$_2$) themselves have properties (accidents or universals$_1$) is paradoxical indeed.[22] One would merely "reproduce" the world of becoming without time in order to "explain" the world of becoming in time. To say the same thing differently, Platonic universals are introduced as part of an explanation how things in the world of becoming come to have properties. If so, one may rightly ask how Platonic universals manage to have properties. For, if they do, nothing is really explained. Ryle, alas, jumps from this sound piece of metaphysical analysis to the conclusion that the ordinary properties of things (accidents or universals$_1$) do not themselves have properties. Clearly, this is an unwarranted move. Equally clearly, it may result from the tendency to identify universals$_2$ with properties of individuals (accidents or universals$_1$). Ryle's elementarism, the "second" source of his nominalism, is thus merely another aspect of the first. Or, if you please, the second pattern rests on the first.

Relations, Russell has taught us, should be assigned the same ontological status as properties, whatever that status may be. In

---

[20] See footnote 17.
[21] See p. 66.
[22] This line of thought shows itself most clearly in PP.

Ryle's case we must nevertheless take special note of them if we are to exhaust the dialectics of our main topic, his philosophy of mind. We noted in other contexts that, according to Ryle, (1) relations are to be classed with universals, propositions, and other members of the non-existent third realm and (2) to treat relations as substances, i.e., as subjects of attributes, leads to antinomies. Thus relations on both counts do not "exist". Yet of course they exist. There are indeed, as at times he dimly perceives, several kinds of them. That is why every now and then he finds it necessary to discuss them, beyond just telling us that they don't "exist". For example, in "Internal Relations" (1935), he argues that one version of the doctrine of internal relations is false, but that there are external relations. (Notice that in the passages he seems, quite consistently, on the verge of giving up substances for bare particulars.)

> ... on this interpretation "relations are internal to their terms" means one of two things....(1) that if something is in a certain relation to something else, their being so related is a logical *sine qua non* of each of the things having *at least one* of its other characters; or it means (2) that if something is in a certain relation to something else, their being so related is a logical *sine qua non* of each of the things having *any* of its other characters.[23]

> Now it seems to me to be demonstrably false that any relation is the logical *sine qua non* of all the other characters of its terms.[24]

> But incidentally it seems to me improper to speak absolutely of the nature of a particular ...[25]

There is a noticeable tendency, notwithstanding the substance metaphysics, to conceive of all relations as external and descriptive. In "Plato's 'Parmenides'", even *exemplification* is thought of as a descriptive relation. This enables Ryle to give a curious argument, based half on Aristotle's Third Man, half on Bradley's infinite regress, to the effect that, like relations, exemplification doesn't "exist":

> Now what of the alleged relation itself, which we are calling 'exemplification'? Is this a Form or an instance of a Form? Take the two propositions 'this is square' and 'that is circular'. We have here two different cases of something exemplifying something else. We have two different instances of the relation of being-an-instance-of. What is the relation between them and that of which they are instances? It will have to be exemplification Number 2. The exemplification of P by S will be an instance of exemplification, and its being in that relation to exemplification will be an instance of a second-order exemplification, and that of a third, and so on *ad infinitum*.

---

[23] Ryle, "Internal Relations", *Science, History, and Theology*, Aristotelian Society, Supplementary Volume XIV, Harrison and Sons, Ltd., 1935, p. 157.

[24] *Ibid.*, p. 158.

[25] *Ibid.*, p. 162.

This conclusion is impossible. So there is no such relation as being-an-instance-of.[26]

The most one can conclude is (what is true) that exemplification is not a descriptive relation – i.e., a connection to be treated like spatial and temporal relations, for example. The more radical conclusion that exemplification does not exist (or "exist") only seems to be proved because Ryle conceives the connection falsely to begin with. We are also faced with the confusion surrounding the notion of *instance of*. Is, for example, a tomato an instance of red or is the red "in" the tomato an instance of red? Failure to be clear on that point may help one to confuse Platonic universals with the ordinary properties of things.

Enough has been said to show Ryle's ambiguity about the ontological status of relations. In a sense no relations "exist"; in another sense external, descriptive relations do, but all other kinds (e.g., internal and logical) do not "exist". How this affects the dialectic of the philosophy of mind we shall see later.

The Epistemological Attack on Representationalism

I now interrupt myself, as it were, to take up Ryle's epistemological attack on representationalism. I use 'epistemological' mainly in order to distinguish this attack from what I call the structural or ontological. Though I shall find some textual evidence for the ontological attack, it is only fair to say that Ryle never consciously undertook to destroy representationalism by bringing to bear an ontology which, of course, he *did* believe to be adequate. That is, the difficulties Ryle actually finds have to do mainly with representationalism as a theory of knowledge, not as a statement of what there is.

The epistemological attack is directed against both internal and external representative realism. In other words, the argument is often against the idea of representation as such. And where the argument is directed only against internal representative realism, we can see, as did Ryle himself, that *mutatis mutandis* the arguments often apply to external representative realism as well.

It is clear that Ryle wants to deny the *existence* of ideas as well as to hold that they are of no use in theory of knowledge. We also see that he *understood* internal representationalism as I characterized it.

It was an assumption rooted in the Cartesian and Lockean theories of mental life that what I am aware of when I am aware of something must always be an "idea." We need not bother our heads about the definition of "idea" (for

[26] PP, p, 138,

nonentities are not necessarily definable), but at least it was held that an idea is a mental something and something existing or occurring inside the mind that is aware of it.[27]

Ryle's criticism of this theory is more or less traditional. The argument has two sides: (1) On the theory we could never know the objects of which it supposed to explain how we know them, and (2) no sense can be made of how an idea can *represent* or resemble, say, a substance. I shall let Ryle speak for himself. As for (1):

The assumption of 'ideas' does not explain how we think about or have knowledge of objects; for they are themselves described as objects about which we think and of which and the relations between which we have knowledge. If there is no difficulty in seeing how we can think about or have knowledge of ideas, then there is none in seeing how we can do so with respect to other objects like the moon or Julius Caesar.[28]

It may be replied that the reason we can know ideas in a way in which we cannot know other objects is because the former are "in" the mind, whereas the latter are not. Anticipating this, Ryle says:

There is a prejudice that minds can only attend to what is part of or attached to their own being, but it seems to be due either to the futile superstition that minds are a species of container or to the popular mistake in logic [?] of supposing that relations are not genuine in the way in which qualities and states are genuine characters of things.[29]

Whether this account of the reasons for the prejudice is correct is here of no interest to us. A similar point is made in another paper, this time with respect to Husserl.

I can see no *a priori* grounds for supposing that perception can only be knowledge where the object perceived and the perceiving of it are conjoined parts of one stream of experience. It seems to me just the old prejudice that the thing known should be in some way very near to the knowing of it.[30]

As for (2), we are told:

Even if there did exist such things as 'ideas' were supposed to be, it is almost impossible so to describe them as to make sense of the assertion that some of them 'resemble' or 'represent' realities . . .[31]

The crucial arguments, then (and I have no quarrel with them), are that neither do ideas explain how we know nor can sense be made of their alleged representative character. Before we see how Ryle applies

---

[27] Phen, p. 78.
[28] Ryle, "Locke on the Human Understanding", *John Locke Tercentenary Addresses*, Oxford University Press, 1933, p. 23. Hereafter referred to as Locke.
[29] *Ibid.*
[30] Phen, p. 82.
[31] Locke, p. 23.

similar arguments against external representative realism, it is worth noting that he has another argument against ideas as such. I merely quote it without comment because I believe it to be of little importance. So, apparently, does Ryle.

> If they [ideas] existed or occurred, there should be empirical evidence of their existence or occurrence. But in fact introspection does not reveal them, and (I put it dogmatically) there is no causal inference to them.[32]

In "Are There Propositions?" the arguments against internal representative realism are referred to briefly and then applied to "objective propositions":

> Just as no theory of Representative Ideas can solve the problem of how knowledge is possible, since it both reduplicates and begs the whole question by assuming (a) that we can know these "ideas," (b) that we can know the realities that they are representative of, and (c) that we can know a particular "idea" to be representative of a particular reality, so no theory of objective propositions can help us in the least to explain how by thinking propositions we can come to know the realities that the propositions are about.[33]

Ryle thus sees clearly that representationalism *as a theory of knowledge* does not stand or fall on the issue whether or not the representing entities are mental. That explains why he puts what we may take to be his own summary of his attack on representationalism in the way he does, i.e., with a reference to intentionality:

> In so far, then, as the proposition theory derives from the theory of intentionality, it seems to be just a new version of the old theory of Representative "ideas" – with the two differences: (a) that the "representatives" are de-psychologized and are now not mental but "neutral" entities, and (b) that they are no longer of the form of *terms* but of complete *judgments*.[34]

As a theory of knowledge representationalism is thus futile. It fails to solve the problem it claims to solve; its solution assumes that what it took to be one is not a problem. That is, it must assume that there is some kind of awareness of the "objects of knowledge" without ideas (which it holds to be impossible) in order to explain why such knowledge or awareness is possible only by awareness of ideas.

But while representationalism may fail as a theory of knowledge, insofar as it assumes *all* knowledge or awareness to consist in awareness of representative entities, it does not follow (1) that there are no such entities as ideas or propositions, nor (2) that we are not at least *sometimes* aware of them. It has indeed been held that what I shall call

---

[32] *Ibid.*
[33] ATP, p. 106.
[34] *Ibid.*, p. 108.

veridical awareness is of the "objects of knowledge" directly, as it were, while *non-veridical* awareness is of ideas or, more often, of something like propositions or objectives. These comments lead to the next section.

The Ontological Attack on Representationalism

The ontological attack is more fundamental. Its point is to show that the allegedly representing entities cannot, or at least do not, exist. This would in itself suffice to show the epistemology to be mistaken, since if the entities the theory requires don't exist the latter cannot be true, while the converse, as we just noted, is false. That is, showing the epistemology to be inadequate, at least as a general theory of knowledge, is not to show that, say, propositions do not exist. Ryle knows this.[35] And now we must glance ahead in order to understand fully why the ontological attack is so crucial.

I shall argue in the next chapter that the main reason Ryle gave up direct realism was that with it he thought he could not solve the problem of non-veridical awareness. That problem is, roughly and briefly, what a non-veridical awareness is *of*, granted that what it seems to be of straightforwardly does not, in the ordinary sense, exist. What, for example, is Jones' false belief that the earth is flat *of*, since there is no state of affairs, or if you prefer, "fact", of the earth's being flat?

Representative realism won't do as a *general* theory of knowledge; yet a watered-down version of it may seem to provide a solution to the problem of non-veridical awareness. It might be claimed, for example, that while true beliefs, real knowledge, and accurate perceptions are straightforwardly of what, in the ordinary sense, is believed, known, and perceived; false belief, hallucination, and daydreams are *of* propositions or ideas. Ryle, we shall see, *was* tempted by this view. Thus, if we are to understand why eventually he became a materialist, we must understand why he could not accept even this watered-down version of representationalism. The most convincing way of showing its inadequacy, also as a "solution" of the problem of non-veridical awareness, is to show that such things as propositions and ideas do not exist. What I called the epistemological attack does not, we recall, refute the watered-down version. Now we see why the ontological attack is fundamental. It not only goes deeper in that it challenges the very existence and not merely the usefulness of propositions or

[35] *Ibid.*, p. 107.

ideas; but we could not without understanding it understand how his other failures drove Ryle to materialism.

Let us briefly recall the early ontology. In a broad sense of 'exist', only substances and *their* properties "exist". In a narrower sense, even more important and still philosophical, only substances "exist". (This narrower sense, we remember, comes from the elementarism pattern.) This is Ryle's nominalism.

Yet he sometimes speaks in an odd way about substances and existence. On the one hand, he may say of something that it doesn't exist because it is not a substance (since only substances exist); on the other hand, he may say that if such and such existed, it would be a substance (since only substances exist). Thus in a passage where he rejects both idealism and representationalism, he says:

Not a few philosophers have tried to evade representationism by denying the existence of the supposed archetypes of the ideas, and thus populating the world with nothing but minds and their ideas. And others have tried to accord to ideas truth of a non-representationist type by such dodges as internal coherence, systematic connectedness, and the like. But the problem which they try thus to solve is a sham one, since the alleged 'contents' for the objective validity of which they proffer such devious defences *have no existence and so no properties or relations*.[36]

An idea, if it existed, would be neither simply a particular, nor simply a property or a collection of such, but rather a particular exemplifying properties. Otherwise they couldn't be, as supposedly they are, like what they represent, e.g., chairs, trees, unicorns, and so on. Thus, unless one takes them to constitute a category of their own, they would have to be "facts". Ryle, *on the whole*, took ideas, as the tradition did, to be members of the ontological category *property*. Assuming that he did, our task is to see why the early ontology rules them out of order. The *first* pattern by which the ontology clashes with ideas goes as follows: Only substances "exist". Ideas are not substances. Therefore, ideas do not "exist". Ideas, after all, are onto-logically dependent; they *are*, don't *have*, properties. The substanti-alism makes itself felt in two ways: (1) Since only substances "exist", ideas are ruled out of order because they are not substances. (2) Because of the nature of *individuals* on the substantialist scheme, ideas cannot be conceived of as qualitied particulars. Put another way, if Ryle (and Descartes) could have accepted the *bare* particular, and an idea to be a qualitied particular, there is no *ontological* reason

---

[36] Locke, p. 23, my emphasis.

why this sort of fact should not exist, even on nominalism. (It would not follow, though, that it does exist.)

I shall next show, by textual evidence from a different context, that this pattern worked in Ryle. Return to the last quotation. The ontological status of ideas in no way depends on their representative function or lack of it. In the following quotation, Husserl's idealism is at issue. But, again, it does not matter that his "essences" do not represent. I shall first quote at considerable length, then discuss the passage.

Rather like Meinong he [Husserl] holds, or used to hold, that universals or essences as well as propositions, are objects of a higher order.

· ·

I fancy that Husserl used to think of them [essences] as independently subsisting and now regards them as intrinsically contents of possible acts of thinking.

· ·

I do not myself believe that phrases such as "being a so and so," "being such and such" and "that so and so is such and such" do denote *objects or subjects of attributes*. For I don't think that they are denoting expressions at all. Consequently, though I can know what it is for something to be a so and so, I think that this knowledge is wrongly described as an "intuition of an essence." For intuition, which I take to be a synonym for knowledge by acquaintance or perception, does seem to be or to involve a relation between two *subjects of attributes*, the perceiver and the thing perceived. *And I do not think that what Husserl calls "essences" are subjects of attributes at all.*[37]

Two points are clear. (1) It matters not to Ryle whether "essences" are "in" the mind or not. (2) In either case, they do not exist. Thus, whether we take Husserl to be an idealist or a Platonist, his "essences" are ruled out of order because they are not substances, i.e., are not subjects of attributes. We noted earlier [38] that Ryle held that it would be antinomous to say that Platonic objects are substances. Now "essences", whether in the mind or not, are said not to be substances and therefore not to exist. Thus at a single blow, Platonism, representative realism, and idealism are refuted, for all three wrongly suppose either that (1) some things exist which are not (or could not be?) substances, or (2) some things are substances which are not (or could not be?). This is the only way I know how to state it. That is why a few paragraphs back I called Ryle's way of speaking "odd". For, clearly, he can be challenged at three points: (1) whether "being a subject of attributes" is a reasonable and adequate criterion of

37 Phen, pp. 72–73, my emphasis.
38 See p. 70

existence, (2) whether in fact properties are not "subjects of attributes" (whether elementarism is true), and (3) whether in fact ideas are simply properties. But that is not my task here.

A *second* somewhat different pattern in Ryle's ontological attack on ideas (and eventually on mind itself) is more directly connected with his anti-Platonism. The Third Realm, that of Platonic entities, does not exist, or rather, none of its members exists[39]. He conceives of internal representative realism as a mistaken attempt to internalize the Platonic, and as such suspect, entities of external representative realism:

> The only reason why people are prone to psychologize ideal entities and treat them as "ideas in the mind" seems to be because they share with mental states and processes the negative property of being inaccessible to sense perception.[40]

Ryle, oddly enough, seems to be prone to the opposite "error". That is, he tends to think of ideas, or even more broadly, *of all mental entities*, as Platonic entites and therefore as non-existent. What I am intimating here is that there is a more direct connection that I have so far suggested between Ryle's anti-Platonism or nominalism on the one hand and his materialism on the other. I shall not and need not put too much stock in this, however. I *shall* not because the textual evidence is thin; I *need* not because we can and shall understand how he came to his materialism, *in part* because of his nominalism, without exploiting the direct connection at which I just hinted. That will not keep me from hinting at it again, however.

I also claim that Ryle tends to identify *ideas* (in contrast to other mental entities) with the Platonic. This weaker claim I shall document. The best way of doing this is through the notion of *concept*. On the philosophical position known as conceptualism, universals are only "in" the mind. A concept is such a universal. Concepts do two jobs. For one, they mediate between the knower and the known. We know something by knowing its concept. For another, concepts account for sameness. Two things have the same properties because they fall under the same concept. Platonic universals do the same two jobs. The first, more important for what we are about, is for Ryle the main job of Platonic entities:

> Somehow or other they [the entities of the Third Realm] alone make anything – even what exists in the world – knowable or thinkable.[41]

---

[39] Notice the lack of double quotes.
[40] ATP, p. 104.
[41] *Ibid.*

A concept is a Platonic universal put into the mind. Ryle tends to think of ideas as Platonic-like because he thinks of them as concepts. Characteristically, he uses 'concept' to mean both an "apprehended property" *and* an "apprehension of the nature of something" (in different papers):

> Now a 'concept' is nothing more or less than an apprehended attribute, property, quality, or character . . .[42]

> If he is succeeding [in conceiving], no clarification is required or possible; and if he is failing, he must find out more or think more about the subject-matter, the apprehension of the nature of which we call his "concept." [43]

Equally characteristically, we are told a few lines after the second of these passages:

> But as I think that it can be shown that it is not true in any natural sense that "there are concepts," . . .[44]

We now see clearly the following pattern: (1) Abstract entities do not exist. (2) Platonic universals are abstract. (3) Ideas are or are like Platonic universals. (4) Hence ideas do not exist. (3) is crucial; it embodies the confusion. This crucial premise is itself supported by the following verbal pattern: (a) Platonic entities are universals. (b) Universals (properties) are concepts. (c) Ideas are concepts. (d) Hence Platonic entities and ideas both being concepts, the latter are or are like the former.

I have claimed but not strictly demonstrated that Ryle identifies concepts, even when he thinks of them as mental, with ideas. Nor do I have the textual evidence required for a strict demonstration. Yet I have been able to quote many passages which make the claim extremely plausible. Ryle speaks of the Third Realm as containing entities which do the same job as those of internal representative realism, viz., ideas. He also speaks of these entities of the Third Realm as doing what, on the traditional view, concepts did. I conclude, with moral certainty, that when thinking of concepts as mental, he thought of them as having the same ontological status as well as the same functions as ideas.

Now it is true that there is a difference between ideas and concepts as traditionally conceived. The former were always the objects of the direct awareness involved in any other kind (e.g., thinking of, remembering, and so on). Concepts, however, were entities *by* which we

---

[42] Locke, p. 19.
[43] SME, p. 141.
[44] *Ibid.*

are aware, and not *of* which we are (ordinarily) aware. (I say "ordinarily" in order not to exclude that under special conditions they might themselves become objects of awareness.) The medievals expressed the distinction between awareness *by* concepts (of something else) and *of* concepts as such, through that between the first and the second intentions. Their realism was intentional, not representative. No such distinction is available to the representative realist, however. Thus he has the familiar problems to which Ryle points and which we noted in the last section. I am suggesting, however, that he did not make the distinction, but thought of concepts on the model of ideas. I have already stated my reasons. Furthermore, I introduced the notion of *concept* more as a heuristic device to explain what seems to me to be Ryle's tendency to think of ideas as Platonic entities than as a reading of his intellectual development.

There is a *third*, though less important, pattern by which the ontology threatens the status of ideas. What has been said so far does not involve the act. The pattern to which I now turn does. Ryle usually thought of a mental act as being or involving an external, descriptive relation between knower and known. In the next chapter I shall argue that this is the main reason why he eventually rejected acts. Right now I merely want to show how this conception of the act might affect the status of ideas. Recall that for Ryle properties are not themselves subjects of properties or relations. Suppose that in awareness there is a relation between a knower and ideas. Then we should have to admit either that properties (ideas) *are* themselves subjects of attributes, i.e., stand in relations, or that ideas are substances. Neither alternative is acceptable to Ryle.

The three patterns I have exhibited are all directed against internal representative realism. One of them, the second, rests on the assumption that there are no Platonic entities. I also hinted at a more direct connection between Ryle's anti-Platonism and his materialism. But apart from that, external representative realism explicitly makes use of what he would call Platonic entities. We need not review his reasons for dismissing such entities; that ontological consideration is, however, sufficient to reject external representative realism. Thus Ryle sees both external and internal representative realism as ontologicallly inadequate, and each ultimately for the same reason – his nominalism *cum* anti-Platonism.

We have seen, then, why Ryle could never accept representative realism either in its pure form or in a modified form where objects such as ideas or propositions are the objects of only some awarenesses. I have suggested that he was resisting the attraction it had for himself. The reason he was attracted was that he saw in it a solution to a problem he couldn't solve otherwise. But before we turn to that problem in the next chapter, I wish to establish some other connections between the early ontology and that which emerges in *The Concept of Mind*.

Direct Connections Between the Early and the Later Ontology

In Chapters I and II, I claimed that the ontology of The Concept of Mind was one of *substances* and their *doings*. In the early ontology there is a similar distinction between *facts* snd *events*. I shall argue that it is the same distinction. Time provides a "criterion" for it:

For events have dates, but facts do not.[45]

What does that mean? Isn't an event just a fact containing a date? Not so for Ryle. What, then, for him is an event?

Jones is a substance. Substance and fact are more or less identified, partly because of the low ontological status of properties, partly because of the non-simplicity of substances. For example:

The word "*fact*" does not denote any new entity or substance; if, for instance, I know that Julius Caesar is dead, the fact that he is dead is not a new substance side by side with the substance we call "Julius Caesar." Julius Caesar's being dead in 1930 is simply part of the being of Julius Caesar and not an entity on its own account.[46]

So Jones is a fact. But it is not the case that Jones just *is*, as it were; he also *does*. He runs, he eats, he talks, and so on. These are all activities of Jones. From this point of view, the world of commonsense could not be exhausted by a list of substances and of spatial relations among them. I hesitate to say "spatial and temporal relations", for the idea, obviously, is that temporal relations obtain not among substances (facts), but rather, among events. That is our cue. Remembering what Jones' activities are we conclude that *an event is a substance doing something.*[47]

The main idea, I believe, is that unless doings are made into a kind of category unto itself, no account of change is possible. Consider an ontology of (simple) particulars and (simple) properties. Even if the

---

[45] *Ibid.*, p. 164.

[46] ATP, p. 111.

[47] As the ontology of *The Concept of Mind* was explicated, a *doing* does not have a substance as a constituent. Here, an *event* is not merely a doing, but rather, a substance's doing or a substance plus its doing.

particulars are continuants, the best one can produce is a universe of things which "tick", having now this property, now that, and so on. Yet phenomenologically change is "continuous". There is therefore a strong temptation to make doings, which are "continuous" and do fill whole time intervals, into an ontological category, even though one may have to admit that they are not "simples".

I don't propose to argue here whether an ontology without such a category can make its peace with the phenomenological facts of change and continuity.[48] Be that as it may, the ontological status of doings (events, activities) in Ryle's early thought is very obscure. It does seem clear, however, that their status is weaker than later on, in *The Concept of Mind*. This later strengthening of their status, I suggest, may plausibly be attributed to the fact that it took Ryle all this time to understand himself. Only when he wrote *The Concept of Mind* did he finally realize that if he were to give mind any ontological status at all, it could only be either that of a disposition or that of a doing. Dispositions, he had convinced himself, do not exist. So he gives mind ontological status by strengthening that of doings.

A fact is a substance; an event is a substance doing something. If I am right, then substances do not have dates, i.e., *are not in time*. This connects very nicely with the ideas discussed near the end of the second chapter.[49]

A doing is an activity of a substance. In "Are There Propositions?" we are told:

> The term *act* is sometimes objected to as implying, what may not be true, that all these things are cases of *doing*, bits of *activity* as opposed to passivity. But even if the term *acts* is taken, as I think it should be, in the wider sense of *actus* rather than *actiones* to denote the actualizations of potentialities rather than the doings of deeds, it is often improperly used.[50]

(The reason it is often improperly used is because some act words, e.g., 'know', 'believe', and 'be of the opinion that', often do not denote occurrences at all.) This "distinction" between *doings* on the one hand and the *actualization of potentialities* on the other is, I suggest, an attempt to avoid falling into idealism. What is to be avoided is a mind which "creates" or "contributes to" its intentions. So the "active" doing of a mind is toned down into "neutral" actualizations of potenti-

[48] See Bergmann, "Some Reflections on Time", *Il Tempo*, Archivio di Filosofia, Padova: Cedam, 1958, and reprinted in his *Meaning and Existence*. The last few pages are of particular relevance to the issue.

[49] See p. 40.

[50] ATP, p. 115.

alities. Later on, when mental acts come to be conceived as doings of the body, there is no need for such caution. Hence, in *The Concept of Mind* the earlier distinction, if there be one, between doings and actualized potentialities, can be safely ignored. For my part, I want neither to defend nor to attack the distinction; I merely want to explain why Ryle first made it and later on could afford to drop it.

One more connection between the early ontology and that of the book is worth pointing out. It, too, has something to do with Ryle's identification of fact with substances. It will be recalled from the second chapter [51] that he is (mistakenly) convinced that granting dispositional statements any categorical (fact-stating) status would commit him to mental entities. Hence he claims that *his* "if-then" analysis exhausts their "meaning". This claim is tied to the broader one that, at least typically, these "statements" are mere inference tickets. In Chapter II I have tied this broader claim to the rejection of "general" facts. In Ryle's ontology, all substances are particulars (*this* cat, *that* tree, and so on). There are no secondary substances (cat, dog, and so on). That puts us on the track of the connection. If the two categories of thing and fact are blurred or identified, then the view that there are only "particular" (This cat is brown) and no "general" facts (Cats are brown) gains some specious support. And, of course, if there are no general facts, then "if-then" statements have no categorical status. Ryle believes, however mistakenly, that to grant this status to those statements is to provide the dualist with an argument. That is the connnection. That this belief is in fact mistaken, whether Ryle or, for that matter, some dualists, may think, I have argued before.[52]

V. INTENTIONALITY AND THE COLLAPSE OF DIRECT REALISM

We have seen why, in view of his early ontology and his epistemological position, Ryle could not accept representative realism in either a strict or a modified form. In particular we now understand why the early ontology had to be brought in: It is crucial for the rejection of the modified form of representationalism. The *main* task of this chapter is to show why Ryle eventually had to give up, or felt that he had to give up, direct realism. Having shown that, I shall have explained *ipso facto* how Ryle came to materialism, provided that materialism doesn't share with either form of realism the problems he thinks he

[51] See p. 37.
[52] See p. 38.

sees in both. But that is only the main task. More specifically I shall proceed as follows: First, I shall furnish a brief statement of the importance of the act and the issue of intentionality. Second, I shall give an exposition of Ryle's early philosophy of mind. Third, I shall show the relevance of the early ontology to Ryle's conception of the act. Fourth, I shall consider Ryle's two "solutions" to the problem of non-veridical awareness. Finally, in the light of what shall have been said, I shall "check" the materialist alternative in order to make sure that it doesn't contain similar problems.

The Act and Intentionality

There certainly do exist mental acts, acts of wondering, remembering, imagining and perceiving. Whether there are, in the same sense, acts of believing, knowing and doubting or whether these are rather dispositions of a certain kind does not matter. What is clearly the case, if I may avail myself of Ryle's distinction between dispositions and occurrences, is that my suddenly remembering that I must pick up some milk on the way home is not a disposition but an occurrence. Nor is it a physical occurrence. Thus even if knowing, e.g., is not an act in this sense, it does not follow that there are no acts. That there are acts is as obvious as that there are chairs.

One of the most important, if one of the most neglected, tasks of philosophy is to give an ontological assay of the act. The neglect has arisen from two sources – the difficulty of the analysis and the tendency to believe that there are no acts. One is tempted to believe that the former is part of the cause of the latter. In any case, since acts *are* there, they must be accounted for in an adequate ontological reconstruction of the world.

The crucial feature of acts, the characteristic which makes them different in an interesting way from all other kinds of objects, is of course their intrinsic intentionality, their "ofness" feature. An act of remembering is always a remembering *of* something. Acts, as Sartre would say, transcend themselves. They "shoot out" beyond themselves to other objects.[1] Acts of course may themselves be objects of acts, but no act is its own object. That acts are intentional is phenomenologically given; even more, what a given act is *of* is phenomenologically given. But that could be taken to say what it does not say. When I remember that my now dead grandfather was very short, my grand-

---

[1] For Sartre, that means that acts somehow lack being. I do not endorse any such doctrine; nor do I recommend it as a way of speaking if it is only that.

father is not of course phenomenologically given. What is phenomeno-logically given is that my remembering is *of* my grandfather. I conclude therefore that there must be something "in" the mind, something directly presented to me, such that I know this act of remembering to be of the fact that my grandfather was short and of no other fact (or object).[2]

When I see a tree, I know that I see a tree. But I have no guarantee that the tree is there. Phenomenologically, there is no difference be-tween seeing a tree that is there and seeing one that isn't there,[3] i.e., hallucinating. If there were a difference, we could always tell *at the time* when our perceptions were not veridical, but we cannot. Though of course *veridical* and *non-veridical* are properties of acts, they are defined logical properties which are not presented to one in the presen-tation of the act. The "ontological" ground of the veridical/non-veridical distinction lies therefore on the side of the object, not on that of the act. Roughly, we should say, an act is veridical if what it is of obtains, exists, is the case; otherwise it is non-veridical. Jones' remembering [4] that Stassen was elected President in 1960 is non-veridical because that state of affairs, Stassen's being elected President in 1960, does not obtain.

Non-veridical acts are nonetheless intentional. Jones' remembering "shoots out" even if, as we ordinarily speak and believe, what it "shoots out" to isn't there. This poses the problem. What are non-veridical acts of? Or, if that seems to beg the question, we may formulate it in this manner: How shall we account for the *ofness* of acts, especially in those cases where, in the ordinary sense, the object of the act is not there?

One may ask at this point: Why is there a special problem in the case of the non-veridical? What does the fact that the object is not there have to do with it? The answer is that the *ofness* of acts has been analyzed by many philosophers as consisting in some kind of *relation* between, say, a believing and the fact or state of affairs believed. Sometimes the believing is itself said to be the relation between what is believed and the mind. This difference makes no difference here. But if this relation is of the same kind (descriptive) as, say, *to-the-left-of,*

---

[2] I sometimes speak as if acts were "propositional", sometimes not. Here it makes no difference.

[3] Some may object that 'see' isn't *used* in a way such that one can see what isn't there, and so for 'remember', 'know', and so on. Since my point is clear, such objectors are invited to substitute any words they wish in those instances where they find my use of those words objectionable.

[4] See footnote 3.

then this view is clearly inadequate, unless there is something to go proxy for the non-existent state of affairs, such as an idea or a proposition, for a relation of this sort cannot be exemplified unless its *relata* exist. *A* cannot be to the left of *B* unless both *A* and *B* exist.

Moreover, since the intentionality of acts is directly presented to us, it again follows that the intentionality cannot consist in a descriptive relation between the mind or the act on the one hand and the object of the act on the other. It also follows that the intentionality cannot consist *solely* in a *logical* relation between the mind and the object. What does follow is that there must be "in" the act some *property* which somehow uniquely identifies its object. Thus if Jones believes [5] that Stassen is President, let us say that there are at least two properties involved.[6] These are *believing* (to distinguish this sort of act from, say, doubting that Stassen is President) and what I shall call the property *that-Stassen-is-President* (to distinguish *this* belief from any other true or false belief). Call the latter kind of property an *intentional character*. This is what we need at a minimum to account for what is phenomenologically given to us with respect to acts. When I believe, I know directly both that I *believe* and *what it is* I believe. These two properties account for these features.

What is the connection between these odd properties of the sort *that-Stassen-is-President* and the (in this case non-existent) fact which is object of the act? Bergmann [7] has claimed it to be a *meaning* connection, a logical relation such that any true statement to the effect that a certain character *means* a certain state of affairs, e.g., '*that-Stassen-is-President* means Stassen is President', is analytic and any false one contradictory. Bergmann also points out that *logical* relations can hold between existent and non-existent states of affairs. For example, the logical connection of *or* holds between the two states of affairs mentioned in the true statement 'It's raining or it's not raining here now'. In spite of this fact of which Bergmann is perfectly aware, he still seems to feel that the dialectic forces one to grant some ontological status to the non-existent states of affairs which are the intentions of non-veridical acts. In any event, for him the intentional

---

[5] Assume that believing is an act, not merely a disposition.

[6] For what I say, the question whether they be properties of a continuant self or of momentary individuals makes no difference.

[7] See Bergmann's "Acts", originally appearing in Italian in *Rivista di Filosofia*, 51, 1960, and subsequently in English in the *Indian Journal of Philosophy*, 2, 1960, and reprinted in his *Logic and Reality*, University of Wisconsin Press, 1964.

feature of acts is "covered" by intentional characters *and* the "meaning" connection.

Others have held that the characters are sufficient. The motive for saying that intentionality is taken care of by these odd properties is of course to avoid having to grant ontological status to non-existent states of affairs. This is the view which Brentano held; it is also the view which Ryle would have Husserl hold, although he, Ryle, never seemed to hold it himself.[8]

Each of these views qualifies as intentional realism. Neither is representationalist, although both hold that there are characters in the mind (properties of acts or the self) which in a weak sense "represent" their unique intentions. Of these two views I am inclined to believe that Bergmann's is the correct one, at least with respect to whether the "meaning" connection is required. But I am quite certain that no ontology can do without intentional characters as well as a class of properties to account for the different species of acts.

This indicates roughly the direction in which the solution to the problems which Ryle could not solve is to be found.

Ryle's Early Treatment of Mind

We already know a good deal about Ryle's early views on mind. He rejects representative realism; asserts that it is a prejudice to think the object known must be "in" or "near" the mind; believes that perception is or involves a relation between two "subjects of attributes". Thus he believed at one time that there are mental acts and that they themselves can be objects of acts:

> ... while I see no reason to doubt that we *can* inspect and recognize states and acts of our own minds, I think that this introspection is not really perception (save in an enlarged sense). I believe that introspecting is merely remembrance controlled by a special interest.[9]

(I shall argue later that, since it makes non-substances the intentions of certain acts, he cannot consistently hold even this view.) Acts,

---

[8] It is also the view held by Lewis in the other essay in this book. He seems to agree that the *meaning* connection is there in a certain sense. But for him, to say that a certain intentional character *means* a certain state of affairs is only to say that there is that intentional character and furthermore that it *is* an intentional character, i.e., that it has the logical property of being an intentional character. For Bergmann the *meaning* connection is yet another entity. That is the difference.

[9] Ryle "Phenomenology", *Phenomenology, Goodness, and Beauty*, Aristotelian Society, Supplementary Volume XI, Harrison and Sons, Ltd., 1932, p. 82. Hereafter referred to as *Phen.*

moreover, with the possible exception of perception, are "propositional". Let Ryle explain this for himself:

I might echo Cook Wilson's strictures on the propriety of imputing real homogeneity to acts of knowing, opining, believing, supposing, wondering, etc., but it is enough for my purposes to point out that there is one common feature, if there are no others, which these various sorts of "thinking" show, namely, that all alike find their expression in *statement* or in sentences in the indicative. If I know something, the something that I know is published in the form "that X is Y" ... Thus in contradistinction from those acts of consciousness, the "accusatives" of which are *things* which can in principle be named and pointed at ...[10]

All imagining is imagining *that* something is the case. The correct form of reply to the question What are you imagining? would be to state a complete proposition, prefaced by a "that." It would be incorrect to reply by naming or describing a thing. That is, imagining is in this respect analogous to knowing, believing, opining and guessing, and not to seeing, fearing, hitting, making or begetting.[11]

Ryle's belief that perception is different from all other sorts of awareness in that it is of "things" while those other sorts are of what can only be expressed by a sentence is, I believe, false or at best misleading. But there is no need for me to argue that, for it makes no difference to what follows. (The reader will be able to see that for himself as we proceed.)

What *does* make a difference, *the* difference as we shall see, is how Ryle views the "connection" between an act and what, if anything, it is of. In one early paper he agreed that all awareness is *of* something:

And we can grant, I think, that it would be both paradoxical and in conflict with the evidence of language to assert that there may be some forms of consciousness which are not consciousness *of* something.[12]

Yet even in this paper he seems to have his doubts, for reasons with which we are by this time very familiar.

But the generalization of the Realist theory of consciousness leads at once to unexpected consequences; for if the physical world is saved, yet a lot more is saved than was originally wanted. All species of thinking are forms of consciousness; but if their objects too are to be emancipated, then "concepts" or universals [!], numbers, laws and relations as well as "judgments" or propositions, which are the objects of acts of conceiving and acts of judging respectively, must be allowed to be genuine entities. The integrity of Newton's world is guaranteed, but the guarantee covers also the world of Plato.[13]

    [10] Ryle, "Are There Propositions?", *Proceedings of the Aristotelian Society*, Vol. XXX, Harrison and Sons, Ltd., 1930, pp. 93–94. Hereafter referred to as ATP.
    [11] Ryle, "Imaginary Objects", *Creativity, Politics and The A Priori*, Aristotelian Society, Supplementary Volume XII, Harrison and Sons, Ltd., 1933, pp. 29–30.
    [12] ATP, p. 93.
    [13] *Ibid.*, p. 97.

Thus Ryle must hold, it appears, that while indeed every piece of consciousness is consciousness of *something*, it is not in every case consciousness of what it straightforwardly seems to be. As we shall see, when we come to consider his first "solution" to the problem of non-veridical awareness, this seems to be exactly what he is saying.

In another paper, not much later, he seems to deny that consciousness is always *of* something. Moreover, he objects to characterizing the intentionality of acts in terms of consciousness for a reason which he himself gives.

He [Husserl] *should* hold (I believe) that what we miscall "the object or content of an act of consciousness" is really the specific character or nature of that act, so that the intentionality of an act is not a relation between it and something else, but merely a property of it so specific as to be a *differentia* or in some cases an individualizing description of it.[14]

From the context it is not clear whether Husserl should hold this view because he, Ryle, believes it to be true, or whether Husserl should hold it in order to make properly the point he, Husserl, wants to make. I would guess the latter, for the following reason. Ryle seems to distinguish what should be distinguished, the claim that every act has the intentionality feature, whether it be veridical or not, on the one hand, and the claim that not every act is intentional on the other. Ryle seems to advocate the latter view several paragraphs later. (I shall document that only when discussing his "solutions" to the problem of non-veridical awareness.)

In another passage from the same paper he says:

Consequently the "intentionality" of mental acts must be defined in terms not of "consciousness of . . ." but of "knowledge of . . ." And as it is, if not self-evident, anyhow plausible to say that what I know to be the case is so whether I know it or not, a phenomenology operating with this modified notion of intentionality would not be obviously bound to terminate in an egocentric metaphysic . . . For it would no longer be essential to any subject of attributes to be "accusative" to a mental act. Intentionality will not now be an internal relation.[15]

The goal of Ryle's strategy is, of course, to avoid idealism. Husserl held, as part of his "egocentric metaphysic", that the "content" or "object" of consciousness is "intrinsically" just that. That makes it, in a traditional sense, a *mental* object. Its being is in its being an object of consciousness. That is idealism. Ryle proposes to avoid this consequence (idealism) in part by defining all "act" words in terms of 'knowing', since objects known are not "dependent" for their existence

14 Phen, p. 79.
15 *Ibid.*, pp. 80–81.

on the knowledge of them. The reason he would make knowledge primary in this way is his belief that *if one knows something (an object or state of affairs), then it "follows" that that object exists or that state of affairs obtains.* This is an obvious mistake. That 'know' is used ordinarily in a way such that we *say* of someone that he didn't "really" know that so-and-so if so-and-so is not the case is of course true. But then such "knowing" does not characterize any act (or disposition). More precisely, 'veridical' is a defined logical character of (some) acts, which character is no more presented to us in our awareness of our acts than the truth of a sentence is presented to us in our seeing or hearing a sentence. No act, knowing included, guarantees that its object exists (or obtains, if you like).

Two comments are relevant at this point:

First. It may be said that "knowing" in contrast to, say remembering, is not an act at all but a disposition. I am inclined to agree. But then it is *obvious* that act terms could not be plausibly defined in terms of 'knowing'. Or rather, insofar as one would be tempted literally to define act words in terms of the *disposition* "knowing", one is already leaning towards materialism.

Second. It may be said that *direct awareness* guarantees the existence of its objects. And in a way that is true, but there is a difference. It is worth noting first of all that direct awareness, even if it does in a sense guarantee the existence of its object, does not provide one with any "certain" knowledge. That is, while my direct awareness yesterday of my wondering "guaranteed" that I was at that moment wondering, the guarantee "runs out" as soon as the direct awareness ends. I have no such guarantee today that I was wondering yesterday. All I have is my (or someone else's) fallible memory to go on. Thus in no case could direct awareness, even granted that it is in a sense infallible, provide a firm basis for the solution to the problems of non-veridical awareness.[16]

But what does it mean to say that an act infallibly guarantees that its object (intention) both is and is as it seems? It surely is not a logical connection[17] such that the act or the statement of its occurrence "entails" the object or the statement of its occurrence. To some the

---

[16] Knowledge could provide such a basis if it were true (1) that all act terms could be defined in terms of 'knowing', and (2) that in the strong sense (and not just the linguistic sense) knowing an object or state of affairs guaranteed the existence of that object or state of affairs.

[17] That is, it is not a logical connection above and beyond the sense in which the connection between any act and its object, whether that object exists or not, may be said to be logical. See Bergmann's "Acts" referred to in Footnote 7.

answer may seem to be this: Suppose I claim to have been directly aware of a remembering yesterday. While there may be good evidence that I did not have such a remembering yesterday, this would also be evidence that I did not have a direct awareness of it. *Granted* that I had such a direct awareness, then the "evidence" is not good enough. But this is not to show the ground of the infallibility; it is merely to restate the fact that we do regard direct awareness as infallible. What is there, if anything, about the world (and not in what we would *say*) such that we are *justified* in saying that a certain form of awareness is infallible?

The answer to our question is really one of metaphilosophy or of philosophical method. That is, to affirm that direct awareness is infallible is only to assert that with respect to the philosophical problems of epistemology, the analysis of perception, and the idealism-realism controversy, one *will* start with that with which he is directly acquainted. Of course, a good number of philosophers have denied that there is any such thing as the given; rather than answering them, I say only that I am here trying to give sense to the claim that direct awareness is infallible, not to prove that there is direct awareness. It is also held to be the wrong kind of skepticism to doubt whether the objects of direct awareness are and are as they seem. Philosophical analysis must begin somewhere. For that kind of skeptic there is no answer, but then neither is he saying anything interesting, for he is, in effect, making knowledge impossible by definition.

Ryle's early view of mind, we now see, is essentially one of direct realism. There are minds in the sense that there are mental substances and in the sense that there are acts. At least some acts (knowledge, perception) are or involve a relation between two substances (the knower and the known). Insofar as he wants to define all act terms in terms of 'knowing', all acts involve such a relation. This takes us into the next section.

The Collapse of the Early View

It has been claimed several times that the crucial element in Ryle's abandonment of realism was his inability to solve the problem of non-veridical awareness. Before discussing this crucial feature, it is worth noticing another way in which the act was threatened, this time directly by the ontology. This way, of course, has something to do with Ryle's notion of relations. Remembering that for him the act is or intrinsically involves a relation permits us to uncover the following two ontological patterns in his rejection of acts. (Whether these patterns actually moved him or not is again beside the point.)

First. Relations are the "heart" of awareness. Not being subjects of attributes, they don't "exist". Hence awareness does not "exist". This is one pattern. It is, we know, but another side of Ryle's nominalism. What is shows is that, even if relations were not in fact subjects of attributes, the "criterion" of existence would still be inadequate. The task is to take the world as it is, then find an ontology that accounts for it. Ryle allows his inadequate ontology to drive him to denying the existence [18] of what is there.

Second. Relations are abstract entities. Abstract entities do not exist. Relations are the "heart" of awareness. Hence awareness does not exist.[19] This is the second pattern. It is more subtle than the first. Relations, it will be recalled, have been put in the "third realm", that of abstract entities. The implicit argument, I suggest, is this: If they "existed", relations would be substances, for only substances "exist". Yet they would be neither mental nor physical substances. Hence they would be substances of a "third realm" in addition to the mental and the physical. Such a realm, or rather, its members, do not exist. Thus we have the apparent paradox that if relations "existed" (i.e., were substances), they would not exist (i.e., be neither mental nor physical). Part of what produces the confusion at this point is the meshing of two notions of ontology. One notion involves putting entities into such categories as substance, relation, universal. The other notion categorizes entities according to whether they are physical, mental, or neither. More broadly, the nominalism-realism issues are meshed with the realism-idealism-materialism issues in the wrong way.

As I have indicated, the main reason why Ryle gave up the act was his inability to solve with it what I have called the problem of non-veridical awareness. In the early papers he tried twice to solve it. The second "solution" robs the act of its intrinsic intentionality. This left only the empty husk of a mental act and thus (in view of his awareness of the inadequacy of the alternative of representative realism in either the strict or modified form) paved the way for the "behavioristic" solution of later years. The problem is, to repeat, what a non-veridical awareness whose apparent intention does not, as we ordinarily speak, exist, is *about.*

Examples of non-veridical awareness are hallucination, imagination,

---

[18] Note the lack of double quotes.
[19] Note the lack of double quotes.

and false belief. These are situations where, as we ordinarily speak, the objects of these mental acts do not exist. The cases of non-veridical awareness constitute the ground for the classical refutation of the view that awareness is or intrinsically involves a *descriptive* relation between knower and known (or believer and believed, doubter and doubted, and so on). For in non-veridical awareness the object (intention) is not there. But a descriptive relation is not exemplified unless what it relates exists. If, therefore, the intention of the act is not there, the relation, if it is descriptive, cannot be exemplified. Hence, since there are non-veridical awarenesses, awareness cannot be or intrinsically involve a descriptive relation between knower and known.[20] This sets the problem. Let us now look at Ryle's two attempts to solve it.

(1) The first occurs in "Are There Propositions?".[21] The "solution" is very curious, one Ryle could not permanently accept. Suppose that A imagines B to be taller than C, whereas in fact C is taller than B. Then, according to this "solution", A is *either* having images of B and C, the former being taller than the latter, *or* A has "in" his mind the sentence 'B is taller than C'. (Sentences, to be sure, are nomental entities; in the context, though, that makes no difference. Ryle could just as well have said "image of the sentence that...") Next we are informed that the object (intention) of this act of imagining is the "hypothetical fact" that these images of B and C or the "sentence" *would* represent B's being taller than C if in fact B were taller than C. Clearly this "solution" rests on what I have called modified representationalism. Just as clearly, this is no solution to the problem. For, somehow, the "fact" of B's being taller than C remains a constituent of the intention of A's imagining. Things have merely been complicated, unnecessarily, by the addition to the intention of the mental entities and the representing relation without thereby "eliminating" what originally seemed to be the intention, namely, the non-existing "fact" of B's being taller than C.

Probably it is worth noticing that even if this were a solution, Ryle for at least two reasons could not have permanently accepted it. (a) It supposes that there are *representing* or would-be representing mental entities. (b) It supposes that on occasion awareness is *of* these representing mental entities. This is what I meant when I spoke earlier of his making non-substances the intentions of certain acts. Ryle, for "reasons" we know to be related to his general ontology, soon came

---

[20] Of course there is sometimes *also* a descriptive relation between an act and its intention.
[21] ATP, p. 123.

to reject these two suppositions. So it is not surprising that he never referred to this early "solution" again, at least not in print.

(2) The second attempt to solve the problem of non-veridical awareness occurs in "Systematically Misleading Expressions" and "Phenomenology". Before discussing it, some preliminary remarks are necessary. I have argued it to be the "essence" of mind that its acts are *about* something. Ryle at one time agreed.

> ... it would be both paradoxical and in conflict with the evidence of language to assert that there may be some forms of consciousness which are not consciousness *of* something.[22]

Yet this is what he comes to deny in the second attempt. And from taking the "intrinsic" *aboutness* out of acts to denying that there are any is but a short step.

The second attempt probably grew out of the rejection of the reference theory of meaning. Against this theory two arguments are adduced.[23] (a) It is nonsense to say of, for example, a desk that it is the meaning of a certain expression, or that the meaning of a certain expression has a cold. This argument is obviously specious. It is also, as I shall shortly show, irrelevant to the main issue.[24] (b) Some expressions have meaning even though they do not refer. Hence their referents, since they have none, cannot be their meanings. This argument is more serious. Nor can one deny its relevance. For the problem is not whether an act *means* what it is about, but rather, whether every act *is* about something or other.

Ryle's second "solution" denies that all acts, non-veridical as well as veridical, are about something. Assume that Jones imagines the moon to be made of green cheese. Ryle "solves" or "dissolves" the problem of *what* it is that Jones imagines by claiming that the *expression* (the linguistic object) 'the object of Jones' imagination' is not only "not *necessarily* a referentially used" expression, but rather, "almost certainly a systematically misleading expression".[25] The only way to make this sort of argument relevant to the original question, "What, if anything, is Jones' imagining about?", is to assume that thoughts, imaginings, beliefs, and so on, are about expressions. That shows how shallow the "solution" really is.

---

[22] *Ibid.*, p. 93.

[23] These arguments are from Ryle, "Systematically Misleading Expressions", *Proceedings of the Aristotelian Society*, Vol. XXXII, Harrison and Sons, Ltd., 1932, pp. 156 and 162–163. Hereafter referred to as SME.

[24] Nor does Ryle seem to believe otherwise.

[25] Phen, p. 79, my emphasis.

A further clue to its shallowness is provided by the 'necessarily' in the phrase just quoted. What that means is perfectly clear. *Since* the objects of Jones' imagination do not in fact exist, the (use of the) phrase 'the objects of Jones' imagination' is not necessarily referential. This agrees with two examples he uses elsewhere. We are told that in 'Tommy Jones is not the King of England' and 'Poincare is not the King of France', 'the King of England' *is* and 'the King of France' is *not* referentially used.[26] I can think of only one reason why this should be so. There is a king of England, but there is no king of France.

All we have been told, therefore, is that there is no problem concerning what Jones' imagining is about. Since the moon is in fact not made of green cheese, Jones' imagining that it is made of green cheese is about nothing, or rather, isn't "about" at all. This, I submit, is not a solution to the problem; it merely states what generates the problem. We have always known that what seems to be the object of Jones' imagination does not, as we ordinarily speak, exist. It does not follow from that, if I may so express myself, that Jones' imagining has no aboutness to it. The problem is, rather, to account for that aboutness.

Thought is "about" something even when its object does not, as we ordinarily speak, exist. It follows that *aboutness* is not a descriptive relation. If one holds, as Ryle does, that all relations are external and descriptive, then one is committed to holding that when the object isn't there, the aboutness "relation" isn't there either (not exemplified). The aboutness is in fact there. Whether that forces one to grant some ontological status to the intentions which, as we usually speak, are not there is a question we need not pursue. We merely insist that this question cannot be settled by pointing out what everyone knows already, namely, that, as we ordinarily use 'exist', the objects of non-veridical awareness do not exist.

Ryle, I suggested, eventually rejected acts because with them he could not solve the problem of non-veridical awareness. We have seen that the two attempts at solutions which he made both failed. The second virtually destroys the act by depriving it of its intrinsic intentionality; for acts, or, for that matter, minds without intentionality are not worth having. So we see Ryle turn to the materialism of *The Concept of Mind*.

<hr>

[26] SME, p. 158.

Materialism and Intentionality

There are two kinds of materialism. One view holds (in a standard form) that acts have all the properties which I have supposed them to have including, let us assume, intentional characters, but that these acts are numerically identical with certain brain or neurophysical states or processes. It may also be held that the "mental" properties, e.g., *believing* or *that-Stassen-is-President* are somehow "reducible" to or "definable" in terms of the obviously "physical" properties of brains. There is no reason to suppose this view to be true. Its crude scientistic roots are obvious, e.g., in an advocate such as J. J. C. Smart. Yet in one sense this view is superior to Ryle's, for at least it does not attempt to deny the existence of certain properties which are obviously there.

The other kind of materialism is Ryle's. Upon his view, mental acts are not identified with brain states, but rather, with actual and potential *behavior*. This view permits one to handle intentionality, after a fashion. I say "after a fashion" because the treatment is, of course, the same as that which a behaviorist psychologist would give to intentionality. For the behaviorist's purpose, which is the discovery of laws enabling him to explain and predict behavior, this treatment is adequate. As a philosophy of mind, it is hopelessly inadequate. Let us reassure ourselves that on such a view, however inadequate as a philosophy of mind, no special problems of intentionality arise. For, only if this is so will I have plausibly "explained" why Ryle was seduced by the view.

'Jones suddenly recalled that the name of his boyhood friend was Gerald'. (I use 'recall' so that he may have "falsely" recalled the name, i.e., so that his recalling may be veridical or non-veridical.) On a behavioristic analysis, this fact (Jones' having recalled, etc.) would probably be treated as a short-term disposition, a disposition to say certain things, for example. We recall that Ryle has considerable trouble with "short-term" dispositions, since they come perilously close to being what he calls occurrences. But here we can ignore his inadequate analysis of dispositions and their alleged difference from occurrences. So we get as a partial analysis: 'Jones has a disposition from times T_1 to T_2 to act in ways x, y, z . . .', which in turn is verbally analyzed as 'Jones would do [27] . . . from T_1 to T_2 if . . . were to happen' or again 'If certain stimuli are given to Jones at any time from T_1 to T_2, certain responses occur'. Now for two comments.

[27] I consider saying as a form of doing, of course.

First. Let us again remember that for the purposes of the psychologist such a treatment is adequate as long as we may suppose that there are no non-parallel interacting minds. For his job is only to find the minimum factors (relevant variables) necessary for the explanation and prediction of behavior. As a behaviorist, he is even forbidden to consider mental factors directly. That some behaviorists, including Watson, thought mistakenly that they had to be philosophical materialists *à la* Ryle is beside the point.

Second. For all practical purposes the *fact* remembered (that the name of his boyhood friend was Gerald) drops out of the analysis. This is as it should be. The only way it remains is that one of the stimulus/response patterns which "holds" from T_1 to T_2 might be something like: If someone makes the sounds "What is your boyhood friend's name?", Jones immediately makes the sound "Gerald". Thus the *problem* of intentionality drops out. Indeed we can still say what Jones' memory is *of*, as can Jones himself, but again, to say that his memory is *of* so-and-so is, on this analysis, simply to say that Jones does or would act in certain ways.

Thus there is *no* problem as to the connection between Jones' "thought" and what it is *of* on a behavioristic analysis and *a fortiori* no special problem as to what the "thought" is *of* if it is non-veridical. The problem Ryle couldn't solve as long as he was a dualist is thus automatically, as it were, "solved" on his materialistic view. There is really no *ofness* in the world and, therefore, no problem as to its proper analysis. There are just physical objects and their actual and potential behavior ("things and events").[28]

I have fulfilled my task. We have seen that Ryle's form of materialism does not contain the problems of intentionality which are inherent in all forms of dualism and which, although they are not insoluble, he could not solve. Materialism, on the other hand, i.e., behaviorism treated as a philosophy of mind, can adequately solve all the philosophical problems of mind which arise within its own limits. This is so because materialism denies the existence of what is obviously there, the mental acts. Nor is this the proper place to reach for Occam's razor. If I may speak concisely, minds are not, in the appropriate sense, *ontological* kinds; hence Occam's dictum does not apply. To deny that there are, for example, imaginings *qua* mental acts in my sense is like denying that there are chairs. And it would obviously be a wrong

---

[28] Their potential behavior does not for Ryle really exist either, of course, since, according to him, dispositions do not exist.

application of Occam's prescription to emerge with the view that chairs don't exist. The error of supposing that minds *are* ontological kinds in themselves and so can be ruled out of order by dialectics is one of the many unfortunate results of the substance ontology. As we saw in Chapter III, both Ryle and Passmore have fallen victim to that error.

Four general comments will serve as a conclusion.

First. In his early as well as his later thought, Ryle often uses his philosophy of language, which in the main he developed in "Systematically Misleading Expressions", to "justify" explicitly what his more or less implicit ontology commits him to. Two examples will show that.[29]

The phrase 'the idea of taking a holiday' in the sentence 'The idea of taking a holiday just occurred to me' is a non-referring phrase. That is the linguistic claim. It is supported by the further claim that the sentence may be restated, i.e., replaced by 'I have just been thinking that I might take a holiday'. Why, I ask, should anyone suppose that this possibility of restatement or replacement shows 'the idea of taking a holiday' to be a non-referring expression? Why would not one be equally justified in inferring that what the second statement stands for has a constituent exactly what is referred to by 'the idea of taking a holiday'? The very question shows that Ryle's linguistic argument will convince no one who is not already convinced of the *"ontological"* claim it is designed to establish.

The second example concerns universals. *Some* statements that appear to be about universals can be so restated that they are seen to be about individuals. This is the linguistic claim. Even if it were justified, does it follow either (1) that *no* statements are about universals (or properties, if you prefer) of (2) that, even if none are, there are no legitimate ontological questions about universals? I think not. 'Red is a color' can indeed be restated as 'Whatever is red is colored'. Does this show that either statement is not about red or, for that matter, about color? Again, I think not.

The examples illustrate what I believe to be a pervading feature of Ryle's style of thought. When apparently talking about language *as such*, he already assumes his general ontology as well as his views on mind. If I am right, then the systematic importance of language in this thought is generally overestimated.

Second. There is in Ryle's thought a tendency toward simplistic

---

[29] SME, pp. 150–151, and p. 161. I have paraphrased the second example.

polarization which affects his general ontology as well as his philosophy of mind. The only ontological alternatives he conceives are Aristotelianism in its most nominalistic variant on the one hand and Platonism on the other. Either only individual substances "exist" or "abstract" entities do. Surely this is simplistic polarization. Neither Platonism nor nominalistic Aristotelianism is adequate. As for general ontology, so for the philosophy of mind. Either there are no minds at all or one must, in addition to acts, countenance ideas, concepts, judgments, and what have you. Again, neither extreme is an adequate philosophy of mind.

Third. A "third realm" whose denizens are either Platonic universals (concepts), or propositions, or truth values, has found a place in many ontologies. Usually the role of such entities is to connect somehow the mental and the "physical" [30] in the knowing situation. But this third realm is unstable. Its entities tend to "fall" either to the mental or to the "physical" side. If they tend toward the "physical", the outcome may be what some call moderate realism; if they tend toward the mental, the result is likely to be conceptualism. This is not the whole story, of course; for entities of the third realm have functions other than that of grounding sameness. For instance, they ground the aboutness of non-veridical awarenesses by providing them with intentions.

Philosophers' minds do work in curious ways. Thus I shall make bold to suggest one more pattern that may have shaped Ryle's thought. In his first attempt at solving the problem of non-veridical awarenesses, the intentions of the latter were mental. Mind was thus made to do the job which more often than not has been assigned to entities of the third realm. But this realm is, rightly, suspect. Thus mind, too, came wrongly to be suspect.

Fourth. Materialism, though absurd, is nowadays very strong. Culturally, the vulgar source of its strength is no doubt the flowering science and the festering scientism of the day. Part of this atmosphere is the idea of a science of man. Ideologists may dispute it or reject it. Intellectually, it is here to stay. Ryle's materialism, we saw, is one strange fruit of his ontology. Nor, alas, is it the only one. We also saw how in his analysis of dispositions he uses the ontology to reject the science of man. Yet the idea of such a science is as sound as materialism is absurd. That does not bode well for the ontology.

---

[30] More accurately, to connect a mind with what it knows. The latter need not be physical, of course. That is why I put 'physical' between double quotes.

BIBLIOGRAPHY

Since I have made use of all of Ryle's works published before *The Concept of Mind*, they are all included in this bibliography. Those that are starred (*) are never directly referred to in the text or in footnotes.

Addis, Laird, "Kant's First Analogy," *Kant-Studien*, January, 1963.

Aristotle, *On the Soul*, from *The Basic Works of Aristotle*, edited by Richard McKeon, Random House, 1941.

Bergmann, Gustav, *Logic and Reality*, University of Wisconsin Press, 1964.

— *Meaning and Existence*, University of Wisconsin Press, 1960.

— *The Metaphysics of Logical Positivism*, Longmans, Green and Co., 1954.

— *Philosophy of Science*, University of Wisconsin Press, 1957.

— "Acts," *Rivista di Filosofia*, 51, 1960 (in Italian) and *The Indian Journal of Philosophy*, 2, 1960 (in English) and reprinted in *Logic and Reality*.

— "The Contribution of John B. Watson," *Psychological Review*, 63, 1956.

— "The Problem of Relations in Classical Psychology," *The Philosophical Quarterly*, 7, April, 1952, and reprinted in *The Metaphysics of Logical Positivism*.

— "Russell's Examination of Leibniz Examined," *Philosophy of Science* (the journal), 23, 1956, and reprinted in *Meaning and Existence*.

— "Some Reflections on Time," *Il Tempo*, Archivio di Filosofia, Padova: Cedam, 1958, and reprinted in *Meaning and Existence*.

Brodbeck, May, "Explanation, Prediction and 'Imperfect' Knowledge," *Minnesota Studies in the Philosophy of Science*, Vol. III: *Scientific Explanation, Space, and Time*, edited by H. Feigl and G. Maxwell, University of Minnesota Press, 1962.

Colburn, N. H., "Logic and Professor Ryle," *Philosophy of Science*, 21, 1954.

Grossmann, Reinhardt, "Sensory Intuition and the Dogma of Localization," *Inquiry*, Vol. 5, No. 3, Autumn, 1962.

Passmore, John, *Philosophical Reasoning*, Charles Scribner's Sons, 1961.

Ross, W. D., *Aristotle*, Meridian Book, World Publishing Co., 1961.

Ryle, Gilbert, *The Concept of Mind*, Barnes and Noble. New York, 1949.

*— *Philosophical Arguments*, Oxford at Clarendon Press, 1945.

— "Are There Propositions?", *Proceedings of the Aristotelian Society*, Vol. XXX, Harrison and Sons, Ltd., 1930.

*— "Back to the Ontological Argument," *Mind*, Vol. 46, 1937.

*— "Categories", *Proceedings of the Aristotelian Society*, Vol. XXXVIII, Harrison and Sons, Ltd., 1938.

— "Conscience and Moral Convictions," *Analysis*, Vol. 7, No. 2, 1940.

— ""If", "So", and "Because"," *Philosophical Analysis*, edited by Max Black, Cornell University Press, 1950.

— "Imaginary Objects," *Creativity, Politics and The A Priori*, Aristotelian Society, Supplementary Volume XII, Harrison and Sons, Ltd., 1933.

*— "Induction and Hypothesis," *Knowledge and Foreknowledge*, Aristotelian Society, Supplementary Volume XVI, Harrison and Sons, Ltd., 1937.

— "Internal Relations," *Science, History, andTheology*, Aristotelian Society, Supplementary Volume XIV, Harrison and Sons, Ltd., 1935.

— "Knowing How and Knowing That," *Proceedings of the Aristotelian Society*, Vol. XLVI, Harrison and Sons, Ltd., 1946.

— "Locke on the Human Understanding," *John Locke Tercentenary Addresses*, Oxford University Press, 1933.

*— "Mr. Collingwood and the Ontological Argument," *Mind*, Vol. 44, 1935.

— "Negation," *Knowledge, Experience and Realism*, Aristotelian Society, Supplementary Volume IX, Harrison and Sons, Ltd., 1929.

— "Phenomenology," *Phenomenology, Goodness and Beauty*, Aristotelian Society, Supplementary Volume XI, Harrison and Sons, Ltd., 1932.

— "Plato's 'Parmenides'," published in two parts in *Mind*, Vol. 48, 1939.

— "Systematically Misleading Expressions," *Proceedings of the Aristotelian Society*, Vol. XXXII, Harrisons and Son, Ltd., 1932.

*— "Taking Sides in Philosophy," *Philosophy*, Vol. 12, 1937.

*— "Unverifiability-By-Me,," *Analysis*, Vol. 4, No. 1, 1936.

— "Why Are the Calculuses of Logic and Arithmetic Applicable to Reality?", *Logic and Reality*, Aristotelian Society, Supplementary Volume XX, Harrison and Sons, Ltd., 1946.

*— Discussion of Rudolf Carnap's *Meaning and Necessity*, *Philosophy*, Vol. 24, 1949.

*— Review of Marvin Farber's *The Foundations of Phenomenology*, *Philosophy*, Vol. 21, 1946.

MOORE'S REALISM

Douglas Lewis

INTRODUCTION

The controversy between the realist and idealist can only be resolved by providing adequate analyses of material objects as well as our awarenesses of them. Moore attempts to resolve the controversy by providing what he considers to be adequate realistic analyses of both. Though he supports what I believe to be the correct side of the controversy, neither of his two analyses is adequate.

The realistic position Moore wishes to secure can be expressed briefly in two statements. (a) Material objects are substances. (b) Material objects exist independently of our awarenesses of them. What Moore means by 'material object' and 'awareness' is perfectly clear and unproblematic. By the former he means such ordinary objects as chairs, tables, rocks and trees; by the latter the various mental states of perceiving, thinking of, remembering, imagining and so on, which occur when we apprehend these objects. Yet what he means by 'substance' and 'independent' is anything but clear and unproblematic. To make clear what he does mean by these terms, and to show that *with these meanings* both (a) and (b) are false, are two major purposes I have set myself in this study.

A third major purpose is to uncover the mistakes which push Moore into the analyses he proposes and, at the same time, keep him from seeing that they are inadequate. Three mistakes may be singled out as particularly important. *One.* Moore fails to distinguish clearly between the evident fact that many commonsensical statements made about material objects are true and the quite different, and not at all evident, claim that a substance analysis of material objects is adequate. Or, to put the point differently, he fails to distinguish between what we know *commensically* to be true about material objects on the one hand and a patently *philosophical* view as to their nature on the other. In short, he takes commonsense itself to be an ontological position. *Two.* Moore is impressed by the fact that in certain contexts we cannot reasonably doubt the veracity of our awarenesses of material objects. He mistakenly believes this to require that there be an intrinsic criterion distinguishing material objects from other objects of which we are sometimes also aware. In other words, he holds there must be an ontological ground in material objects for the certainty we have of our judgments about them. *Three.* Moore is unable to see any alternative to the view that an awareness of a material object consists of a mind, or mental individual, and a material object jointly exemplifying a descriptive relation. Attempting to cast all our awarenesses of things into this mold, he is unable to account adequately for perceptual error.

In the course of making clear what Moore's realistic analyses are and of showing in what ways they are mistaken, other analyses, quite unlike his, of material objects as well as of our awarenesses of them will be proposed. Basically, material objects will be analyzed as patterns of what Moore calls sense-data; awarenesses, as individuals exemplifying what I shall call intentional characters. What has been called traditionally a reconstruction of material objects and an account of the intentionality of our awarenesses of them are the two crucial features around which an adequate realistic position must be secured. The way I try to secure them may not be adequate in all details. Yet, it alone suffices to illuminate the inadequacy of Moore's realism.

I. THE REFUTATION OF IDEALISM

Throughout his philosophical career Moore never doubted that there are rocks and mountains, and chairs, and tables. Moore never doubted that there are human beings who perceive rocks and chairs. Nor did he ever doubt that there are rocks and chairs when there are no human beings perceiving them. Yet, though he was certain of all this, he was not certain that realism was true. Nor is there anything paradoxical in this. The truth of such commonsensical assertions as that this is a chair and that I am perceiving a chair (when I am perceiving one) is unproblematic. What is problematic is the correct analysis of what is expressed by these assertions. As to their correct analysis Moore was never sure. He was strongly inclined to believe, though not always for the right reasons, that for any analysis to be correct it must be *realistic in character*. He devoted himself in much of his philosophical writings to the task of giving such an analysis. That he never succeeded is a

measure of his failure. In this chapter I am not concerned with Moore's
various attempts to secure realism. Rather, I am concerned with the
different though related task which he set himself of refuting idealism.

To refute idealism is not to secure realism. To refute idealism is to
show that no analysis of the states of affairs expressed by sentences
like 'I am perceiving a chair' *which is idealistic in character* is the true
one. To secure realism is to give an analysis of such states of affairs
which is in the appropriate sense realistic. The value of Moore's refutation of idealism is wholly negative. Though he was not clearly
aware of this in his early paper, he soon realized he had not secured
realism. The volume of his later writing devoted to that task is evidence of this. As to what characteristics an analysis must have to be
realistic I need not concern myself here. The question to be answered
is, when is an analysis idealistic? A short quotation from Moore will
help to suggest an answer.

In "The Refutation of Idealism" [1] Moore states that nothing he
will say has the slightest tendency to prove that the general conclusion
which idealism asserts, namely, that reality is spiritual, is false. What
he intends to dispute is the truth of a premise which occurs in all
arguments idealists have ever considered necessary for establishing
their general conclusion. If the premise which occurs in all these
arguments is false, and if any one of the arguments is a necessary and
essential step in establishing the conclusion, then the truth of the
conclusion remains the barest supposition. The premise in question is
esse is *percipi*. What does it mean to say that *esse* is *percipi*? Though,
as Moore says, this proposition is very ambiguous it is,

... at once equivalent to saying that whatever is, is experienced; and this, again,
is equivalent, in a sense, to saying that whatever is, is something mental.

He continues immediately by saying:

But this is not the sense in which the Idealist *conclusion* must maintain that
Reality is *mental*. The Idealist *conclusion* is that *esse* is *percipere;* and hence,
whether *esse* be *percipi* or not, a further and different discussion is needed to
show whether or not it is also *percipere*. And again, even if *esse* be *percipere*,
we need a vast quantity of further argument to show that what has *esse* has
also those higher mental qualities which are denoted by spiritual.[2]

Here Moore distinguishes three senses of 'mental'. Idealists maintain
that whatever is, is mental in that sense (whatever it be) which is

---

[1] G. E. Moore, "The Refutation of Idealism," *Mind*, N.S. XII (1903), 433–453; reprinted
in *Philosophical Studies* (London: Routledge and Kegan Paul, Ltd., 1922), pp. 1–30. All page
references are to the latter.

[2] *Ibid.*, p. 6.

meant by saying that reality is spiritual. But in order to show that whatever is, is mental in this sense, the idealist considers it necessary to show that whatever is, is also mental in the different sense of 'mental' in which to be mental is to be an experienc*ing*, or synonymously, to experience. And in order to show that whatever is, is mental in this second sense, the idealist considers it necessary to show that whatever is, is also mental in a third sense in which to be mental is to be experienc*ed*.

By distinguishing among these senses of 'mental' one can characterize an idealistic analysis in the following way. An analysis is idealistic when *every* constituent of what is analyzed is claimed to be in some sense mental. The idealist maintains that in a state of affairs such as that expressed by the sentence 'I am perceiving a chair' every constituent is mental either in the sense that it itself experiences (that is, is an experiencing), or in the sense that it is experienced, or in some more exalted sense of 'mental', or several or all of these senses together. What Moore attempts to show in his paper is (1) that not everything in the world experiences, that is, is an experiencing, and (2) that not everything in the world either experiences or is mental in that sense in which being experienced is alleged to make it mental. Whether or not everything is mental in some other sense or senses of 'mental' he does not profess to know. All he claims to be able to show is that everything is not mental in either sense (1) or (2).

Has Moore, then, refuted idealism? If his arguments are conclusive, then he has shown that two idealistic analyses are inadequate. This is not, of course, equivalent to showing that all other claims which idealism makes about the world are false. But Moore is not concerned to refute idealism in the broad sense in which it includes such claims as that reality is spiritual, in some unanalyzed sense of 'spiritual'. Rather, he is concerned to show that the idealistic analyses upon which such other claims are based are false. If these analyses are false then all other claims which idealism makes about the world are the barest suppositions. Moore implicitly holds that the two analyses which he considers are the only ones upon which idealists have ever based their other claims. If this is true and if his arguments against these analyses are conclusive then in the only sense of 'idealism' in which idealism is of philosophical interest he has refuted it.

Are these two analyses the structural roots of all idealistic positions? In this chapter I could not hope to establish any claim so broad as that they are. To establish this one would have to exhibit the structural root of every idealistic philosophy. Though I shall not show that the claim is true, I believe that it is. Moore states that the first analysis which he considers is the structural root of Hegelian idealism. I assume that he is correct in this. The second analysis, or more accurately, one variant of it, is the heart of Berkeleian idealism. This I shall indicate briefly later.

This chapter follows the following plan. First, I shall state what the first idealistic analysis is and discuss Moore's argument against it. The crucial point which he makes against this idealistic analysis is, briefly, that in every situation in which there is experiencing of anything there are *two* constituents involved. The experiencing and the experienced are two things and not one. Second, I shall state and discuss the second analysis and Moore's argument against it. The crucial point here is that the experiencing and the experienced do not stand to each other as a thing to its qualities or as two qualities (necessarily) tied to each other. What is experienced is not mental either in the sense of being a quality of the whole of which experiencing is also a quality. Third, I shall make some general comments about Moore's paper, and discuss some limitations of it.

Before I turn to the first part, however, an introductory comment will help to distinguish the central question at issue from certain other questions which, though related to this one, can, for our purposes, be safely brushed aside. Moore does not attempt to analyze any situation so complex as that of someone's perceiving a chair. He considers a much simpler situation which he calls "the sensation of blue." Though there are certain ambiguities in the expression 'the sensation of blue' to which I shall attend presently, this paradigm has at least two advantages over other more complex ones. First, this simple paradigm indicates that what is at issue is not the analysis of *what* is experienced, that is of the intention of experiencing, whether the experiencing be sensing or perceiving, but rather what the relation is between the sensing or perceiving on the one hand and what is sensed or perceived on the other. That there are two questions here and not one is, I think, clear. Nor is that to say that there are no connections between them. Certain analyses of what we would ordinarily call material objects preclude certain analyses of the relation between them and the mind. To give one illustration, a philosopher who holds that material objects, chairs for example, are substances, in the traditional sense of 'substance', will not hold that they stand in a relation of dependence on the mind, in the sense that they can exist only when perceived. Substances are independent in a sense, among others, which excludes this kind of dependency.[3] On the other hand a philosopher who holds that material objects are, roughly, collections of simple qualities will find this alternative open to him. Second, the paradigm indicates that what is at issue is not the analysis of a mind. The question as to whether a mind is a substance, in the traditional sense of 'substance', or a series of acts of awareness or something else can safely be left to one side. Idealism stands or falls depending upon whether the relation between the object experienced and what experiences it is as the idealist claims it is, and not whether the latter is a substantial mind (an enduring entity or continuant) or a mental act (or series of such). A brief mention of Berkeley's idealism will illustrate this point. For Berkeley what experiences is a substance; a substantial, enduring, active mind. The objects experienced are ideas; that is, qualities of the mind. In what I have called the second analysis Moore characterizes the idealist as maintaining that the experienced and the experiencing stand to each other as quality to substance. The pattern is the same. The implicit analysis of a mind is what differs.

Though the simple paradigm – " the sensation of blue" – serves to distinguish the question of the analysis of the connection between act and object from those of the analyses of material objects and of minds, it may nevertheless foster some confusions itself. The paradigm suggests that there might be an experience whose sole object was blue; that one might sense blue, for example, apart from blue specks. That one never experiences blue apart from blue things is, of course, perfectly clear. Nor did Moore ever suppose that one does. In the brief discussion of his refutation paper in "A Reply to My Critics" [4] he expressly denies it. The point is, again, that to mention a simple entity as the object of experience rather than the complexes in which it occurs avoids any discussion of the analysis of such complexes. The paradigm is, nevertheless, misleading in this respect. Also, the use of the sensation of blue as opposed to the perception of blue or the thought of blue may lead one to suppose that it is with sensing, as contrasted with these other acts, that Moore is specifically concerned. This may lead one to suppose that he is denying that sense-data or their properties are mental. But this is not the issue. Moore is not concerned with

3 This sense of 'independent' is explicated in Chapter II. See pages 127–128.

4 P. A. Schilpp, ed., *The Philosophy of G. E. Moore*, 2nd ed. (New York: Tudor Publishngi Co., 1952), p. 659.

the analysis of the connection between any specific kind of act and its particular kind of intention. Rather, he is concerned with the analysis of the connection between the act and its intention independently of what specific kind of act it is. As he himself says:

> The distinction between sensation and thought need not detain us here. For, in whatever respects they differ, they have at least this in common, that they are both forms of consciousness or, to use a term that seems to be more in fashion just now, they are both ways of experiencing.[5]

Whatever differences there may be between sense-data and material objects can be ignored when discussing the connection between either of them and the experiencing of them.

I turn now to the first idealistic analysis. Some idealists maintain that everything in the world is mental in the sense in which to be mental is to experience, or, to be an experiencing. To put the point more idiomatically, they maintain that everything in the world is conscious. What exactly is the claim which these idealists are making about the world, and how did they come to make it? Moore characterizes how they came to make this claim as follows. (The characterization is, of course, not an historical account of how they came to hold the view, but a description of the structure of it.) First, they claim that *esse* is *percipi*, that is, that whatever is, is also necessarily experienced. Second, they confuse with this claim or take as a reason for it another, namely, that whatever is, forms, together with the experiencing of it, an organic unity. By an organic unity they mean a complex (a whole) which is such that,

> ...whenever you try to assert *anything whatever* of that which is a *part* of an organic whole, what you assert can only be true of the whole.[6]

These idealists maintain, in other words, that everything in the world is mental in the sense that every *thing*, every experienced object enters into a complex of which experiencing (consciousness) is also a constituent. But these complexes are so "simple" that their constituents cannot be named; that is, nothing whatever can be said about the constituents. The simplest things one can talk about are organic unities. But to claim that the simplest things one can talk about are organic unities is equivalent to claiming that organic unities have no constituents. These idealists are therefore both asserting and denying that an organic unity is complex in one and the same sense of 'complex'; they both affirm and at the same time deny that the experienced

---

[5] "The Refutation of Idealism," *op. cit.*, p. 7
[6] *Ibid.*, p. 15.

and the experiencing are distinct. To point out this contradiction is, as Moore says, sufficient to refute the view.

The above paragraph states succinctly the Hegelian idealistic analysis and Moore's argument against it. A few comments may help to illuminate certain points in the paragraph. The idealist claims that *esse* is *percipi*; that whatever is, is also necessarily experienced. What exactly is the idealist saying about the world when he makes this claim? Moore gives two formulations of '*esse* is *percipi*' which are not equivalent to each other. Which of these formulations expresses more accurately the fact to which the idealist wishes to call attention? One of them is exemplified in the following quotations.

Esse is *percipi* asserts that wherever you have [esse] you also have *percipi*, that whatever has the property [esse] also has the property that it is *experienced*.[7]

We have therefore discovered the ambiguity of the copula in *esse* is *percipi*, so far as to see that this principle asserts two distinct terms to be so related, that whatever has the *one*, which I call *esse*, has *also* the property that it is experienced.[8]

And about *esse* Moore says "'real' is a convenient name for a union of attributes," and in this context he uses the phrase "the other qualities included under *esse*." [9]

In these quotations it is clear that Moore is using the words '*esse*' and '*percipi*' to designate two properties that are in some way related to each other. He claims that by '*esse* is *percipi*' the idealist is asserting that of any entity whatsoever, if it has the property existence, then it also has, and must have, the property being experienced. Existence and being experienced are two properties necessarily tied to each other. But it is clear to me that the idealist is not attempting to say anything at all about the (alleged) properties existence and being experienced. Whether or not existence is a property is, in this context, wholly irrelevant. And there are passages in which Moore seems to understand *esse* is *percipi* quite differently from the above. The following two quotations are representative. Referring to a passage he has just quoted from a paper on idealism by Mr. Taylor, Moore says:

---

[7] *Ibid.*, p. 10. The exact quotation is:

Esse is *percipi* asserts that wherever you have x you also have *percipi*, that whatever has the property x also has the property that it is *experienced*.

By 'x' Moore means a property, which he later calls *esse*, which does not include *percipi* as a constituent. This subtlety does not affect the sense of the passage; hence I have ignored it.

[8] "The Refutation of Idealism," *op. cit.*, p. 11.

[9] *Ibid.*, p. 10.

... I *shall* undertake to show that what makes a thing real cannot possibly be its presence as an inseparable aspect of a sentient experience.[10]

And as a kind of summary of his discussion of '*esse* is *percipi*' he says:

Idealists, we have seen, must assert that whatever is experienced, is *necessarily* so. And this doctrine they commonly express by saying that 'the object of experience is inconceivable apart from the subject.' [11]

In these quotations Moore claims that by '*esse* is *percipi*' the idealist is asserting that every entity must have the property being experienced. But to say of any entity that it must be experienced is, of course, to say of that entity that there is an experiencing necessarily tied to it. In other words, in these quotations he takes the principle to assert that every entity, every exist*ent*, is necessarily tied to the experiencing of it. This second formulation of '*esse* is *percipi*' seems to express what the idealist wishes to say about the world more accurately than the first.

There is nevertheless an ambiguity in this formulation. It is not clear whether 'existent' applies to the experiencing, as well as the object experienced, or not. If it does then every experiencing will itself be necessarily tied to an experiencing of it, and so on *ad infinitum*. Some idealists may have meant this. But others did not mean their principle to apply to the experiencing itself. Berkeley, for example, held that the *esse* of ideas is *percipi*, but that the *esse* of minds is *percipere*. After the discussion in which Moore himself clarifies some of the other ambiguities in *esse* is *percipi* (a section of the paper I do not discuss) he makes the startling statement:

We have, then in *esse* is *percipi*, a *necessary synthetic* proposition which I have undertaken to refute, And I may say at once that, understood as such, it cannot be refuted.[12]

At the beginning of his paper Moore had claimed that it was this premise which occurred in all idealistic arguments at least one of which was necessary in establishing the idealist's general conclusion that he was going to refute. Why does he say, then, that understood as such, it cannot be refuted? One thing that he may mean by this is that he cannot point to or indicate any thing which is not being experienced. When one succeeds in pointing out something to another that thing is being experienced by him, either imagined or thought of or perceived or experienced in some other way. But this point is rather obvious.

10 *Ibid.*, p. 8.
11 *Ibid.*, p. 12.
12 *Ibid.*, p. 11.

A more subtle point that Moore may be making here is that *esse* is *percipi* understood as such does not constitute a philosophical analysis of the connection between the experiencing and the object experienced. That every *thing* is necessarily tied to the experiencing of it; that, in other words, nothing can, in some ordinary sense of 'can', exist unperceived may be understood as merely a commonsensical claim about the world. Understood as such it is patently false. But it cannot be refuted just as its denial, that there are things existing unperceived, cannot be proved. This is one of those unproblematic common-sense truths with which we begin. What Moore wants to refute is not this claim, but *esse* is *percipi* understood as expressing a certain analysis of the connection between the experienced object and the experiencing of it. The Hegelian idealist does not merely assert that every *thing* is necessarily tied to the experiencing of it. He also asserts the different claim which, as Moore says, he either confuses with the first or takes as a reason for it, namely, that every *thing* is necessarily tied to the experiencing of it in the *particular way* that the experienced and the experiencing form an organic unity. This is the claim which Moore refutes in the argument I stated above. To repeat that argument briefly: according to the Hegelian idealist the tie which connects the experiencing and the experienced is so "close" that the two entities tied become one.

Approximately in the middle of "The Refutation of Idealism" Moore makes another rather startling statement. He says:

But at this point I propose to make a complete break in my argument.
. . . .
I pass, ... from the uninteresting question 'Is *esse percipi*?' to the still more uninteresting and apparently irrelevant question 'What is a sensation or idea?'[13]

There is in one respect a complete break in Moore's argument. He drops the discussion of what I have called the first idealistic analysis and goes on to discuss the second. But in another respect there is a continuity between the two sections which must not be overlooked. The question which he asks himself about sensations is essentially the same as the question he asked himself about *esse* is *percipi*, namely, what is the connection between the elements in a sensation; what is the connection between the sensing and the object sensed, between the experiencing and the object experienced? In a sense, then, Moore fails to appreciate the structure of his own paper. He is

[13] *Ibid.*, pp. 16–17.

misled into thinking he is making a *complete* break, in part, I submit, by his own misleading formulations of *esse* is *percipi* which I discussed above.

What is a sensation or idea? A sensation is a complex which consists of at least two elements. There is the element which all sensations have in common and which makes them sensations, the element which Moore calls 'consciousness'. And there is the element in virtue of which one sensation differs from another, the element which he calls "the 'object' of sensation," or, alternately "the object of consciousness." The sensation of green and the sensation of blue are alike in that both contain the element consciousness, and different in that one contains the element green and the other the element blue.

There is at the outset in Moore's discussion an ambiguity in his use of the word 'sensation'. He sometimes uses 'sensation' to refer to the whole of which consciousness and an object are elements. But he also uses 'sensation' to refer to that part of the whole which is common to them all, namely, consciousness. For example, in the phrase "the object of sensation" 'sensation' is used to refer to that element which he otherwise calls 'consciousness', but in the phrase "in every sensation ... we must distinguish two elements" 'sensation' is used to refer to the whole. I shall consistently use 'sensation' to refer to the whole and not to any of its elements. If one uses 'sensation' in this way the phrase "the object of sensation" must be discarded. Green, for example, is not the object *of* any sensation at all. Green is an object *in* a sensation. If green is the object *of* anything, it is the object of that other element in the sensation, consciousness.[14]

This ambiguity occurs again, in a different form, when Moore states what the relation is which the idealists have maintained connects these elements. According to him, idealists have held that the relation of object to consciousness in any sensation is that of "content of." The object in any sensation stands to consciousness as its content. Moore explains what is meant by saying that one thing is the "content" of another in a passage which I shall quote at length.

First of all I wish to point out that "blue" is rightly and properly said to be part of the content of a blue flower. If, therefore, we also assert that it is part of the content of the sensation of blue, we assert that it has to the other parts (if any) of this whole the same relation which it has to the other parts of a blue flower

---

[14] Choosing to use 'sensation' for the whole of which consciousness is an element rather than for consciousness itself is not gratuitous. That Moore thinks of a sensation as a complex including consciousness and an object has an effect on his later analysis of acts (see Chapter IV, pages 158–164) and ultimately on his realism (see Chapter V, pages 177–178).

... And we have seen that the sensation of blue contains at least one other element besides blue – namely, what I call "consciousness," which makes it a sensation. So far then as we assert that blue is the content of the sensation, we assert that it has to this "consciousness" the same relation which it has to the other parts of a blue flower: we do assert this, and we assert no more than this. Into the question what exactly the relation is between blue and a blue flower in virtue of which we call the former part of its "content" I do not propose to enter. It is sufficient for my purpose to point out that it is the general relation most commonly meant when we talk of a thing and its qualities; and that this relation is such that to say the thing exists implies that the qualities also exist.[15]

This paragraph does not state perfectly clearly what the "content" analysis of a sensation is. There is a blur in it which is masked by an ambiguous use of the phrase 'content of'. In the first part of the paragraph 'content of' is used to refer to a relation which obtains between the two elements in the sensation. Blue, the content, is said to stand in the relation of "content of" to the other element in the sensation, consciousness. This is the relation which is mentioned by Moore when he says that "so far as we assert that blue is the content of the sensation, we assert that it has to this 'consciousness' the same relation which it has to the other parts of a blue flower." But in the latter part of the paragraph 'content of' is used to refer, not to a relation which obtains between the two elements in the sensation, but between one of the elements in the sensation, namely, blue, and the sensation itself. This is the relation which is mentioned by Moore when he says that "into the question what exactly the relation is between blue and a blue flower in virtue of which we call the former part of its [the flower's] 'content' I do not propose to enter," and again when he says that "this relation is such that to say the thing exists implies that the qualities also exist." It is the relation which Moore mentions at the beginning of this quotation and not the one which he mentions at the end which is crucial to the "content" analysis of a sensation. What the idealist wants to give an analysis of is the connection between the elements in a sensation, and not the connection between one of these elements and the whole of which it is an element. I shall, accordingly, use the phrase "content of" to refer to the connection between these elements. With regard to *this* relation it is not the case "that to say the thing exists implies that the qualities [the contents, that is] also exist." The thing, the substance – that element in the complex which is not a content – does not depend for its existence upon its content. The converse (or nearly the converse) is, however, the case. To say that a quality, or content, exists implies that a thing also exists. There

[15] "The Refutation of Idealism," *op. cit.,* pp. 21–22.

cannot be a content which is not a content of something; there cannot be a quality which does not qualify something. This is part of what is meant by 'content' and 'quality' in this context.

This last point is an important one which I shall pick up again presently. But first there is another ambiguity with regard to the word 'content' which must be mentioned which Moore himself points out. To say that blue is *the* content of the sensation of blue may be misleading. Moore explains the sense in which it may mislead in the following quotation.

The term "content" may be used in two senses. If we use "content" as equivalent to what Mr. Bradley calls the "*what*" – if we mean by it the *whole* of what is said to exist, when the thing is said to exist, then blue is certainly not *the* content of the sensation of blue: part of the *content* of the sensation is, in this sense of the term, that other element which I have called consciousness . . . But there is another sense in which "blue" might properly be said to be *the* content of the sensation – namely, the sense in which "content," like EIDOS, is opposed to "substance" or "matter." For the element "consciousness," being common to all sensations, may be and certainly is regarded as in some sense their "substance," and by the "content" of each is only meant that in respect of which one differs from another.[16]

Here Moore says that consciousness may be taken to be either one or another of two kinds of entities. Consciousness may be taken to be a substance, that is, an entity different in kind from blue, or it may be taken to be itself a content, that is, an entity of the same kind as blue. If consciousness is taken to be a substance then blue stands to it in the relation of "content of" discussed above. If consciousness is taken to be itself a content then blue does not stand to it in this relation, but in some other relation not discussed by Moore. He suggests that either of these two alternatives is open to the idealist within the general framework of the "content" analysis of a sensation.

What, then, is the second analysis which idealists may give of such situations as the sensation of blue which is *idealistic in character?* What do these idealists mean when they say that everything in the world is mental? First, these idealists maintain that in any such situation as the sensation of blue there are two constituents and not one. The sensing and the object sensed, the experiencing and the object experienced, consciousness and blue, are two distinct elements which form a complex. Second, they maintain that the experiencing and the object experienced are related to each other either as a substance to its qualities or as two qualities (necessarily) tied to each other. These are

[16] *Ibid.*, pp. 22–23.

the two variants of the second idealistic analysis. The object experienced is taken to be a quality of, or a content of, the experiencing of it. Or, it is taken to be a quality of, in a different sense of 'quality of', the complex of which the experiencing is also a quality. When the idealist says that everything in the world is mental, what he means if he takes the first variant of this analysis (which is the one in which I am most interested), is that everything is either itself an experiencing – a mental entity in an unproblematic commonsensical sense of 'mental' – or it is a quality of such an entity. To say that whatever is, is mental in the sense of being experienced is just to say that whatever is, is a quality of the experiencing of it. To say that whatever is experienced, *must* be experienced is just to say that qualities must qualify an experiencing.

I said at the beginning of this chapter that this analysis is the structural root of the Berkeleian idealism. Though I do not wish to discuss Berkeley's idealism in detail a few comments will help to justify this claim. For Berkeley there are two kinds of existents, minds and ideas. Minds are perceiving, active beings; unextended, indivisible substances or spirits. Ideas are passive, inert, sensible qualities or collections of such; colors, sounds, figures, tastes, orders and so on. How are these two kinds of entities related to each other? Ideas, Berkeley says, are "in" the mind, which is the same thing as to say, ideas are "perceived by" the mind. What is this relation between ideas and the mind which Berkeley refers to by the word 'in' and the phrase 'perceived by'? Two crucial characteristics of this relation show that it is the relation which Moore refers to by the phrase 'content of' or 'quality of'. First, there can be no idea which does not stand in this relation to a mind. There are no ideas which are not "in" a mind or "perceived by" it. Ideas are the kind of entity which must be "in" or "perceived by" something which is itself not an idea. There being is to be perceived. This characteristic they share with what Moore calls "contents" or "qualities." But secondly, ideas stand to minds in precisely the relation in which philosophers vulgarly hold, as Berkeley says, sensible qualities stand to matter. To quote part of section 91 of the *Principles:*

It is acknowledged on the received principles, that extension, motion, and in a word all sensible qualities, have need of a support, as not being able to subsist by themselves ... So that in denying the things perceived by sense, an existence independent of a substance, or support wherein they may exist, we detract nothing from the received opinion of their *reality*, and are guilty of no innovation in that respect. All the difference is, that according to us the unthinking beings perceived by sense, have no existence distinct from being perceived, and cannot therefore exist in any other substance, than those unextended, indivisible substances, or *spirits*, which act, and think, and perceive them: whereas philosophers vulgarly hold, that the sensible qualities exist in an inert, extended, unperceiving substance, which they call *matter* . . .[17]

This is precisely the view which Moore attributed to the idealists in the passage which I quoted at length above. To put the point in Moore's words, when the idealist claims that blue is the content of a sensation he claims that blue has to consciousness the same relation it is rightly and properly said to have to the other parts of a blue flower. That this is the pattern of Berkeley's idealism is, I think, undeniable.[18]

So far I have stated what the second idealistic analysis is. The next question is, what is Moore's argument against it? His argument consists, essentially, in stating that there is a unique element in every sensation which all idealists ignore. A sensation is a complex consisting of consciousness, that is experiencing, and an object experienced, in the paradigm, blue. According to him, the object experienced may be the content of the experiencing, though we have no reason to suppose that it is. But whether it is the content of the experiencing or not it is *also* related to the experiencing in another way, and the unique element in all sensations which accounts for the fact that consciousness and object are related in this *other* way is the element which idealists have overlooked. What is this "other way" in which experiencing and the object experienced are related? Moore expresses the fact that consciousness and objects are thus uniquely related to each other by saying that in the sensation of blue consciousness is *of* blue. He also uses the word 'awareness' for consciousness and says that every sensation is an awareness *of* an object. But aside from using 'of' to express this relationship he makes only two claims about it. (1) The connection between consciousness and object is perfectly distinct and unique, one which is *not* that of thing or substance to content, nor of one part of content to another part of content. (2) The connection is such that at least one of the terms which it connects is always a kind of experiencing, either perceiving, sensing, knowing, or some other kind. He also expresses this second claim by saying that it is the presence in a

---

[17] George Berkeley, *A Treatise Concerning the Principles of Human Knowledge;* reprinted in *The Works of George Berkeley,* ed., A. A. Luce and T. E. Jessop (London: Nelson and Sons Ltd., 1949), II, 80–81.

[18] For a more thorough analysis of the role this pattern plays in Berkeley's idealism, see E. B. Allaire, "Berkeley's Idealism," *Theoria,* XXIX (1963), 1–16; reprinted in E.B. Allaire *et al., Essays in Ontology* (The Hague: Martinus Nijhoff, 1963), pp. 92–105.

sensation of the element which accounts for the fact that consciousness and object are thus uniquely related which "makes the sensation
of blue a mental fact." (p. 24) This element is, in other words, *the*
characteristic feature of mind.

Do these two claims constitute a conclusive argument against the
second idealistic analysis? I believe that they do. To show that an
analysis is inadequate it is sufficient to point out that there is a feature
of the states of affairs being analyzed of which the analysis does not
take account. In this case the states of affairs being analyzed are
those such as sensing a blue speck, or perceiving a chair. In each of
these situations there is a unique element which might appropriately
be called the intentionality of consciousness. This feature is omitted
in the idealistic analysis. Hence it is inadequate. Moore's argument
may be stated as follows. Idealists analyze the sensation of blue into
consciousness and blue related either as substance to quality or as two
qualities (necessarily) tied to each other. There is in the sensation of
blue a unique element in virtue of which consciousness and blue are
related in neither of these two ways. Therefore, the idealist's analysis is
inadequate, that is, it does not take into account an element which is
there. The argument is valid. The first premise is true. Is the second
premise true? Moore does not offer any argument for it. But it is the
kind of premise for which no argument need be given. That there is an
intentional feature in such states of affairs as contain these various
forms of consciousness is as unproblematic as that there are chairs
and tables which exist unperceived. These are not claims whose truth
has to be proved. These are truths for which any adequate analysis
must account.

Has Moore, then, refuted idealism? I said at the beginning of this
chapter that he implicitly holds that the two analyses which he considers are the structural roots of all idealistic positions. And I said
that if he offers conclusive arguments against these two analyses, then
he has refuted idealism. I have tried to show that his arguments against
these analyses are conclusive, and hence, that he has refuted idealism.
One may object that to refute idealism does not consist merely in
offering conclusive arguments against these two idealistic analyses,
but that it includes, in addition to this, at least showing that these two
analyses are the basis of all idealistic claims. The objection is merely
verbal. There are several things any one of which the phrase 'refute
idealism' may be taken to mean. A refutation of idealism may be taken
to consist of offering conclusive arguments against these idealistic

analyses, showing that these two analyses are the basis of all idealistic claims, *and* showing that all other idealistic claims are false. Or, a refutation of idealism may be taken to consist of all this as well as giving a diagnosis of why idealists came to hold these views. Or it may be taken to consist of all of *this* plus giving a realistic analysis. To refute idealism may be any of these five tasks. All I claim is that Moore has refuted idealism in the first sense which I have given to that phrase.

Though Moore has refuted idealism, he has not secured realism. To secure realism is to give an analysis which is in the appropriate sense realistic. One may object that in pointing out that there is an intentional element in consciousness, that the experiencing and the object experienced in such situations as the sensation of blue are related in such a way that the experiencing is *of* blue, he has given a realistic analysis. But this is not the case. To state that there is a feature of such situations which the idealist has overlooked is one thing. To give an analysis of such situations which accounts for this feature is another. That there is an intentional element in the sensation of blue is the fact with which we begin. An adequate analysis of the sensation must state what kind of element this is, what kind of connection consciousness and object have to each other, the similarities and differences of it to other connections, and so on.

In conclusion I shall make four general comments about Moore's paper. Two comments concern limitations of the paper, and two concern insights in it. One limitation I have already discussed. Moore has refuted idealism in one sense, though he has not refuted idealism in several others. Nor has he secured realism. This limitation is in a sense its strength. By limiting himself to a discussion of the structure of idealism, he has brushed aside other issues which, though important, take one beyond the scope of a single paper. The other limitation I leave until last.

The two insights are these. Moore sees that the characteristic feature of mind is intentionality, the element which accounts for the fact that experiencing is always "of" an object. The vision is, to be sure, veiled. At one place he says that the element which makes a sensation a mental fact is consciousness (p. 20); at another, that it is the "third" element, the relation which connects consciousness to its object (p. 29). He cannot give an analysis of a sensation which accounts for this feature. But however blurred the insight is it is crucial to his refutation of idealism. For the idealist, mind in some way or other affects everything it touches, which is, indeed, everything. And as Moore forcefully says:

> ... we [must] recognise that this awareness [mind, that is, as Moore understands it] is and must be in all cases of such a nature that is object, when we are aware of it, is precisely what it would be, if we were not aware ...[19]

The denial of this claim, which he so emphatically insists upon, is, I suppose, the fount of all idealistic philosophy.

The second insight is expressed in the passage immediately following the one just quoted.

> ... it becomes plain that the existence of a table in space is related to my experience of *it* in precisely the same way as the existence of my own experience is related to my experience of *that*.

The relation between a material object and the perception of it, between the sensing of a blue sense-datum and the awareness of it, is the same in each case. To quote one other sentence:

> ... "blue" is as much an object, and as little a mere content, of my experience, when I experience it, as the most exalted and independent real thing of which I am ever aware.[20]

This is an insight which Moore later lost. In most of his attempts to give a realistic analysis of perceptual situations such as perceiving a chair, he analyzed perceiving a chair as sensing a sense datum, with the sense-datum a representative of the chair in some way or other. In other words he took the connection between perceiving and the chair to be *different* from the connection between sensing and a sense-datum. In the former case the relation, between perceiving and the chair, was mediated by an additional entity. In the latter case the relation, between sensing and the sense datum, was not. The question of how the sense datum was related to the chair plagued Moore the rest of his philosophical life. This is a difficulty he may have avoided altogether if he had held fast to the point which he made here.

The second limitation occurs in the form of a blur. Moore distinguishes between act and object, between the seeing and the seen, between the knowing and the thing known. That there is this distinction is the crucial point he makes against the first idealistic analysis. He also draws *a* distinction between the mental and the non-mental. Mental entities are those entities which stand *to* other entities in the intentional – the 'of' – connection. In other words perceiving, sensing, knowing, being aware of, in general, all the various forms of conscious-

---

[19] "The Refutation of Idealism," *op. cit.*, p. 29.
[20] *Ibid.*, p. 27.

ness, are mental entities. But these are two distinctions and not one. The object of an intentional entity may itself be an intentional entity. As he himself says:

> To be aware of the sensation of blue . . . is to be aware of an awareness of blue; awareness being used, in both cases, in exactly the same sense.[21]

Yet, though he understood the distincton between these two dichotomies he nevertheless blurred them together. He maintained that the existence of the simple and unique relation not only "justifies us in distinguishing knowledge of a thing from the thing known," but "indeed in distinguishing mind from matter" (p. 26), and he concluded:

> There is, therefore, no question of how we are to "get outside the circle of our own ideas and sensations." Merely to have a sensation is already to *be* outside that circle.[22]

But all Moore has succeeded in getting us outside of is the circle of our own acts. What he has shown is that not everything is an act or a property of an act. That is not sufficient to distinguish mind from matter. To distinguish mind from matter, in other words, to secure realism, one must draw other mental/non-mental distinctions among the non-intentional entities. This Moore did not do in his paper. Indeed, though he spent much of his philosophical career at this task, he never succeeded adequately in doing it.

II. REALISM AND MATERIAL OBJECTS

Idealism is the philosophical view which asserts about the world that everything is mental. The idealist claims among other things that chairs are mental. Clearly he is using 'mental' in a peculiar sense, for in any of the ordinary senses of the word chairs are not mental. It is the task of the philosophical analyst to discover what a philosopher means when he makes such an extraordinary claim and having made this discovery to show that what he means either is or is not the case. The task, in other words, is to find an ordinary (commonsensical) explication of the extraordinary (philosophical) claim and then to show that the statement expressing this claim is either true or false as the case may be.

In "The Refutation of Idealism" Moore in effect provides two commonsensical explications of 'chairs are mental'. He says that

---

[21] *Ibid.*, p. 25.
[22] *Ibid.*, p. 27.

when the idealist claims that chairs are mental he means either that chairs are inseparable aspects of the experiencing of them, that is, that they form together with the experiencing of them an organic unity, or that chairs are contents of or qualities of the experiencing of them. Neither of these two explications is true. The first is contradictory; the second misdescribes the connection between chairs and the experiencing of them. And since the two analyses in terms of which the idealist's extraordinary claim has been explicated are the only analyses in terms of which it can be explicated idealism is an inadequate philosophical view.

Realism is the philosophical view which asserts about the world that though there are mental things, there are also things which are not mental. Chairs, for example, are not mental. Taken on the face of it this claim is a truism. Chairs are clear-cut examples of objects which are not mental. Indeed, they are what we ordinarily call material or physical objects, and material objects are at least one kind of non-mental thing. However, in asserting that chairs are not mental, or, a stronger claim, that chairs are material objects the realist is not merely uttering truisms. Rather, he is using the phrases 'not mental' and 'material object' philosophically. He is opting, however implicitly, for certain analyses of the connection between things like chairs and the perceiving of them as well as of chairs themselves. Or, to put the point linguistically, he is opting for certain analyses of what is expressed by sentences like 'I perceive a chair' on the one hand, and by 'This is a chair' on the other. The philosophical analyst must discover what analyses the realist holds; he must, in other words, explicate the philosophical uses to which he is putting his words. It is with some of the analyses which provide the explications of the realist's philosophical assertion that "there are also things which are not mental" that I shall be concerned in this chapter.

'Realism' is an ambiguous term when it is used as a label for a philosophical view. Calling a philosopher a realist may mean that he holds a certain analysis of what we ordinarily call material objects, that is, of chairs, tables, rocks, and so on, or it may mean that he holds a certain analysis of the perception of material objects, for example, of perceiving a chair.[1] Though holding a realistic analysis of material objects is structurally incompatible with holding an idealistic analysis of the perception of material objects, a point mentioned in Chapter I,

---

[1] 'Realism' is also the term which is used to refer to the view that there are universals. I am not concerned with realism in this sense.

page 106, a philosopher may be realistic with regard to his analysis of perception without holding a realistic analysis of material objects. Realism in the first sense is stronger than realism in the second. This chapter will be limited to a discussion of analyses of material objects. A realistic analysis of perception will be discussed in Chapter IV.

The realistic analyses of material objects are the substance analyses. Moore inclines toward a substance analysis of material objects, that is, toward realism in the stronger sense. I say that he inclines toward realism, rather than is a realist, because, though there are passages in which such an analysis is implicit, he never explicitly embraces it. The characteristic hesitation with which he opts for any philosophical position is present in this context as it is in all others. Though he never explicitly embraces a realistic analysis of material objects, and, indeed, is not certain that such an analysis is the true one, he is, nevertheless, driven strongly toward it. What drives him is commonsense, or, more accurately, a confusion between certain commonsensical claims and an analysis of them. Consider the following four commonsense truths. Call them the crucial commonsense truths.[2] (C1) Material objects exist when there are no human beings who are perceiving them (or thinking of or acquainted with them in any other way). (C2) Material objects undergo a variety of changes and yet remain the same objects. Leaves change their color in autumn; the figures on a balloon change their size and shape as air is blown into the balloon; houses are redecorated and additions built onto them. Yet it is the same leaves which are now red which were green; it is the same figures which have grown from a small to a voluminous size; the house which now has a porch is the same one which last year had none. (C3) Vast numbers of ordinary perceptual judgments, expressed by such predicative sentences as 'This is a chair', 'That is a door', 'That is a pencil', and 'This chair is brown', 'That door is solid oak', 'That pencil is cylindrical', are true. (C4) Though we can be mistaken when we make such perceptual judgments as these we nevertheless make them exceedingly commonly with the greatest certainty. Moore is strongly inclined to believe that these commonsense truths themselves either amount to, or at least presuppose, a realistic analysis of material objects. When he argues against an analysis which he considers to be inadequate he argues

---

[2] By calling these truths crucial I mean that each is the center of a philosophical controversy concerning materials objects. The first concerns the mind-independence of material objects; the second the problem of the continuant. The third concerns the nexus between material objects and the characters which they have, and, indirectly, the distinction between appearance and reality. The fourth raises the problems of perceptual error and certainty.

against it on the ground that it cannot account for one, or several, of these truths. In giving such an argument it is not surprising, then, to find that he himself unwittingly adopts a realistic analysis of material objects.

It is a mistake to suppose that the commonsense view of the world what is expressed by true sentences – is itself a philosophical view. It is also a mistake to suppose that any particular commonsense claim presupposes any particular analysis of it. What I shall show in this chapter is that Moore does adopt a realistic analysis of material objects. In Chapter III I shall show that one can give an analysis which accounts for these commonsense truths which is not realistic in this sense. In other words, I shall show that commonsense is not itself realistic, or does not presuppose realism, in the sense in which Moore thinks that it is.

The plan of this chapter is as follows. First, I shall briefly outline a substance analysis of material objects, using Aristotle's analysis as a paradigm. In presenting this analysis I shall show how in terms of it C2 and C3 are accounted for. A comparison with the non-substantialist analyses of Berkeley and Bergmann will be needed for later reference. The differences between the Aristotelian and Lockean analyses of material objects, both substance analyses, will be mentioned. Second, I shall state the sense in which substance analyses of material objects are realistic analyses. Or, in other words, I shall explain what 'realism' means when it is used as a label for an analysis of material objects. The explanation consists, basically, in showing how on a substance analysis C1 is accounted for. Third, I shall substantiate my claim that Moore is opting for an analysis of material objects rather than merely reiterating commonsense, and show the extent to which this analysis is a substance analysis. C4 will be mentioned in this context at the end of the chapter.

In the Aristotelian analysis of material objects, a chair, a table, and a stone are each composites of two kinds of entities, namely, a substance and the various accidents and attributes which inhere in it.[3] The substance is that entity which has or supports the accidents; it is the bearer of the characteristics which can be predicated truly of a thing. Accidents are those entities which inhere in or are supported by a substance. In a sentence such as 'This chair is brown, the phrase 'this chair' refers to a substance and 'brown' to an accident which

---

[3] I ignore the traditional distinction between accidents and attributes, consider only accidents.

inheres in it. The relation of predication indicated by 'is' in this sentence is the linguistic reflection of the inherence tie between the substance and its accident. That substances and accidents are different ontological kinds is reflected linguistically by the fact that 'chair' cannot occur as a predicate in a predicative sentence. The substance is that which has the accident and cannot be an accident (or attribute) of anything else. How Aristotle analyzes the apparent exception expressed by 'This is a chair' will be discussed below.

In the Berkeleian analysis of material objects, there is only one kind of entity, namely, accidents, or, as he calls them, sensible qualities.[4] Berkeley analyzes what is expressed by 'This chair is brown' as a complex of sensible qualities, this chair, of which brown is a member. In 'This chair is brown' 'is' is not the linquistic reflection of an inherence or exemplification connection, but a member of or part-whole connection. Brown is a part of or member of the collection of sensible qualities which constitute this chair. A chair is not an entity distinct from the sensible qualities which are predicated truly of it. Rather, it is just the combination of all such qualities. The substance, present in Aristotle's analysis of material objects, is eliminated in Berkeley's.

On both of these analyses the truth of such perceptual judgments as expressed by sentences like 'This chair is brown' can be accounted for. For Aristotle 'This chair is brown' is true if the substance referred to by 'this chair' has the accident, brown, inhering in it. For Berkeley the sentence is true if the collection of sensible qualities referred to by 'this chair' has brown as a member. That such sentences as this are, on many occasions on which they are uttered, true is a commonsensical matter of fact. Both of these analyses of material objects, though radically different, can, *prima facie*, account for this fact.

On the Aristotelian analysis of material objects a substance, though simple relative to the accidents which it has, is itself a composite of form and matter. Chair, the form or nature of all those material objects which are chairs, is distinguished from the matter in each. The matter makes a chair a particular instance of chair rather than some other particular instance (in other words, matter individuates). A form is an unanalyzable constituent of every material object. Its role in the Aristotelian analysis is two-fold: it serves both a causal and a logical

---

[4] Traditionally, accidents were thought of as particularized characteristics; that is, the kind of entity which is unique to the substance which has it. Qualities are often thought of as universals; that is, the kind of entity which two things can share. This difference between accidents and sensible qualities I ignore. Aside from this difference each plays the same role in these analyses.

function. Causally the form is said to produce or create all the various accidents which the material object has. Logically the form determines what accidents the material object can and cannot have. There are, in other words, certain necessary connections between the form and the spatio-temporal series of accidents which inhere in the substance. For Berkeley there are no forms. He rejects the anthropomorphic causal function of form. But more significantly he replaces the simple constituent chair, in the example, by a cluster of characteristic shapes, sizes, tactual qualities, and so on (what one ordinarily identifies as the characteristic features of chairs), which have both spatio-temporal and lawful, not necessary, connections with other clusters of qualities. The entire pattern of sensible qualities is *a* chair, and chair is the cluster of characteristic sensible qualities which is lawfully, and spatio-temporally, related to the whole. For Berkeley what is expressed by 'This is a chair' is analyzed as a pattern of lawfully connected sensible qualities of which a certain characteristic cluster is a member. For Aristotle what is expressed by 'This is a chair' is analyzed as a substance of which the form, chair (which informs the other constituent in the substance, matter), is a constituent. For Aristotle 'is' in 'This is a chair' is not the linguistic reflection of the same ontological connection as in 'This chair is brown'. In other words, brown (an accident) and chair (a form) are not of the same ontological kind, just as brown and this chair (a substance) are not. For Berkeley 'is' in 'This is a chair' is the linguistic reflection of the same ontological connection as it is in 'This chair is brown'. In both cases it reflects the member of or part-whole connection. For Berkeley, then, brown (a simple quality), chair (a cluster of such qualities), and this chair (a pattern of simple qualities and a cluster of such) are all of the same ontological kind. The differences among them are differences of complexity, not of kind.

In the Aristotelian assay of material objects the substance is not only the bearer of the characteristics which can be predicated truly of a material object (i.e., the supporter of accidents) as well as the ground of the material object being the kind of thing that it is (i.e., a natured entity), it is also a continuant. The substance is an entity which endures through the change of its accidents. For Aristotle a situation such as a chair having its color changed from brown to red is analyzed as a substance, a chair, with the accident, brown, inhering in it at an earlier time and the accident, red, at a later one. That the red chair is the *same* chair as that which was brown is accounted for by there being a constituent in the situation which remains through the change.

In an analysis which does not contain continuants there is no constituent in a material object which accounts for this sameness. There being only one chair in the situation must be accounted for by the spatio-temporal relations and lawful connections among the constituents in the material object.

Gustav Bergmann offers an analysis of material objects which accounts for this sameness in this way.[5] In his analysis, as in Aristotle's, there is an ontological distinction between the qualities which a thing has and that which has them. Predication, in other words, is taken to be the linguistic reflection of a connection between two kinds of constituents in a thing, and not of a membership or part-whole connection. The paradigm of predication for Aristotle is 'The chair is brown' whereas for Bergmann whose "substances" are momentary the paradigm is 'This is brown'. But this difference reflects a difference in their account of natures or forms, not of predication. For both there is a substantial element in a thing – a bearer of qualities. The difference between an analysis with continuants and one with momentary entities is that on the former view the substantial element endures through the change of its qualities (accidents) whereas on the latter view it does not. To account for the red chair being the same chair as that which was brown Bergmann must maintain that the substantial element (or elements) which is red and that (or those) which is brown are constituents of *a* pattern of substantial elements, that is, of one chair. Bergmann analyzes *a* chair as a pattern of momentary substantial elements (individuals), which are lawfully connected with and spatially and temporally related to each other in a way in which they are not so related to any others. In the analysis of what is expressed by 'This is a chair' there is a cluster of individuals (referred to by 'this') exemplifying those qualities which one identifies as the characteristic features of chairs (the chair percept or perceptual core of a chair), which are lawfully connected with and spatio-temporally related to other individuals which together with the former constitute this chair. Chair is a highly complex character including the shapes, tactual qualities, and so on, of the chair percept as well as the lawful connections and spatial and temporal relations mentioned. A chair is a pattern of individuals which exemplify this character.

[5] See Gustav Bergmann, "Remarks on Realism," *Philosophy of Science*, XXIII (October, 1946), 261–273; reprinted in *The Metaphysics of Logical Positivism* (New York: Longmans, Green and Co., 1954), pp. 153–175, and section V of "The Revolt Against Logical Atomism," *The Philosophical Quarterly*, VII (1957), 323–339, and VIII (1958), 1–13; reprinted in *Meaning and Existence* (The University of Wisconsin Press, 1960), pp. 39–72.

Though both Berkeley and Bergmann offer non-substantialist analyses of material objects Locke, though differing from Aristotle in several respects, proposes a substance analysis. For Locke a material object consists of the several simple qualities of extension, figure, motion and solidity in various determinations which inhere in, are united together, and supported by a substantial element or substratum. The substratum is that which has the qualities; it is, in other words, the subject of the qualities which are predicated truly of a thing. That the material object contains only the so-called primary qualities and not the secondary qualities can be ignored.[6] The substratum is also a continuant; it is that entity which unites together the various qualities, which manifest themselves to us in a succession of experiences or ideas, as qualities of one rather than of a series of material objects. The substratum is, however, not natured for Locke as it is for Aristotle. Chair, which for Aristotle is a simple constituent of the substance, is a characteristic configuration of extension, figure, motion, and so on. This configuration of qualities (or accidents) does not play the anthropomorphic causal role which form plays for Aristotle. It does not cause or produce the other accidents in a material object. Nor does this characteristic configuration of extension, figure, motion, and so on, play the logical role which form does in the Aristotelian analysis. It does not determine which other accidents can, and which cannot, belong to the substance.[7]

Traditionally, those philosophers who gave substance analyses of material objects were called realists. What this label signifies is that upon these analyses material objects are the kind of entity which *cannot* depend for their existence upon the acquaintance, perception, knowledge or any other kind of awareness of them.[8] On a substance

---

[6] According to the scientific account of material objects current in Locke's day, the classical atomic model, material objects were thought of as configurations of atoms having only the primary qualities, those to which quantitative measurement was applicable. Colors, therefore, were not qualities of atoms. To give an analysis of material objects which denies that colors are qualities of them is to mistake the scientific account for what it is not, an ontological analysis. For the passages in which Locke presents his analysis of material objects, see his *An Essay Concerning Human Understanding*, ed. A. C. Fraser (Oxford, 1894), II, 390–423. (Bk. II, Ch. xxiii.)

[7] That this feature of form is lacking in the Lockean analysis is reflected in Locke's worry about whether minds can be extended and bodies think.

[8] To characterize an analysis of material objects as realistic one must bring in mind. This does not contradict my claim that to give an analysis of material objects and to give an analysis of the perception of material objects are two things and not one. Mind is introduced here perfectly commonsensically. Realistic analyses of material objects are distinguished from non-realistic ones on the basis of how they account for the commonsense truth (C1) *about material objects* that material objects exist when there are no human beings who are perceiving them.

analysis material objects are independent of minds in two senses. (1) Material objects cannot depend upon the mind in the sense of being qualities of the mind (or of the perception, knowledge, acquaintance, and so on, of them); that is, on a substance analysis material objects are analyzed such that not every constituent of them can be a quality of a mind. (2) Material objects cannot depend upon the mind in the sense that they exist only so long as they are the objects of acts of perception, or other kinds of awareness of them; that is, on a substance analysis material objects are analyzed such that not every constituent of them can exist only so long as it is in the intention of an act. On a substance analysis there is a constituent in material objects which *cannot* exist *only* while the material object is the object of perception, and so on. This analysis *guarantees* that material objects exist when they are not perceived. The question which one must ask about this use of 'realism' is: what is the ontological feature of material objects which, on a substance analysis, guarantees that they are mind-in-dependent in these two senses? This is a question which I shall answer below, but first I shall comment briefly on the analyses of material objects which are not realistic.

Both the Aristotelian and Lockean analyses are realistic; they are both substance analyses. Berkeley's analysis is clearly not realistic. There is no constituent in a material object which guarantees that it exists unperceived. Indeed, on Berkeley's analysis of *perception* material objects *cannot* exist unperceived. A material object is a collection of sensible qualities, and it is dependent upon minds in the sense that each member of the collection is a quality of a mind. On the Berkeleian analysis material objects are not mind-independent in either sense (1) or (2). But not only is the Berkeleian analysis not realistic; neither is Bergmann's. On Bergmann's analysis there is a substantial element in material objects which makes them independent of minds in sense (1). In other words, his analysis is not compatible with an idealistic analysis of the perception of material objects. But this substantial element or individual is not an independent existent in the sense in which the traditional substance is. On his analysis there is no constituent in a material object which must exist whether or not the object is perceived. Material objects are mind-independent in the first sense, but not in the second.

Why call an analysis which satisfies these two requirements realistic and withhold this label from one which does not? The reason is that on any analysis for which (1) and (2) hold, material objects are ontologically of a kind which exist when there are no human beings who are perceiving them, or knowing them, or aware of them in any other way. The commonsense truth that material objects exist when there are no human beings who are perceiving them – a commonsense truth about material objects for which any adequate analysis must account – is accounted for in the strongest possible way. It is guaranteed by being grounded in an ontological feature of material objects. An analysis which satisfied (1), but not (2), does not account for this truth *about* material objects by grounding it in the ontological analysis of them. An analysis such as Bergmann's accounts for this truth by distinguishing contextually, or externally, among the objects of perception, between those which satisfy a certain criterion and those which do not.[9] In this analysis the non-mental or *realistic* character of material objects is not as strong as it is in a substance analysis; hence it is not realistic.

What is the ontological feature of material objects which, on a substance analysis, guarantees that they are mind-independent in these two senses? The constituent in material objects which is common and peculiar to substance analyses is the continuant, namely, that entity which endures through the changes which material objects undergo. In any situation in which a thing changes, for example, its color, its shape, or its size, that entity which has the color, its shape, or its size, endures through the changes. Material objects such as chairs, tables, trees and so on, undergo a great variety of changes. Just commonsensically, it is evident that there are many changes of things which go unnoticed. But since the continuant is that entity in a material object which undergoes these changes as well as accounts for its being the same object despite the changes, it is also that consituent which makes a material object the kind of thing which exists when it is not perceived.

Though it is the continuant in the traditional substance analyses which grounds the mind-independence of material objects, an analysis of material objects can be proposed in which there are continuants which nevertheless do not carry this independence feature. If the duration of the continuant is limited so that it endures only those changes which occur within the span of one's attention – as for example the change in brightness of the spark of a firecracker which one notices at a glance – then in such an analysis there are continuants

[9] For Bergmann the criterion is coherence. See his "Realistic Postscript," *Logic and Reality* (The University of Wisconsin Press, 1964), pp. 302–340.

which exist only while there are human beings who are perceiving
them. In this analysis the account of gross physical changes will have
to be altered. The continuant will not provide the ontological ground
of the material object's being the same object despite its changes.
This sameness will be accounted for, as it is on the analysis with
momentary entities, by the spatio-temporal relations and lawful
connections between these "mind-dependent" continuants. It is the
fact that the continuant accounts for this sameness on the traditional
substance analysis, that it makes material objects ontologically of a
kind which exist when there are no human beings who are perceiving
them.

Moore does not consider any analysis of material objects adequate
which fails to account for the fact that they exist unperceived. By not
clearly distinguishing between this commonsense truth on the one
hand and the analysis which accounts for this truth on the other, he
is able to slip (unknowingly) from the methodological program of
rejecting any analysis which fails to account for this truth to the
ontological position of adopting an analysis which guarantees it in
an ontological feature of material objects. In other words, he fails to
distinguish between the commonsensical claim that material objects
exist when there are no human beings who are perceiving them and
the philosophical claim that they are the kind of thing which exist
when there are no human beings who are perceiving them. He inclines,
therefore, toward a substance analysis of material objects.

My claim that Moore is opting for a realistic analysis of material
objects rather than merely reiterating commonsense will be substantiated by considering some passages in his early writing.[10] In Chapter
VI of *Some Main Problems of Philosophy* [11] he discusses the consequences for the status of material objects of what he calls "Hume's
second rule." The rule states, in effect, that we cannot know of the
existence of anything whatever except what we have directly apprehended, namely, our own acts of consciousness, sense-data, and images
of sense-data, and what is like what we have directly apprehended,
for example, sense-data-like entities, that is, unsensed sense-data. He
claims that if this rule, and Hume's other rules, were true, we could
never know of the existence of any material objects. But, he says,

---

[10] The drive toward a substance analysis does not operate only in his early writing. The
role it plays in some later papers is discussed in Chapter III.

[11] G. E. Moore, *Some Main Problems of Philosophy* (London: George Allen and Unwin,
Ltd., 1953).

... curiously enough many of those who hold them have thought that they were not denying our knowledge of material objects. They have thought that, to allow that we do know of the things, which they say that we do know of, is *the same thing* as to allow that we do know of the existence of material objects. They have thought that they were not denying our power to know anything which Common Sense supposes itself to know.

Moore wants to show that

... these views *do* deny our power to know of the existence of material objects; and that in doing so they do flatly contradict Common Sense.[12]

The discussion is about our knowledge of material objects, but the point which Moore wants to make does not concern our knowledge of material objects, but material objects themselves. He wants to show that if these views were true, then some, if not most, of the common-sensical statements which we make about material objects and *which are in fact true* would be false. In other words, he wants to show that the analyses of material objects implicit in these philosophical views are inadequate on the ground that they cannot account for what we know commonsensically to be true about material objects.

This is the heart of Moore's philosophical method. The test of the adequacy or inadequacy of a philosophical claim, once we understand clearly what it means (in other words, after we have explicated it), is whether it does or does not controvert commonsense. Though this is his method, he does not always adhere to it. In the instance at hand the ground upon which he rejects the analysis implicit in these views is not that they contradict or deny any commonsense truths, but that they contradict another analysis which he (implicitly) holds to be adequate. My concern is not to defend any of the analyses which he describes either in Chapter VI or in Chapter VII of *Some Main Problems of Philosophy* in the forms in which he describes them. He correctly rejects all these analyses as stated. Rather, it is to show that he does not reject them for the right reasons. He ought to reject them, according to his own method, on the ground that they deny what we know commonsensically to be true. He does reject them on the ground that they contradict an analysis which he himself unwittingly adopts.

The following passage makes this clear. Referring to the view that material objects are nothing but a pattern of sensed and unsensed sense-data, he says:

But nevertheless it seems to me [this view] would *not* allow me to know of the existence of exactly that, in which I believe – the material object, the pencil.

[12] *Ibid.*, ch. vi, p. 113.

For all these things similar in shape to parts of the pencil, which it would allow me to know of, are, it must be remembered, patches of *colour* of a certain shape, patches of *hardness,* and *smoothness* or *roughness* of a certain shape ... Yet these patches of colour and of hardness and smoothness certainly do not constitute the *whole* of the material object in which I believe. Even if there are *here* now all sorts of colours, which I do not see, and all sorts of tactual qualities, which I do not feel, yet the pencil, in which I believe, certainly does not consist *solely* of colours and of tactual qualities: what I believe when I believe that the pencil exists is that there exists something which really is cylindrical in shape, but which does not consist *merely* of any number of patches of colour or of smoothness or hardness, or any other sort of sense-data which I have ever directly apprehended ... I certainly believe that there is in that place *something else besides*. This something else, even if it be not the *whole* material object, is certainly a *part* of it.[13]

Here Moore claims that the analysis of a material object into a pattern of sense-data fails to take into account an element which is there. A pencil, for example, is not a mere collection of sense-data, but something which, besides including some, if not all, of the sense-data, includes something *else* which has these sense-data. In a pencil "there exists something [other than a sense-datum] which really *is* cylindrical in shape." (My italics.) At just the point at which Moore introduces this other element he shifts in his use of 'sense-data' from referring to *patches* of color of a certain shape, *patches* of hardness, etc. to colors and tactual qualities. This shift in usage is not accidental. It betrays the fact that at just this moment, at least, he thinks of sense-data as qualities, that is, as a kind of entity which must be exemplified by something which is not a quality (not a sense-datum). Nor is this something else a series of individuals each exemplifying one or several qualities. This is what he may reasonably be taken to reject when he says that a material object "does not consist merely of any number of *patches* of colour or of smoothness or hardness."(My italics.) This something else is *an* element which *is* cylindrical as well as hard and colored in a certain way, if the pencil is taken also to include these qualities.[14] In other words, it is a substance in at least part of the traditional sense of that word. It is the bearer of the qualities which are predicated truly of a thing as well as a continuant. For Moore, a pencil is a complex consisting of a substance together with at least some of the sense-data as its attributes.

A short quotation from Chapter VII confirms this diagnosis, if more confirmation is needed.

13 *Ibid.,* ch. vi, pp. 118–119.
14 In *Some Main Problems of Philosophy* Moore often speaks as if material objects have only the characters which are usually called primary qualities. This makes colors, for example, not qualities of the object. This is to make the same mistake that Locke made. See footnote 6.

Every material object, then, I admit, must *have* at least one property, which is in this extended sense a sense-datum: it must have shape. But though it *has* shape, it is not itself the shape which it has: just as a coloured patch must have a shape, and yet the patch itself is quite a different thing from the shape which it has. And what I mean to say of all material objects is that no one of them *is* a sense-datum of any kind whatever, though they all must *have* a shape, which is a sense-datum. Anything whatever which is a sense-datum, of any kind at all, or a collection of sense-data, cannot *be* what I mean by a material object.[15]

There is a difference between this second passage and the passage I quoted earlier. In the second Moore says that a material object *is* that which has the shape. In the former he says that if that which has the shape is not the *whole* material object, it is certainly a part of it. This difference reflects the ambiguity in the traditional use of 'substance' which I mentioned above (p. 124). Considering a shape, say cylindrical, as contrasted with a pencil, the pencil is said to be a substance and cylindrical an accident of it. But considering the pencil itself, apart from any accidents it may have, what is traditionally taken to be the matter of the pencil may be called a substance and pencil the form or nature of *it*. Depending upon which way 'substance' is used, one will say (as in the earlier quotation) that a pencil is a complex consisting of a substance together with at least some of the sense-data as its attributes, or (as in the latter one) that a pencil is a simple, that is, a substance and at least some of the sense-data are its accidents.[16]

The question to ask about what Moore says in these quotations is this. When one says, speaking both truly and commonsensically about a pencil, that it is cylindrical, is one attributing an accident to a substance?[17] Does the commonsensical sentence 'This pencil is cylindrical' in any way presuppose this analysis? The answer is that it does not. The analysis of a pencil being cylindrical into a substance having an accident is no more forced upon us in order to account for the truth of 'This pencil is cylindrical' than any other. This analysis is not shown to be adequate merely by asserting, in a particular tone of emphasis, the commonsensical and true assertion that the pencil really is cylindrical. Moore assumes that predicating truly some characteristic of a material object presupposes that the material object is an entity which bears the character in question. But this

---

[15] *Some Main Problems of Philosophy, op. cit.*, ch. vii, pp. 130–131.

[16] I use 'attribute' here instead of the traditional terms 'form' or 'nature'. Moore's substances are certainly not natured in the causal and logical senses of 'nature'. There is, however, a reason for calling Moore's substances natured. See below, page 134.

[17] 'Property', 'quality', 'character', can be used for 'accident'. Universals are not at issue here. See footnote 4.

assumption is mistaken. There are other analyses which can account for predication as well as this one.[18] He might have attempted to show that this analysis is adequate by showing that, while it accounts for this truth, no other analysis does so. But in the passages quoted, he has not shown that there are any commonsensical claims which we all know to be true which alternative analyses have failed to account for. Yet this is what he set out to show. What he has shown is merely that he himself adopts a certain analysis of material objects. This analysis is by no means evidently an adequate one, and must itself be subjected to the tests to which all others must be subjected.

One final comment about the extent to which Moore opts for a substance analysis will conclude this chapter. When we make ordinary judgments such as that this is a pencil, or that this pencil is cylindrical – judgments which, as Moore says, we make exceedingly commonly – not only are the sentences expressing these judgments in most cases true, but also we make the judgments with the greatest certainty. Moore believes that in order for the sentences expressing these judgments to be true there really must be something (an entity) which has the property mentioned in the judgment. And since chairs, doors, and pencils are rather permanent pieces of the material world's furniture that entity must be a continuant. That these two features of substance are present in his analysis I have shown. But there is another feature of substance which attacts him. If the property mentioned in the judgment that this is a chair were a form in the substance, the certainty with which we make the judgments would be grounded in what is judged. Chair, considered as a simple constituent of a chair, could be presented to the perceiver on the occasion in which he makes the judgment that this is a chair. Though Moore does not explicitly embrace forms, his desire to secure the certainty of such judgments is great. Forms presented to the perceiver would provide an ontological ground in the material object for the certainty of the judgment. The role that this desire plays in his thought will be discussed further in the next chapter.

III. A NON-REALISTIC ANALYSIS OF MATERIAL OBJECTS

In the preceding chapter I stated that Moore confuses certain commensense truths about material objects with an ontological analysis of them, specifically, with a realistic analysis. By this I mean

---

[18] The Berkeleian analysis, as can be seen from the discussion above, is one.

that he takes these commonsense truths either to amount to, or at least to presuppose, a realistic (substance) analysis of material objects. In that chapter I showed that Moore fails to distinguish clearly between commonsense and a substance analysis by presenting some passages in his early writing in which this failure is apparent. I did not, however, show that his failure to make this distinction is a confusion. In other words, I did not show that commonsense is not itself realistic, or does not presuppose a realistic analysis.

In this chapter I shall propose an analysis of material objects which is not realistic, but which is nevertheless adequate. By calling it adequate I mean that it accounts for the crucial commonsense truths. The crucial commonsense truths are those which are the focal points of philosophical problems concerning material objects. These truths were discussed in Chapter II in the context of a substance analysis.[1] I shall mention them again here. (C1) Material objects exist when there are no human beings who are perceiving them (or thinking of or acquainted with them in any other way). (C2) Material objects undergo a variety of changes and yet remain the same objects. (C3) Vast numbers of ordinary perceptual judgments, expressed by such sentences as 'This is a hand' and 'This hand is pale white', are true. (C4) Though we can be mistaken when we make such perceptual judgments as these we nevertheless make them exceedingly commonly with the greatest certainty. The main task of this chapter is to establish the claim that on the nonrealistic analysis of material objects which I shall propose these truths can be accounted for, and hence that Moore's failure to distinguish the commonsensical claims about material objects from a substance analysis of them is indeed a confusion.

There is also a secondary task. There is a difficulty with regard to the analysis of material objects which Moore cannot overcome. He discusses this difficulty in all of the philosophical writings in which he attempts to give an analysis of material objects. He cannot overcome the difficulty because of his implicit substantialism. Indeed, the implicit substantialism – the failure to distinguish a realistic analysis of material objects from commonsense – prevents him from arriving at an adequate analysis of material objects not only in his early writing, but throughout his philosophical work. The secondary task of this chapter is to establish this fact.

Moore's difficulty concerning the analysis of material objects

[1] See Chapter II, page 122 and footnote 2.

is that he cannot answer the following question: *In what sense is the object presented to one in a perceptual situation representative of the material object which one may be correctly said to perceive in this situation?* Call this question Q. Either one of two kinds of answers is possible, *viz.* (a) that the presented object is representative of the material object in the sense of being a constituent of it, or (b) that the presented object is representative of the material object, not in the sense of being a constituent of it, but in the sense of being distinct from and standing in a certain relation to it. To both of these two kinds of answers Moore finds insurmountable objections; in short, he cannot give a satisfactory answer to Q. I shall propose a non-realistic analysis of material objects in terms of which the answer to this question is (a), and I shall show that on this analysis this answer is satisfactory.

There is a sense in which Moore understands the nonrealistic analysis of material objects which I shall propose. In "Some Judgments of Perception," [2] a paper in which he states his difficulty quite clearly, he also states succinctly, yet clearly, this analysis. He even realizes that the objection to giving (a) as an answer to Q can be met in terms of it, and hence that his difficulty can be overcome. Yet he will not accept the analysis. The combination of these factors produces a curious tension in his writing. I shall show that the source of this tension is his failure to distinguish clearly a realistic analysis of material objects from commonsense.

This chapter is divided into three sections. In section I I shall, first, explain carefully what the question is which Moore is asking about material objects, and, second, propose a non-realistic analysis of material objects in terms of which (a) is a satisfactory answer to it. In section II I shall state the objection to (a) which Moore thinks is insurmountable, and then proceed to show that it is in fact not insurmountable, but can be answered. In other words, I shall show that in terms of my analysis (a) is satisfactory. In section III I shall show that it is Moore's implicit substantialism which prevents him from overcoming his difficulty in the way in which I have overcome it. Remember that the main task of this chapter is to establish the claim that a non-realistic analysis of material objects is adequate, that is, that it accounts for the crucial commonsense truths. In section II, in the course of the demonstration that on the non-realistic analysis I

---

[2] G. E. Moore, "Some Judgments of Perception," *Proceedings of the Aristotelian Society*, N.S. XIX (1918–1919), 1–29; reprinted in *Philosophical Studies*, op. cit., pp. 220–252. All page references are to the latter.

propose Moore's objection to (a) can be answered, I shall show that two of the crucial commonsense truths (C2 and C3) can be accounted for. In section III, in the course of the demonstration that his implicit substantialism prevents him from overcoming the objection he falsely believes to be insurmountable, I shall show that the remaining two crucial commonsense truths can be accounted for.

I

Moore finds insurmountable objections to both of the two possible answers to the question: *In what sense* is the object presented to one in a perceptual situation *representative* of the material object which one may be correctly said to perceive in this situation? In order to give a satisfactory answer to this question one must get clear on exactly what it is that is being asked. The question presupposes a distinction between an object presented in a perceptual situation and the material object which is perceived in it. Moore is quite certain that there is a distinction. He expresses it in the following two passages.

Two things only seem to me to be quite certain about the analysis of such propositions [as 'This is a hand'] ... namely that whenever I know, or judge, such a proposition to be true, (1) there is always some *sense-datum* about which the proposition in question is a proposition – some sense-datum which is *a* subject (and, in a certain sense, the principal or ultimate subject) of the proposition in question, and (2) that, nevertheless, *what* I am knowing or judging to be true about this sense-datum is not (in general) that it is *itself* a hand, or a dog, or the sun, etc., etc., as the case may be.

. . . .

In other words, to put my view in terms of the phrase 'theory of representative perception', I hold it to be quite certain that I do not *directly* perceive *my hand;* and that when I am said (as I may be correctly said) to 'perceive' it, that I 'perceive' it means that I perceive (in a different and more fundamental sense) something which is (in a suitable sense) *representative* of it ....[3]

... in all cases in which I make a judgment of this sort, [as, for example, that this is a hand] I have no difficulty whatever in picking out a thing, which is, quite plainly, in a sense in which nothing else is, *the* thing about which I am making my judgment; and that yet ... I am, quite certainly, *not*, in general, judging with regard to it, that *it* is a thing of that kind for which the term, which seems to express the predicate of my judgment, is a name.[4]

[3] G. E. Moore, "A Defence of Common Sense," *Contemporary British Philosophy*, 2nd Ser., ed. J.H. Muirhead (London: George Allen and Unwin Ltd., 1925), pp. 191–223; reprinted in *Philosophical Papers* London: George Allen and Unwin Ltd., 1959), pp. 32–59. All page references are to the latter. The quoted passage occurs on pages 54–55.
[4] "Some Judgments of Perception," *op. cit.*, p. 229.

In both of these passages Moore distinguishes between an object presented to one in a perceptual situation, what in the first passage he calls a sense-datum and in the second *the* thing about which I am making my judgment, and the material object, the hand, for example, which one may be correctly said to perceive in this situation. That there is a distinction between a presented object and the material object of which it is representative is, I think, clear. The way in which Moore expresses this distinction may nevertheless be misleading. A series of comments about the two passages will help to prevent one from being misled.

One. Though Moore says in the first passage that two things seem to him to be quite certain about the analysis of such propositions as 'This is a hand', (1) and (2) are not statements about the analysis of such propositions (that is, of what is expressed, for example, by 'This is a hand') at all. They are commonsense statements which describe situations in which one perceives such things as hands.

Two. Being both commonsensical, (1) and (2) do not prejudge any issue with regard to the analysis of a material object or of the perception of a material object. The first assertion seems to raise the question of the status of sense-data. Yet it merely gives the appearance of doing this. The question as to the sense-data is whether sense-data are mental or non-mental, and, if mental, in what sense of 'mental'. Moore in (1) neither offers an answer, nor prejudges the answer, to this question.[5] All he claims is that in a perceptual situation there is always something there which is, as he says in the second passage, *the* thing about which I am making my judgment (should I make a judgment in such a situation) or which is, as he says in the first passage, the referent of the subject term in the sentence expressing this judgment. Here is what he himself says about his use of 'sense-datum' in "Some Judgments of Perception."

If we want to define ... a sense-datum, in a manner which will leave it not open to doubt what sort of things we are talking of, and that there are such things, I do not know that we can do it better than by saying that sense-data are the sort of things, *about* which such judgments as these always seem to be made – the sort of things which seem to be the real or ultimate subjects of all such judgments.[6]

[5] In "The Nature of Sensible Appearances," *Methods of Analysis*, Aristotelian Society Suppl. Vol. VI (1926), 179–189, Moore argues at length that he is not using 'sense-datum' in a sense which prejudges the answer to this question. He distinguishes his use of 'sense-datum' from C. D. Broad's use of 'sensum', the crucial difference being that it is part of the very meaning of 'sensum' that sensa are directly apprehended and are not constituents of material objects at all.

[6] "Some Judgments of Perception," *op. cit.*, pp. 231–232.

In this sense of 'sense-datum' it is perfectly clear that there are sense-data. It is perfectly clear that when we make perceptual judgments there is always something which is what we are judging about. The use of 'sense-datum' as a name for this entity is perhaps unfortunate. The phrase 'presented object', which Moore also uses in "Some Judgments of Perception," may be less subject to misunderstanding.

Three. The phrase 'presented object' may itself not be perfectly clear, however, for there are many entities presented to one in any perceptual situation in addition to the object which Moore calls *the* thing about which I am making my judgment. One is not only presented with this object, but also with various properties which this object has, other objects about which one is not judging, their properties, and so on. The presented object in question is only that one among the variety of entities presented which is the referent of the subject term of the sentence which expresses the judgment which one may make on this occasion.

Four. Moore speaks in these passages both of making a *judgment*, *knowing* or *judging* that a proposition is true, and of *perceiving* a material object. There is, I believe, a clear-cut difference between making a judgment on the one hand, and perceiving on the other.[7] I shall ignore the question as to whether in a perceptual situation in which one may be correctly said to perceive a hand one also makes the judgment that this is a hand, and, if one does, what the connections between making the judgment and perceiving are. I shall assume that in such perceptual situations one perceives a hand, by which I mean (a) that there is actually a perceiving occurring, and (b) that this perceiving is *of* a hand, that is, that the sentence 'This is a hand' expresses (refers to) what the perceiving is of.

Five. Moore's phrase "... when I am said (as I may be correctly said) to 'perceive' [a hand]" may be misunderstood in two ways. (a) One may think that what he means by this is merely that there is an ordinary use of 'perceive' which is such that one may, without linguistic impropriety, say "I perceive a hand." There is, of course, such a use. But when he says that I may be correctly said to perceive a hand he is not calling attention to this fact. What he means (and in this he is correct) is that the sentence 'I perceive a hand' is, on some occasions in which it is uttered, true. That is, there are situations in which human beings perceive hands. (b) Moore does think (and in this he is *not* correct) that I may be correctly said to perceive a hand

---

[7] See page 148, comment *Two*, for an example.

only when there is a hand there to be perceived. In other words, he believes that if, on a given occasion, I may be correctly said to perceive a hand then the sentence expressing what the perceiving is of, namely, 'This is a hand', is true. Moore fails to distinguish "I may be correctly said to perceive a hand" and "I may be correctly said to perceive veridically a hand." He believes that the second is a redundant form of the first.[8]

Six. When Moore says that the presented object is not itself a hand, or a dog, or the sun, as the case may be, he is drawing attention to two commonsense facts. (a) There is, to put it roughly, "more" to a material object than what is in one's field of presentation on any occasion in which one perceives a material object. There is the other side of a hand, for example, which is not presented to one on any given occasion. (b) There are, again to put the point roughly, numerically many more objects presented of which one may say truly 'This is a hand' than there are hands. One is in a vast number of perceptual situations in which one perceives one's own right hand, and though of each of the vast number of presented objects one can say truly 'This is my right hand', yet all of the presented objects are representative of the same, i.e., one, hand.

Seven. (1) and (2) are not only both commonsensical, but also true. Hence, on any adequate analysis of material objects one must be able to account for them. That is, an adequate analysis of material objects must reflect the difference between what is presented and is representative of the material object and the "whole" material object which one may be correctly said to perceive.

Eight. That one can be correctly said to perceive a material object must itself be accounted for. On an adequate analysis of the *perception* of material objects one must account for the sense in which one perceives a material object even though, on any occasion in which one is perceiving, the presented object is not itself a material object.

The non-realistic analysis of material objects which I am about to propose reflects the difference between the presented object and the material object and provides a clear answer to the question, in what sense is the former representative of the latter? Consider a hand. There is in a hand a pattern of individuals, that is, a pattern of momentary

---

[8] One may object that I am the one who is mistaken here, and not Moore. I defend my claim in Chapter IV in which I discuss the analysis of perception. For everything that is said in this section and in section II of this chapter the distinction is not crucial. Only cases of veridical perception are being considered. The distinction becomes crucial for the last point I make in Section III, pages 154–155. This point is, not surprisingly, propaedeutic to Chapter IV.

substantial elements (see Chapter II, p. 126). I say that there is a pattern of individuals because these individuals are spatially and temporally related to each other in a sense in which they are not so related to any others; these individuals *jointly* exemplify a complex spatio-temporal relation – call it *P* (for pattern). I shall say that an individual is *in* a pattern if it is one among those individuals which jointly exemplify *P*. There are, of course, many individuals in a pattern. There are, as well, many patterns. There are as many patterns as there are hands. Each individual which is in a hand is not only *in* a pattern, but also exemplifies the material object character, hand. Hand is a complex character including certain shapes, sizes, tactual qualities, and so forth (the characteristic features in terms of which one identifies something as a hand), the complex spatio-temporal relation *P*, and lawful connections. A hand is a pattern of individuals which each exemplify this character.

When one is in a perceptual situation in which one perceives a hand what the perceiving is of, the object (intention) of the perceiving, may be referred to by the sentence 'This is a hand.' The commonsense fact that there is, in such a situation, something presented which is the referent of the subject term in the sentence expressing what the perceiving is of is accounted for, on this analysis, by there being an individual (or set of individuals [9]) which exemplifies several characters some of which, at least, one identifies as characteristic features of hands. The commonsense fact that the presented object is not itself a hand is accounted for by this individual (or set of individuals) not being identical with the set of individuals which constitute the pattern.

On this analysis, an answer is immediately forthcoming to the question, in what sense is the presented object representative of the material object? The presented object is representative of the material

---

[9] Whether there is one or a set of individuals is a matter of detail. If there are several, as there certainly are given the complexity of material objects, then, if there is nothing obstructing the vision of the object, as a ribbon lying across one's hand (see "The Nature of Sensible Appearances," *op. cit.*, p. 180), there is one which is such that all others stand in the spatial relation of part of to it. As Moore says in "Some Judgments of Perception," *op. cit.*, p. 238:

I am, of course, at this moment, seeing many parts of the surface of this inkstand. But all these parts, except one, are, in fact, themselves parts of that one. That one is the one of which we should naturally speak as "*the* part of the surface that I am now seeing" or as "*this* part of the surface of this inkstand." There is only one part of the surface of this inkstand, which does thus contain, as parts, all the other parts that I am now seeing.

This is a purely spatial sense of 'part' in which to say that *a* is a part of *b* is to say that *a* stands in the spatial relation of part to *b*. This is the sense in which the area which is the upper half of this sheet of paper is a part of the area which is the whole sheet. For two other senses in which Moore uses 'part' in the paragraph from which this quotation was taken, see pages 146–147.

object in the sense of being a constituent of it. The individual (or individuals) which exemplifies the characters characteristic of hands, and which is presented in a perceptual situation in which one may be correctly said to perceive a hand, is, if the perception is veridical, one (or several) among those individuals which jointly exemplify P, and which are, therefore, each constituents of the same, i.e., one, hand.

A few comments about the proposed analysis of material objects and the answer to Q given in terms of it may help to forestall certain objections to and misunderstandings of both. Also they will add body to the exposition of the analysis and the answer. First, one may claim that the distinction between the material object character on the one hand and the complex spatio-temporal relation on the other is super-fluous, and suggest that 'hand' is a name for the spatio-temporal relation which all the individuals which constitute a hand jointly exemplify rather than the complex character which I say each exempli-fies. This would seem to be more consistent with Moore's statement (quoted above, page 137) that the presented object is *not* "a thing of that kind for which the term, which seems to express the predicate of my judgment [that this is a hand], is a name." The distinction between the material object character and the spatio-temporal relation is crucial for the analysis of perception, which is the subject of Chapter IV.[10] Here I shall say only that an individual exemplifies a material object character if and only if that individual is one among those individuals which jointly exemplify the spatio-temporal relation which is a constituent of that character. If an individual exemplifies the character, hand, for example, then it is a constituent of a pattern of individuals which constitute a hand, and if it is a constituent of a pattern, then it exemplifies the character. One can say, with a certain inaccuracy, that to say of an individual that it exemplifies a material object character and to say of it that it is a constituent of a pattern are two ways of expressing the same fact. To exemplify a material object character and to be a constituent of a pattern amount to the same.

Second, when one is in a perceptual situation in which one may be correctly said to perceive a hand, and the perception is veridical, then the individual (or individuals) with which one is presented ex-emplifies the material object character, hand, of which P is a constitu-ent. One may object that this is tantamount to obliterating the dis-tinction between the presented object and the material object which I insisted in comment *Seven* was commonsensical and must be pre-

[10] See Chapter IV, pages 173-174.

served. But this is not the case. I have so used 'presented' (consistent with Moore's use in "Some Judgments of Perception") that though one is presented with an individual which – in a case of veridical perception – exemplifies hand, one is not presented with the fact that the individual exemplifies this character. In other words, I have so used 'presented' that, in the case of the veridical perception of a hand, one is presented with an individual or (several), with a character (or several) characteristic of hands, and with this individual exemplifying this character. One is not presented, *in this sense of 'presented'*,[11] with the material object character, hand, nor with the fact that the individual exemplifies this character. The difference between characters characteristic of hands, and the character, hand, itself, in virtue of which the former is presented and the latter not, is that each constituent of the former (if it is complex) is exemplified by the individual which exemplifies this character, whereas each constituent of the latter is not so exemplified. It is the distinguishing mark of material object characters that they are just those characters which include as a constituent a relation which is not exemplified by the individuals which are in one's field of presentation when one perceives the material object. A material object is just the kind of entity all of whose constituents are not presented on any occasion in which it is perceived. It is this distinguishing mark of material object characters which, on this analysis, accounts for the commonsense facts about material objects discussed in comment *Six*.[12]

Third, P is a highly complex spatio-temporal relation whose definition is, no doubt, very complicated, and not in any sense easy to construct. I shall not attempt to define P. Two comments about the relation, however, may help to illuminate it. (a) Consider a perceptual situation in which one first perceives one's own right hand with the palm up, and subsequently with the palm down. At first one is presented with an individual which exemplifies that character which is common

---

[11] There is a sense in which one is presented with the character, hand, namely, it is a constituent of what is intended by the intentional character which is a constituent of the act of perceiving a hand. The relevant distinctions are made in Chapter IV.

[12] Consider an individual, presented on some occasion, which exemplifies the character square. Let M be a complex character exemplified by this individual. Let '$M(x)$' be short for '$Sq(x) \cdot (\exists y) L (y, x)$'. '$L$' refers to the relation to the left of. Assume that y is not presented on the occasion in which x is presented. M is a paradigm of a material object character. Were one to perceive an M (veridically), one would be presented with an individual which does exemplify the material object character, M, a constituent of which, L, is not exemplified. It is the characteristic difference between 'Sq', 'L' on the one hand and 'M' on the other that sets such characters as red, square, to the left of, between, red square off from such characters as hand, chair, ashtray, cloud.

to the palms of all right hands, call it palm-shaped. (There are, of course, other characters which this individual exemplifies, a color, if one is perceiving by sight, a size, etc. which I ignore. I assume that one is presented with one individual, rather than several.) Later one is presented with an individual which exemplifies the corresponding character common to the backs of all right hands, call it back-hand-shaped. The spatio-temporal relation which these two individuals jointly exemplify is a constituent of P. (b) This relation must not be confused with the "connection" between the palm of one's own right hand and the back of it. The palm and the back of one's own right hand are each material objects which are spatially and temporally related to and lawfully connected with each other. These spatio-temporal relations and lawful connections are what constitute both as parts of one's own right hand. But the individual which is palm-shaped and the individual which is back-hand-shaped are not parts of a hand in this sense; they are not themselves material objects. They are constituents in a hand and it is the spatio-temporal relation which they jointly exemplify which makes them constituents of one, rather than of different hands.

II

In "Some Judgments of Perception" Moore presents a lengthy argument in which he states what he considers to be an insurmountable objection to the view that the presented object is representative of the material object in the sense of being a constituent of it. Following are the crucial passages in this argument.

> The fact is that we all, exceedingly commonly, when, at each of two times, ... we see a part of the surface of a material thing, in the sense in which I am now seeing this part of the surface of this inkstand, ... make, on the second occasion, the judgment "*This* part of a surface is the *same* part of the surface of the same thing, as that which I was seeing ... just now." How commonly we all do this can scarcely be exaggerated.

> Now when we do this ... we, of course, do not mean to exclude the possibility that the part in question may have changed during the interval ... That is to say, the sense of sameness which we are here concerned with is one which clearly does not exclude change ... We can, therefore, divide cases, in which we judge, of a part of a surface which we are seeing, "This is the same part of the surface of the same material thing as the one I saw just now," into cases where we should also judge "But it is perceptibly different from what it was then," and cases in which ... we are certainly not prepared to assert that it is *perceptibly* so.

But now let us consider the cases in which we are not prepared to assert that the surface in question has changed perceptibly. The strange fact ... is that ... if, at the later time, I am at a sufficiently greater distance from the surface, the presented object which corresponds to [i.e., is representative of] it at the time seems to be perceptibly smaller, than the one which corresponded to it before. ... It seems, in short, that when, in such a case, I judge: "This surface is not, so far as I can tell, perceptibly different from the one I saw just now," I cannot possibly be judging of the presented object "*This* is not, so far as I can tell, perceptibly different from that object which was presented to me just now," for the simple reason that I *can* tell, as certainly, almost, as I can tell anything, that it is perceptibly different.

Moore concludes,

It ... [is] absolutely impossible that the surface seen at the later time should be identical with the object presented then, and the surface seen at the earlier identical with the object presented then, ...[13]

In other words, it cannot be the case that the presented object is representative of the material object in the sense of being a constituent of it.

Moore's argument may be stated succinctly as follows: (The numbers refer to the three paragraphs quoted.) (1) I may, and, indeed, do perceive the same object on several occasions. I may perceive the same hand, for example, on two different occasions. I may even perceive the same surface of the object, for example, its palm. (2) I can distinguish, without the slightest difficulty, cases in which the object has changed perceptibly from the former occasion to the latter, as when, the hand having been burned, the palm is now swollen and red whereas it was flesh-colored and lean before, from those in which no perceptible change has occurred. (3) Nevertheless, the object may appear differently on the two occasions even in those cases in which no perceptible change has occurred in the object. In other words, there is something in the latter situation which *is* perceptibly (qualitively) different from the corresponding thing in the former situation, even though the material object is perceptibly (qualitatively) unchanged. The conclusion is that the presented objects, being qualitatively different, cannot both be identical with one and the same constituent of the material object, namely, the one usually called its surface.

(1), (2) and (3) are all commonsensical. (1) merely asserts the obvious fact that one can perceive the same material object many times, and together with (2) that it is the same object whether it has altered or been altered in any way or not. (3) draws attention to the distinction between an object's being, for example, red – when a hand is burned

[13] "Some Judgments of Perception," *op. cit.*, pp. 241–244.

– and its appearing red – when it is seen under unusual lighting. What Moore is claiming in his conclusion is that no analysis of material objects which takes the presented object to be a constituent of the material object can preserve this distinction. Or, to speak as I spoke before, he concludes that the objection to taking the presented object as a constituent of the material object is insurmountable. I shall show that this is not so by showing that on the non-realistic analysis of material objects which I have proposed all the distinctions which must be made to meet this objection can be made, or, what amounts to the same, that (1), (2) and (3) can all be accounted for.

In the paragraphs just preceding this argument Moore uses the word 'part' in several senses. That creates an ambiguity in his argument. Consider the following two passages:

> ... I can imagine that some people would be willing to assent to the proposition that this sense-datum really is, in some sense or other, a "part" of this inkstand, and that what I am judging with regard to it, when I judge "This is an inkstand," is, in effect, "There is an inkstand, of which *this* is a part," ...

> [I am here using the word "part" in] the sense in which the trunk of any tree is undoubtedly a part of that tree; in which this finger of mine is undoubtedly a part of my hand and my hand a part of my body. ... it is, so far as I can see, the only proper sense in which a material thing can be said to have parts.[14]

In the first passage Moore uses 'part' in the sense in which I have used 'constituent'. But when he goes on to explain the sense in which he is using 'part' – a word which is, as he says, "often used extremely vaguely in philosophy" (p. 237) – he says that he is using 'part' in the sense in which the trunk of any tree is a part of that tree. This is a rather complex sense of 'part' involving spatial and temporal relations and lawful connections between two material objects. Clearly, the sense-datum (the presented object) is not a "part" of the material object in this sense, for the presented object is not itself a material object. The presented object stands in spatial and temporal relations to other individuals in the material object. But these individuals and spatial and temporal relations are not themselves spatially and temporally related to and lawfully connected with each other. The individuals and spatial and temporal relations are constituents of the material object – a unique sense of 'part' in which every material object has parts.

The ambiguity with which Moore uses 'part' creates an ambiguity in his argument. In the first paragraph, a paragraph in which he uses the phrase 'this part of the surface of this inkstand', he may

14 Ibid., pp. 237-238.

reasonably be taken to be using 'part', or more accurately, 'part of the surface', in the sense of 'constituent'.[15] When one perceives a hand (to change the example) one is presented with an individual which exemplifies several characters at least one of which is a characteristic feature in terms of which one identifies something as a hand. When one perceives a hand with the palm up the presented individual exemplifies some character which one might call the character of being palm hand-shaped. That one is perceiving a hand with the palm up may be expressed by saying that one is perceiving (among other things) part of the surface of a hand; namely, that part of the surface (that constituent of the hand) which is palm hand-shaped. In the second paragraph, a paragraph in which he uses the phrase 'the part in question may have changed during the interval' he is considering the kinds of changes which material objects undergo, for example, the changes which occur to palms of hands when they are burned. Here he is using 'part' in the sense in which one material object is a part of another; the sense in which the palm of a hand is part of a hand. That he is using 'part' in this paragraph to refer to material objects which are parts of other material objects and not to individuals which are constituents of material objects is perfectly clear, for otherwise his distinction between "cases where we should also judge 'But it is perceptibly different from what it was then', and cases in which ... we are certainly not prepared to assert that it is perceptibly so" would make no sense. 'It' in 'but it is perceptibly different' refers to a material object, whether it be a hand, or the palm of a hand, or part of the palm of a hand in the sense in which the base of the palm of a hand is part of the palm of a hand.

This ambiguity in the use of the word 'part' is reflected in an ambiguity in the use of the word 'same'. In the first sentence of the argument Moore uses 'same' in two senses. He says *"This* part of a surface is the *same* part of the surface of the same thing, as that which I was seeing ... just now." The non-italicized occurrence of 'same' in this sentence means that the two presented objects are representative of one, rather than of different material objects. The italicized occurrence of 'same' means that the two presented objects have some characteristics in common, for example, being palm hand-shaped. These are two senses of 'same' and not one, for two presented objects may have characteristics in common and yet be representative of

---

[15] I have already explained that 'part' as it occurs in 'part of the surface' is a purely spatial sense of 'part' and refers to a spatial relation exemplified by two individuals one of which is a part of the other. See footnote 9.

different material objects. Two presented objects may both be palm hand-shaped; the one representative of one hand and the other of some other hand. To say that they are representative of the same hand, that is, of one rather than of different hands, is to say that they *jointly* exemplify a spatio-temporal relation which is a constituent of the material object character, hand. To say that the two presented objects have some characteristics in common is not to say that they jointly exemplify any character, but that there is at least one character which each exemplifies.

If one distinguishes between what is referred to by 'part' and 'constituent' and between the various kinds of sameness one can hold that the presented object is a constituent of the material object and also account for the difference between a material object's being, for example, red and its merely appearing red under unusual lighting. Consider two perceptual situations, call them A and B respectively, in each of which one perceives a hand with the palm up. I make the following assumptions. (1) The presented object in each situation is representative of the same, *i.e.*, one, hand. In other words, in B one perceives the same hand as one perceives in A. (2) The hand undergoes no perceptible change. It is pale white on the first occasion and remains so throughout the time span being considered. (3) In both situations one is perceiving by sight and in A one perceives the "real" color of the hand, pale white, and in B one perceives the hand under unusual lighting and therefore it appears red. The task is to provide an analysis of a material object having a character, for example, of a hand's being pale white. The following series of comments provide this analysis. *One.* In A one may be correctly said to perceive veridically a pale white hand. This means that there is actually a perceiving occurring, that the sentence 'This is a pale white hand' refers to *what* the perceiving is of, and that the sentence is true. *Two.* One may *not* be correctly said to perceive a pale white hand unless the presented object which is representative of the hand exemplifies the color, pale white. In B one may not be *correctly* said to perceive a pale white hand. The sentence 'This is a pale white hand', were one to utter it on this occasion, would be true. Nevertheless it would not express what is perceived, but rather the judgment which one may make in this situation. This is as clear an example of making a judgment as opposed to merely perceiving as I can think of. *Three.* The phrase 'pale white hand' in 'This is a pale white hand' refers to a complex character exemplified by the presented object. The fact that the presented object exemplifies this complex character is however not itself presented. (See p. 143.) Rather, in A one is presented with an object's being white and in B with an object's being red. Therefore, in B the sentence 'This is pale white' is false, though the sentence 'This is a pale white hand' is true. It follows that the analysis of a hand's being pale white is not that the presented individual exemplifies both the character, hand, and the character, pale white. In other words 'x is a pale white hand' is not short for 'x is a hand and x is pale white'. *Four.* Pale white hand is a complex character of exactly the same structure as hand. Pale white hand is a complex character including characters characteristic of hands, the complex spatio-temporal relation P, lawful connections, *and* the character pale white. A pale white hand is a pattern of individuals a certain number of which each exemplify the character, pale white. Which individuals and how many is a matter of detail. The pale white individuals are those which are not perceived under unusual lighting, and are not in those spatio-temporal segments of the hand in which the hand is burned, sunburned, and so on. Note that it is not essential that the presented individual exemplify the character, pale white. In B the hand is pale white though the presented individual is not. *Five.* The distinction between a material object having a certain character and its merely appearing to have a certain character is immediately forthcoming. A hand is pale white if the presented object exemplifies the complex character, pale white hand. A hand is pale white though it appears red if the presented object exemplifies both the complex character, pale white hand, and the character, red. That there is no contradiction in the presented object exemplifying both of these characters is clear from what is said in comments *Two* and *Three* above. In such a situation one may not be correctly said to perceive a pale white hand though the sentence 'This is a pale white hand' is true. 'This is a pale white hand' expresses what one may judge in such a situation. 'x is a pale white hand' is not short for 'x is pale white and x is a hand'. A hand may both be pale white and appear so. In this case (the most usual) the presented object exemplifies both the complex character, pale white hand, and the character, pale white. This is the case in A described above.

Moore objects to this account of the difference between a material object having a certain character and its merely appearing to have this character on the ground that,

... if [a non-realistic analysis of material objects] were true, the sense in which a material surface is 'round' or 'square', would necessarily be utterly different from that in which our sense-data sensibly appear to us to be 'round' or 'square'.[16]

Why is this objectionable? A material object and a presented object are different kinds of entities. The former is a pattern of the latter. One would expect the sense in which a material object is round to be different from the sense in which a presented object is round. But Moore's objection is not that they are different; his objection is that they are "utterly different." He expresses this by saying:

[On this view] you must give a Pickwickian interpretation ... to the assertion that they (i.e., coins) are *circular*. ... To this view my objection is only that ... they are "circular" in a sense that is not Pickwickian. I have [a] ... strong ... propensity to believe that they are really circular, in a simple and natural sense. ...[17]

There is nothing "Pickwickian" about the sense in which a coin is circular. A coin is circular in the simple and natural sense that at least some of the individuals in the pattern of individuals which constitute the coin exemplify the character, circular. A presented object is circular in the sense that it exemplifies the character, circular. The analyses are different because coins and presented objects are different. The difference is just what one would expect. There is nothing utterly different about them.

Moore considers the possibility that his difficulty may be overcome, that is, that the objection to taking the presented object as a constituent of the material object may be met, if one denies the "assumption" that presented objects have the characters that they are presented as having. He says in "Some Judgments of Perception":

What now seems to me to be possible is that the sense-datum which corresponds to ... a penny, which I am seeing obliquely, is not really perceived to *be* different in shape from that which corresponded to the penny, when I was straight in front of it, but is only perceived to *seem* different – that all that is perceived is that the one *seems* elliptical and the other circular; that the sense-datum presented to me when I have the blue spectacles on is not perceived to *be* different in colour from the one presented to me when I have not, but only to *seem* so. ...[18]

What Moore is suggesting here is that in a perceptual situation such as *B* described above in which one perceives a hand, which is in fact pale white, but which appears red because of the unusual lighting,

[16] "A Defence of Common Sense," *op. cit.*, p. 58.

[17] G. E. Moore, "The Status of Sense-data," *Proceedings of the Aristotelian Society*, N.S. XIV (1913–1914), 355–380; reprinted in *Philosophical Studies, op. cit.*, pp. 168–196. All page references are to the latter. The quoted passage occurs on page 193.

[18] "Some Judgments of Perception," *op. cit.*, p. 245.

the object presented to one is not really red, but only *seems* red. In other words, he is saying that in such a situation there is nothing that is red; there is only something which seems red. This simply will not do. It is simply undeniable – it is not an "assumption" at all – that in such a situation the presented object is red. What seems red is the hand of which the presented object is representative. To say that the presented object is not really red, but merely seems so, is to make seems a simple unanalyzable connection between presented objects and characters on a par with exemplification. It is to hold that presented objects and characters may not only be connected by the nexus of exemplification but also by the nexus of seems. That this solution to the difficulty is untenable hardly seems to me to require any argument.[19]

III

At the beginning of this chapter I said that there is a sense in which Moore understands the non-realistic analysis of material objects which I propose. I said that in "Some Judgments of Perception"

---

[19] In "Realistic Postcript," *Logic and Reality, op. cit.*, p. 319, Bergmann makes essentially the same suggestion.

Second Case. I perceive$_2$ an oval coin. Surprised that there should be such a thing, I reach for it, examine it, perceive$_3$ it to be round. The 'Op' of the original perceiving$_2$ is false. How about its 'Mp'? Let a be the particular (area) "in" it that was presented to me. 'a is round', I have now reason to believe, is true; 'a is oval', false. The latter is a conjunction term of 'Mp'. That makes Mp, too, a mere possibility. But *the external particular in Mp is real.*

To say that a is oval is a mere possibility is to say that a does not exemplify the character, oval. One is presented in this situation with a; one is also, of course, presented with oval, though one is not (on this account) presented with an individual which exemplifies this character. But to say that a is oval is a mere possibility is to say that a and oval are connected by some nexus which makes this fact a possible fact. This is to give ontological status to a nexus between individuals and characters, other than exemplification, in precisely the same sense in which Moore gives ontological status to seems.

The second case is a case of perceptual error. I have not discussed a case of perceptual error in this chapter, but such a case can be easily handled. Consider a situation in which one perceives an oval coin. In this situation one may be correctly said to perceive an oval coin, which means (1) that there is actually a perceiving occurring, and (2) that 'This is an oval coin' refers to what the perceiving is of. 'This is an oval coin' is, of course, false; that is what makes this situation a case of perceptual error. 'This' refers to an individual presented in this situation: call it a. a exemplifies the character, oval; that is, 'This is oval' is true. It is *not* the case, however, that a exemplifies the character, oval coin; that is, 'This is an oval coin' is false. *That a does not exemplify the character, oval coin, means that oval is not exemplified by the appropriate individuals in the pattern of individuals which constitute the coin which must exemplify it for the coin to be oval.* It does not mean that the presented individual does not exemplify oval. That it does is undeniable.

he states succinctly, yet clearly, this analysis. The passage occurs near the end of the paper.

> [According to this view] when I judge "This is an inkstand," I am judging this presented object to possess a certain property, which is such that, if there are things, which possess that property, there are inkstands and material things, but which is such that nothing which possesses it is itself a material thing; so that in judging that there are material things, we are really always judging of some *other* property, which is not that of being a material thing, that there are things which possess *it*.[20]

He even realizes that his objection to taking the presented object   as a constituent of the material object can be answered in terms of this analysis. Of his paper as a whole he says:

> Indeed, this paper may be regarded, if you like, as an argument in favor of the proposition that some such view *must* be true. Certainly one of my main objects in writing it was to put as plainly as I can some grave difficulties which seem to me to stand in the way of any other view.[21]

Nevertheless, he himself will not accept this analysis. Why will he not accept it? The answer is suggested in the sentence immediately preceding the passages just quoted.

> [Philosophers who propose a non-realistic analysis of material objects] hold, in short, that though there are plenty of material things in the Universe, there is nothing in it of which it could truly be asserted that *it* is a material thing: that, though, when I assert "This is an inkstand," my assertion is true, and is such that it follows from it that there is in the Universe at least one inkstand, and therefore, at least one material thing, yet it does not follow from it that there is anything which is a material thing.[22]

Moore here insists that no analysis of material objects is adequate unless there is *an entity* which is this inkstand, *an entity* which is my right hand, *an entity* which is this piece of paper. Any analysis upon which material objects are patterns of entities, however related to each other and tied together, is objectionable to him merely because it makes them patterns of entities and not single ones. Why does he insist on this kind of simplicity? If one can account, on a non-realistic analysis, for the sense in which 'This is a hand', asserted of a presented object, is true as well as the sense in which this hand is pale white (that is, C_3), and if one can account for the sense in which this is the same hand as I saw just now whether it has changed perceptibly or not (that is, C_2), why persist in the view that this hand is a single

---

[20] "Some Judgments of Perception," *op. cit.*, pp. 250–251.

[21] *Ibid.*, p. 251.

[22] *Ibid.*, p. 250.

entity, and not a pattern of such? Two reasons suggest themselves, each of which I shall discuss in turn.

Moore believes that if a material object is analyzed as a pattern of entities its mind-independence will be lost, that is, that C1 will not be accounted for. Remember what has been said in Chapter II (pp. 127–129): On a realistic (substance) analysis of material objects the mind-independence of material objects is guaranteed by their being *onto-logically* of a kind which must exist when not perceived, or thought of or known in any other way. The continuant in the material object is the ontological ground of this independence. On a non-realistic analysis of material objects there is no such entity which grounds their mind-independence. That is, of course, what I have meant by calling the analysis non-realistic. The mind-independence of material objects can nevertheless be accounted for. One can show that the non-realistic analysis proposed is perfectly compatible with the common-sense truth about material objects that they exist when there are no human beings who are perceiving them. To show that the analysis and the truth are compatible is to show that, in this respect, this analysis is adequate. There are two considerations which show this.

First, on this analysis material objects are not dependent upon minds in the sense in which for Berkeley they are dependent upon them. The constituents of material objects are not qualities of or contents of the mind. In his early writing Moore raises arguments against non-realistic analyses on the ground that they make material objects dependent upon minds in this sense, but in his later writing he no longer considers these arguments to have any force. In "Some Judgments of Perception" he says:

I am quite unable to see that [certain arguments] have any [force; namely,] ... all those which assume ... that this sense-datum is a sensation or feeling of mine, in a sense which includes the assertion that it is dependent on my mind in the very same sense in which my perception of it obviously is so.[23]

What makes the material object independent of minds in this sense is the presence in it of the individual. For, individuals are ontologically of a kind which *can* exist when they are not presented to anyone. Whether or not there are any individuals which do so exist is, of course, another question.

Second, when one is in a perceptual situation in which one may be correctly said to perceive a material object, and the perception is veridical, the individual with which one is presented exemplifies

[23] *Ibid.*, p. 240.

a material object character. If it exemplifies such a character, then *there are* other individuals, not presented on this occasion, which exemplify certain characters and stand in spatial and temporal relations to each other and to the presented individual. *If the perception is veridical*, then there are individuals which are not presented in this perceptual situation. There is however no guarantee that all of these individuals are not presented in other perceptual situations. That they are not is simply a matter of fact. Nor does one have any guarantee that one's own perception is veridical. That the vast majority of one's perceptions are veridical one knows from experience – by turning the object over, looking again, and so on. The non-realistic analysis of material objects proposed so assays material objects that the possibility of their existing unperceived is guaranteed ontologically. That there are entities which fulfill this possibility is a mere matter of fact. Moore's insistence that an analysis must guarantee this truth ontologically is unjustifiable. *The task is to provide an analysis which accounts for this truth; not one which makes it a certainty.*

This brings me to the second reason why Moore persists in the view that a material object is a single entity, and not a pattern of such. In the vast majority of perceptual situations in which material objects are perceived, though mistakes may be made, one is quite certain of what one perceives. In other words, one is quite certain that the sentence referring to *what* the perceiving is of, for example, 'This is a hand', is true. On a non-realistic analysis of material objects this certainty seems to be in jeopardy. It seems that C4 will not be accounted for. Perception is always open and subject to error. And this "openness" does not result merely from the fact that the sentence expressing what is perceived is synthetic – that it is logically possible that this is not a hand – but rather that for the presented individual to be a hand there must be other individuals, not presented, which exemplify certain properties, stand in certain spatial and temporal relations to other individuals, and so on. The openness of perception consists in the fact that merely to be in a perceptual situation in which one perceives a hand does not guarantee that there is a hand there to be perceived. For the presented individual to exemplify the character, hand, other states of affairs must obtain with some constituents of which one is not presented.

Moore's desire to ground the certainty of perception in the object perceived is re-enforced by his view that all perception is veridical. Remember what was said earlier (p. 139): Moore believes that one may be correctly said to perceive a hand only when there is a hand there to be perceived; he fails to distinguish "I may be correctly said to perceive a hand" and "I may be correctly said to perceive veridically a hand." One who fails to make this distinction will hold that one is certain that this is a hand in exactly the same sense in which one is certain that one is perceiving a hand. But since one is certain that one is perceiving, when one is perceiving, in the sense that one cannot mistake one's perceiving, say for imagining or doubting, then one will hold that one cannot make a mistake regarding what one perceives. If one makes this confusion it may seem reasonable to suppose that no analysis of material objects is adequate unless the certainty regarding one's perceiving is grounded in the object perceived. But one can be correctly said to perceive a hand, and yet be mistaken with regard to what one perceives. In a perceptual situation one is certain, in the sense that one can make no mistake, both that there is a perceiving occurring, and that the perceiving is *of* a hand. Yet one is not certain in this sense that the perceiving is veridical. That one is "certain" that one's perceptions are veridical is a matter of experience – one's expectations have been habitually fulfilled. One cannot reasonably expect an analysis of material objects to guarantee a certainty which we do not have.

In order to account for the certainty which one does have in perception an analysis of the perception of material objects must be given which accounts for the fact that one cannot be mistaken both with regard to the fact that, in a perceptual situation, there is a perceiving occurring, and when one is perceiving a hand, that the perceiving is of a hand. To account for these truths one must turn to the analysis of perception. This analysis I shall undertake in the next chapter.

IV. PERCEPTION AND MATERIAL OBJECTS

In this chapter I shall attempt to give an analysis of what occurs in one's mind when one perceives a material object, say, a chair. In other words, I shall attempt to give an analysis of what might be expressed, somewhat inaccurately, by the sentence 'A perceiving of a chair occurs in my mind'. But I shall *not* attempt to give an analysis of what is expressed by such sentences as 'I am perceiving a chair' or 'Jones is perceiving a chair'. To give an analysis of the latter involves more than is involved in the former, since the latter requires the analysis of minds, or selves, while the former requires only the analysis of acts. An act is a constituent of a mind; perhaps, acts are the only constituents of minds. Yet, to give an analysis of an act is not to give an analysis of a mind. There are many acts, not only of perceiving, but of remembering, believing, imagining, and so on, all of which are "mine" or "in my mind." What makes them "mine" is a question different from the question what an act is. Nor is this the only difference between the analyses of acts and of minds. Some of "my" acts are constituents of what might be called my state of consciousness or conscious state at some moment; some others are not. I perceive a chair, later I remember my having perceived it, then come to doubt this memory. When I am in the state of doubting, the act of doubting is, or is a part of, my conscious state; the remembering and the perceiving are not. The question what makes the doubting, but not the remembering or the perceiving, a conscious state of mine, or a part of one, is a question different from the question what an act is. To put this second difference between the analyses of minds and acts in terms of perception, the analysis of someone's perceiving a chair involves analyzing not only what perceiving a chair is, but also what is it to be in a state of perceiving one.

A perceiving of a chair is an act. When one is in that state of mind which may be expressed by saying that one is perceiving a chair there is an act of perceiving a chair in one's mind. One's state of consciousness consists, at least in part, of an act of perceiving. It must be explained, then, what an act is. But when one perceives a chair one's conscious state does not consist merely of an act of perceiving a chair. There is also what might be called an act of presentation. What one is presented with in an act of presentation I have called in Chapter III, following Moore, presented objects or sense-data. It must also be explained, then, what the connections are, as well as the similarities and the differences, between an act of presentation (Moore calls it an act of direct apprehension) and an act of perceiving, and how together they account for the various problems centering around the analysis of perception.

Moore provides an analysis of acts of direct apprehension. I shall begin by presenting this analysis. He cannot, however, provide an adequate analysis of acts of perceiving. The crucial constituent in such acts which he overlooks is what I call an intentional character. I shall first show how he is led to his analysis of direct apprehension, and how, being thus led, he overlooks intentional characters. Next I shall explain what an intentional character is. Then I shall turn to Moore's analysis of perception, explaining the crucial differences between direct apprehension and perceiving, and discussing what Moore has to say specifically about perceiving. That will bring out how, though he distinguishes these two, he yet assimilates certain instances of perceiving to direct apprehension in order to avoid the problem of perceptual error. Finally, I shall put the pieces together and present what I consider to be an adequate analysis of perception.

In "The Status of Sense-data" Moore mentions several classes of "mental events" all of which he calls sensory experiences. He says about these experiences that each consists of an entity being experienced. And about the experienced entity he says:

The entity which *is* experienced must in all cases be distinguished from the fact or event which consists in its being experienced; since by saying that it is experienced we mean that it has a relation of a certain kind to something else. We can, therefore, speak not only of *experiences* of these five kinds, but also of the entities which *are experienced in* experiences of these kinds; and the entity which is experienced *in* such an experience is never identical with the experience which consists in its being experienced.[1]

The distinction Moore makes here between an experienced entity and "something else," both of which, he says, are constituents of a sensory experience, is the crucial one he made when refuting the Hegelian idealists in "The Refutation of Idealism," a point discussed in Chapter I, pp. 108–109. In that paper the distinction is stated as follows:

In every sensation or idea we must distinguish two elements, (1) the "object," or that in which one differs from another; and (2) "consciousness," or that which all have in common – that which makes them sensations or mental facts.[2]

But not only does Moore distinguish object and consciousness, the entity experienced and the sensory experiencing (of it), he also maintains in "The Status of Sense-data" that these two constituents of a "mental fact" or "event" stand in a unique relation to each other. Every object experienced in a sensory experience,

... has to *something* the fundamental relation which I wish to express by saying that it is directly apprehended, and ... the event which consists in its being directly apprehended by that something is certainly a mental act of *mine* or which occurs in my mind. ...[3]

In every sensory experience there are not merely two constituents, but three: namely, (1) an object, (2) *something* which directly apprehends this object, and (3) the relation called direct apprehension.

[1] "The Status of Sense-data," *op. cit.*, p. 169.
[2] "The Refutation of Idealism," *op. cit.*, p. 20.
[3] "The Status of Sense-data," *op. cit.*, p. 174.

Moore calls the complex which consists of these constituents an act of direct apprehension. An act of direct apprehension consists of a mental individual directly apprehending an object.

Here Moore provides an analysis of an act, specifically, of an act of direct apprehension, or, as he also calls it, a sensory experience. This analysis I believe to be mistaken. Presently I shall give reasons for my belief. First, though, I wish to make clear what exactly Moore's analysis is. The second constituent, (2), the *something*, is a mental individual, or, as he calls it in "The Refutation of Idealism," an awareness. He calls this second constituent "something" rather than "mind" because he does not wish to prejudge the analysis of minds, or selves. As he himself says in a passage, part of which was quoted above:

> ... though the event which consists in [the object] being directly apprehended by that something is certainly a mental act of *mine* ... yet the something which directly apprehends it may quite possibly not be anything which deserves to be called "I" or "me." It is ... quite possible ... that the entity which directly apprehends, in those acts of direct apprehension which are mine, is numerically different in every different act; and that what I mean by calling all these different acts *mine* is either merely that they have some kind of relation to *one another* or that they all have a common relation to some other entity, external to them, which may or may not be something which deserves to be called" me." [4]

As was pointed out at the beginning of this chapter, I, too, am not concerned with the analysis of mind. So I shall, following Moore, call the "something" which directly apprehends (or, more accurately, the something which is a direct apprehending) an awareness or mental individual. All awarenesses and the characters they exemplify, including the relations, if any, in which they stand to each other and to other entities which are not awarenesses, and only such entities, are mental in the sense that they are constituents of mind.[5] They are what is "in one's mind" when one directly apprehends something, or perceives it or imagines it, and so on. What the constitution of a mind is, I shall not, as I have said, discuss.

The object, (1), the entity which is directly apprehended by the awareness, is called a sensible, or alternately, a sense-datum or presented object. A patch of blue, or a blue sense-datum, is an example. To call this entity a *constituent* of an act of direct apprehension is both confusing and, if generalized for all acts, leads to a difficulty which I shall discuss below. The confusion is that it makes a "non-

---

[4] *Ibid.*, pp. 174–175.
[5] Awarenesses stand to each other and to individuals which are not awarenesses in temporal relations. Temporal relations are, however, not mental. They constitute an exception.

mental" entity a constituent of mind. A sensible or sense-datum is non-mental in the sense that it is neither an awareness nor a character of an awareness. (This is the crucial point which Moore makes against the Berkeleian idealists, a point discussed in Chapter I, pp. 114–116.) It is not "in the mind" or a constituent of the mind in the sense in which an awareness and its characters are. There are contexts in which Moore uses 'act' – for example in his discussion of belief in *Some Main Problems of Philosophy* [6] – to refer to a complex which includes only those constituents of what he here calls an act which are mental. He nevertheless uses 'mental fact' and 'mental event' synonymously with his first use of 'act'. That makes a "mental fact" a complex which includes a non-mental constituent. Such uses of 'mental' should be avoided. I shall set them off by surrounding the word with double quotes.

The third constituent of an act, (3), the relation of direct apprehension, serves two functions in Moore's analysis. It serves, first, to distinguish an act of direct apprehension, that is, a sensory experience, from acts of perceiving, imagining, believing, remembering, and so on. There is a clear difference between an act of direct apprehension on the one hand, and, for example, an act of remembering on the other. There must, therefore, be a constituent of the one act which is not a constituent of the other. Direct apprehension is the constituent common to all sensory experiences which is not shared by acts of any other kind. It therefore accounts for this difference. If direct apprehension is a relation, this would naturally suggest that, say, remembering is a relation common to all acts of remembering. This suggestion seemed initially plausible to Moore. The relation of direct apprehension serves, second, to account for another feature of acts of direct apprehension, which in Chapter I I called the intentionality of consciousness. According to Moore, an act of direct apprehension consists of an awareness and an object connected in a unique way which may be expressed by saying that the awareness is *of* an object. There must, therefore, be a constituent in the act which accounts for the fact that the awareness and object are thus uniquely connected. This constituent, according to Moore's analysis, is the relation of direct apprehension.

I hold that this analysis of acts of direct apprehension is mistaken in two respects. But I shall state these two mistakes in a manner that applies to all acts, and not specifically to acts of direct apprehension.

[6] See below, page 161, and footnote 9.

The reason for this will be immediately apparent. (a) An act consists of an awareness and its object. The object of the awareness is a constituent of the act of which the awareness is a constituent. (b) The constituent in an act which accounts for the fact that its awareness is *of* an object is a relation jointly exemplified by the awareness and the object. Moore holds (a) and (b). I claim that they are false. But I shall not argue that they are false by showing that they are so in the special case of direct apprehension. I shall show, rather, that (a) and (b) certainly are false for some kinds of acts and merely assume that in these two respects all acts are alike. Next I shall show that by holding (a) in the case of direct apprehension Moore is naturally led also to hold (b) in this case, as well as that (a) and (b) together force him to distinguish acts of two ontological kinds, namely, acts of direct apprehension on the one hand and all other acts on the other. This distinction between two kinds of acts leaves him without means of analyzing adequately the second kind.

The first mistake occurs already in "The Refutation of Idealism." [7] There he says that an object experienced is always distinct from the experiencing of it; object and consciousness are two things and not one. But he not only makes this claim; he also makes the quite different, and, in a sense, stronger one that the object experienced is itself a constituent of the experience which consists in its being experienced. Sensation, for example, which he calls a "mental fact," *consists* of consciousness *and* the object of consciousness. This model of "mental facts," or acts presents a difficulty when applied to acts other than of direct apprehension. In *Some Main Problems of Philosophy* Moore has become aware of this difficulty. Consider what he says about pure imagination – the imagining of imaginary entities – in Chapter XI of that book.

We should insist most strongly that there really is no such thing [as a centaur]; that it is a pure fiction. But ... I certainly can imagine a centaur; we can all imagine one. And to imagine a centaur ... is plainly quite a different thing from imagining a griffin; whereas, it might seem, if both were nothing – pure nonentities, there would be no difference between imagining the one and the other.

Further on he says:

I am as sure as you can be, that there is no such thing as a centaur: that is the side I want to take: I wish to maintain that, in the proper sense of the words,

---

[7] Following is a quasi-historical account of how Moore's conception of acts changed from "The Refutation of Idealism," published in 1903, through *Some Main Problems of Philosophy*, a series of lectures delivered in 1910–1911, to "The Status of Sense-data," published in 1914. His views of acts remained essentially unchanged after that paper.

there really *is* no such thing and never has been. But I am not at all sure, how to get over the opposite argument. Mustn't you admit that, when you imagine a centaur, you are imagining *something*?[8]

There are two commonsense claims which are made in these passages which are both true, but which seem to Moore to be incompatible. (a) There is no such thing as a centaur. (b) When one imagines a centaur one's imagining is different from what it would be if one were imagining a griffin. Given his model of "mental facts," he cannot account for (b) without rejecting (a). In order to distinguish the two "mental facts," imagining a centaur and imagining a griffin, there must be a constituent of the one which is not a constituent of the other. If the imagined centaur is a constituent of one's imagining a centaur, (b) is accounted for; but then (a) is false, that is, there *is* such a thing as a centaur.

The same difficulty arises in the case of belief. In Chapter XIV of *Some Main Problems of Philosophy* Moore presents an analysis of belief which he formerly held, but which, at the time he presents it in this chapter, he knows to be inadequate.

... the analysis of beliefs is this. It says that, in the case of every belief without exception, whether it be true or whether it be false, we can always distinguish two constituents – namely, the *act* of belief, on the one hand, and the *object* of belief or what *is* believed on the other. The *act* of belief is something which is of the same nature in absolutely all cases. Whether I believe that twice two are four, or something so different as that lions exist, the *act* of belief which I perform is of exactly the same kind in both cases. What constitutes the difference between the two cases, is that the *objects* of belief are different.[9]

The difficulty which arises on this analysis of belief is the same as that which arises in the case of pure imagination. In the case of a false belief there is no object believed; what is believed does not obtain. But there is a clear difference between any two false beliefs, for example, believing that twice two is five and believing that centaurs exist. On this analysis the difference cannot be accounted for. In Moore's words:

... if you consider what happens when a man entertains a false belief, it doesn't seem as if his belief consisted merely in his having a relation to some object which certainly *is*. It seems rather as if the thing he was believing, the *object* of his belief, were just *the* fact which certainly is *not* – which certainly is not, because his belief is false.[10]

[8] *Some Main Problems of Philosophy*, *op. cit.*, Ch. xi, pp. 212–213.
[9] *Ibid.*, Ch. xiv, p. 258. Here Moore uses 'act' to refer only to the mental constituents of belief in contrast to his use of the word in "The Status of Sense-data" where it refers to both the mental and non-mental constituents of sensory experiences.
[10] *Some Main Problems of Philosophy op. cit.*, Ch. xiv, p. 263.

In the case of sensory experiences the model of acts, or "mental facts," with which Moore begins does not lead to the difficulty it produces in the cases of imagination and belief. One of the differences between sensory experience on the one hand and imagination and belief on the other is that in all instances of the former there is an object experienced whereas in *some* instances of the latter there is no object. Moore begins in "The Refutation of Idealism" with the distinction between object and consciousness, between the entity experienced and the experiencing of it, which enables him to refute the Hegelian idealists. Nevertheless, he fails to distinguish clearly, if at all, between the fact that object and consciousness are two things and not one on the one hand, and the model according to which a mental act *consists* of object and consciousness on the other. Consequently, the success of the (correct) distinction between object and consciousness seems to lend support to the (incorrect) model. Later, after the model has been seen not to be applicable to all mental acts, he distinguishes acts of two kinds rather than give up the model. One kind are those to which the model may be applied without leading to this difficulty, *e.g.*, sensory experiences. The other kind are those to which the model may not be so applied, belief and imagination. This division of acts into two kinds is made explicitly in "The Status of Sense-data." Consider what he says:

> This ... relation [direct apprehension], which I sometimes have to sensibles of all sorts of different kinds, images as well as others, is evidently quite different in kind from another relation which I may also have to sensibles. After looking at this black mark, I may turn away my head or close my eyes, and then I ... may have a visual *image* of the mark ... [to which I] have exactly the same kind of relation which I had just now to the mark itself. But ... to the mark itself it is quite certain that I have *not* now got the same kind of relation as I had just now ... And yet I certainly may *now* have to that mark itself a kind of relation, which may be expressed by saying that I am *thinking of* it or remembering it.[11]

The difference between direct apprehension on the one hand and thinking of and (or) remembering on the other is thus not merely that direct apprehension is that constituent common to all acts of direct apprehension while remembering is that common to all acts of remembering. Direct apprehension and remembering are "relations" which are "quite different in kind." Remembering is indeed not a relation at all.[12] But if direct apprehension and remembering are quite different

---

[11] "The Status of Sense-data," *op. cit.*, p. 173.

[12] As Moore says about belief in *Some Main Problems of Philosophy*, *op. cit.*, Ch. xiv, p. 263, when a belief is false, and, hence, there is no object believed "it is impossible for [the believer] or for anything else to have any kind of relation to it. In order that a relation may hold between two things, both the two things must certainly be."

in kind, then so are the acts of which they are constituents. In other words, according to Moore, acts of direct apprehension and acts of remembering differ structurally or ontologically from each other. While each of the former consists of an awareness and an object jointly exemplifying a relation, none of the latter consists of three such constituents.

The second mistake is closely related to the first. After distinguishing two kinds of acts, Moore is unable to provide an analysis that accounts for the connection between an awareness and its object in those cases in which the connection is certainly not a relation. The model with which he begins suggests that in those acts to which it may be applied the connection between an awareness and its object is a relation. As to those acts to which the model does not apply he simply does not know what the connection is. In "The Refutation of Idealism" he maintains that in each act there is a constituent which accounts for its being an awareness of an object. Specifically, with regard to sensation, or sensory experience, he argues that the presence of this constituent in a sensation is what the idealists ignore. All those ideal-ists who do make some distinction between an object experienced and the experiencing of it, maintain that these two entities are related either as quality to substance or as two qualities (necessarily) tied to each other. By pointing out that in every sensation there is a unique constituent in virtue of which object and consciousness are connected *in some other way* Moore has shown that the idealistic analysis is inadequate. But he maintains not only that there is a unique consti-tuent in sensation which makes a sensation an awareness *of* an object; he also maintains that this constituent is the same *in kind* in all acts. This is stated in a passage which I quoted in Chapter I.

The existence of a table in space is related to my experience of *it* in precisely the same way as the existence of my own experience is related to my experience of *that*.[13]

In "The Status of Sense-data" Moore provides an analysis of sen-sation, or sensory experience, in which the connection between awareness and object is a relation jointly exemplified by these two. The unique constituent in every sensory experience which idealists overlook is, *according to this analysis*, the relation of direct appre-hension. But proposing this analysis of direct apprehension amounts to giving up the attempt to find a constituent in every act, which

---

[13] "The Refutation of Idealism," *op. cit.*, p. 29.

accounts for the fact that each is an awareness of an object, *which is the same in kind* in all acts. A belief, an imagination, a remembering, and so on, simply do not each consist of an awareness and an object jointly exemplifying a relation.

Every act contains a constituent, the same in kind in all acts, which accounts for the fact that each is an awareness of an object. A perceiving a chair, an imagining a centaur, a thinking of my grandmother's house, a remembering a black mark which I saw just now, a direct apprehension of my remembering are all acts. The first is a perceiving, the second an imagining, the third a thinking of, and so on. All of these acts are alike in that each is an awareness of some object; the first is an awareness of a chair, the second an awareness of a centaur, and so on. They differ in that the object of the awareness in some of these acts exists; the object of the awareness in some others does not. The object of the awareness in the act of thinking of, for example, exists – there is such an object; the object of the awareness in the act of imagining does not – there is no such object. To put the point paradoxically, though each of these states of affairs consists of an awareness of an object, it does not follow that each consists of an object and the awareness of it; though each awareness is of an object, it does not follow that there is such an object as that which the awareness is of. To use a phrase which I used before acts are always intentional in character; an act always intends something. But *what* an act intends, the object or intention of the act, may not exist. There may be no such thing as that which a particular act intends; this particular act intends this "non-entity" nevertheless.

It follows that the constituent in an act which accounts for the fact that it is an awareness of an object cannot be a relation jointly exemplified by the awareness and its object. For some acts there are no objects. And if the constituent in question is the same in kind in all acts, as I believe it to be, then it cannot be a relation in any. Moore, as we have seen, gives up the task of finding a constituent the same in kind in all acts. Though he knows that acts are always intentional, he cannot understand how they can be so in those instances in which there is no such object as that which is intended. In other words, he cannot give an analysis which accounts for this fact. He gives up, for example, the attempt to analyze belief.[14] But though he gives up this attempt, he

---

[14] In a passage in *Some Main Problems of Philosophy*, *op. cit.*, Ch. xiv, p. 266, so characteristic of his candor, Moore says:

[The analysis of belief] ... into the act of belief on the one hand and the thing believed on the other ... gives us no help at all towards solving our original question – the question

does not give up the attempt to analyze perception. He analyzes perception on a model similar to, though not exactly the same as, the model on which he analyzes sensory experience. Yet insofar as he cannot give an adequate analysis of belief, he cannot give an adequate analysis of perception. The constituent in an act which is crucial in accounting for the fact that one can believe what is not the case, is equally crucial in accounting for the fact that there is perceptual error. I must explain, then, as clearly as I can what this constituent is.

Consider again the case of pure imagination – the imagining of imaginary entities. There is no such thing as a centaur; there is no such thing as a griffin. Yet one can imagine a centaur as well as imagine a griffin, and, clearly, to imagine the one is quite a different thing from imagining the other. Equally clearly, the difference between them is not merely that they are numerically different instances of imagining. There is also a qualitative difference between the two more like the difference between red and green than that between two instances of red. (That is why, on p. 161, I stated (b) as I did.) Nor is the difference between the two that one contains a centaur as a constituent and the other a griffin, for there are no centaurs and griffins to be constituents even of imaginings.[15] The difference is, rather, that there is a constituent of each of these two instances of imagining, a different constituent in each instance, each of which accounts, respectively, for the fact that the one is an imagining of a centaur and the other an imagining of a griffin.

Moore fails to distinguish clearly between the following three claims: (a) I am imagining a centaur; (b) There is no such thing as a centaur; and (c) There is a centaur which I imagine. (a) and (b) are both truths. In (a) two claims are made about my awareness, namely, (1) that my awareness is an imagining and (2) that my awareness is of a centaur. In (b) a claim is made, not about my awareness, but about *what* I am aware of, the intention of my awareness, namely, that it doesn't

as to what exactly is the relation between a true belief and the *fact* to which it refers. ... Possibly some positive analysis of a belief *can* be given, which would enable us to answer this question; but I know of none which seems to be perfectly clear and satisfactory. I propose, therefore, to give up the attempt to analyse beliefs.

The task of giving an analysis of belief is one to which he never returned in his published writings.

[15] To say, as we ordinarily do, that centaurs exist only in the imagination, is not to say that a centaur is a constituent of one's imagining. It is an elliptical way of expressing both the fact that there are no centaurs, and the fact that we can nevertheless imagine them. Perhaps it is a reference to intentional characters, which I discuss below. The relevant intentional character is not a centaur at all, but that *existent* in imagination which accounts for the fact that one can imagine them even though there are none.

exist – that there is no such thing. (c) is ambiguous. Taken as a statement about centaurs it is a falsehood for it contradicts (b). Taken as a statement about my awareness it is just another, though misleading, way of stating (a) and, hence, a truth. Since (a) is a truth, (1) and (2) must be accounted for. Since (c), taken as a statement about centaurs, is a falsehood, (1) and (2) cannot be accounted for by saying that a centaur is a constituent of the act of imagining which is in my mind when I imagine a centaur. (1) and (2) are accounted for by saying that when I imagine a centaur the act of imagining (of mine) consists of, first, an awareness, second, imagining which is a character of this awareness, and, third, another character, which I shall call an intentional character, (being) of-a-centaur. It is a fact about one's act of imagining when one imagines a centaur that the awareness is of a centaur, that is, there is an awareness which exemplifies the intentional character, (being) of-a-centaur. A centaur is not a constituent of this fact. Also, it is a fact *about the intentional character*, (being) of-a-centaur, that the presence of this character in one's conscious state when one imagines a centaur accounts for the fact that one's awareness is of a centaur, that is, to use a phrase of Moore's, (being) of-a-centaur brings a centaur "before one's mind," or makes it "an object to one's mind." This is not to say that a centaur is a constituent of this fact. Rather, it is a logical (or ontological) fact about an intentional entity to the effect that it accounts adequately for the intentionality of consciousness in this instance. An intentional character is just that *kind* of entity that can bring something before one's mind even when there is no such thing at all. It is just this peculiarity of intentional characters that accounts for the fact that one can think of what is not the case – that one can imagine purely imaginary entities.[16]

Two comments about this analysis of acts will help to avoid misunderstanding. Two reasons why Moore does not accept intentional characters will then be suggested. *First*. The hyphens in the phrase '(being) of-a-centaur' indicate that the character, (being) of-a-centaur, is simple, that is, that it does not contain, for example, a centaur, or even the character, centaur, as a constituent. The difference between imagining a centaur and imagining a griffin is as immediate as that between red and green. One may doubt that one ever just imagines a centaur, and believes, rather, that one always imagines some particular centaur, or a centaur in some particular determination, or something

---

[16] I gather from Professor Bergmann that this account of the intentionality of acts is virtually the same as Brentano's.

about some particular centaur. If one believes this one is in danger of confusing the images which one may have when imagining a centaur and the imagining of the centaur itself. Nevertheless, if one imagines a large white centaur eating lilies in a garden then one's act of imagining contains the intentional character, (being) of-a-large-white-centaur-eating-lilies-in-a-garden, which is simple in the same sense in which (being) of-a-centaur is simple. The difference between imagining a large white centaur eating lilies in a garden and imagining a small gray one eating rose petals is as immediate as the difference between imagining a centaur and imagining a griffin.

Second. One may wonder whether, when imagining a centaur, one is not also aware of one's imagining it. Whether or not one is so aware is a question of fact which should not be prejudged by the analysis of imagination. It may be that while one imagines a centaur one is also aware of imagining it, or it may be that one only becomes aware of one's imagining upon reflection, not while one is actually imagining. But whatever the case may be, the following three states of affairs are all obviously quite different. (a) I am imagining a centaur. (b) I am aware of imagining a centaur. (c) I am *both* imagining a centaur *and* aware of imagining it. (c) seems to me to be what most often, if not always, occurs when one imagines a centaur. The (partial) analysis of this state of affairs is as follows: There are in one's mind two acts, an act of imagining and an act of direct apprehension. The act of imagining consists of an awareness, imagining which is a character of this awareness, and the intentional character, (being) of-a-centaur. The act of direct apprehension consists of an awareness, direct apprehending which is a (non-relational) character of this awareness, and the intentional character, (being) of-an-imagining-a-centaur. To use a phrase which I used at the beginning of this chapter, these two acts are, or are at least a part of, one's conscious state when one both imagines a centaur and is aware of imagining one. What makes these acts a conscious state, or a part of one, I am not attempting to answer. That is why I called the analysis partial.

Moore considers acts to be simple in a respect in which they are in fact complex. According to him two beliefs, for example, or two imaginations, or two sensory experiences, differ qualitively from each other only with respect to their objects. As he says about belief in a passage which I quoted (p. 161): "Whether I believe that twice two are four, or ... that lions exist, the *act* of belief ... is of exactly the same kind on both cases. What constitutes the difference between the two cases, is that the *objects* of belief are different." Moore is not denying that there is a numerical difference between the two acts of belief, that the awareness which is a constituent of the one is (numerically) different from that which is a constituent of the other. He is denying that there is any qualitative difference in the acts. (I use 'act' as Moore does in the quoted passage.) All the qualitative difference in these two cases lies on the side of the object. This, as we have seen, is mistaken. These two acts differ, not only numerically, but also qualitatively. Each contains a different intentional character, the former belief is an awareness of twice two being four, and the latter that character which accounts for the fact that the latter belief is an awareness of the existence of lions. Moore's not seeing that clearly is one reason for his not accepting intentional characters.

Moore cannot understand what the connection between an awareness and its object could possibly be if it is not a descriptive relation. The view that is some acts, *e.g.*, sensory experiences, the connection between an awareness and its object can be accounted for by a descriptive relation jointly exemplified by these two is naturally suggested by the model of acts, or "mental facts," with which he begins. What the connection is in those cases, *e.g.*, belief, for which such an analysis is clearly inadequate Moore simply does not know. In the analysis of acts I propose the connection is twofold. (a) An awareness exemplifies an intentional character. (b) The intentional character "brings the (awareness') object before the mind" or "makes this object an object to the mind." The phrases "brings the object before the mind" and "makes the object an object to the mind" do not express the fact that there is a descriptive relation between the intentional character and the object, for the simple reason that there is no such relation. An intentional character can bring before the mind what does not in any sense exist. The connection between an awareness and its object is perfectly distinct and unique. Moore's not seeing that is the second reason for his not accepting intentional characters.

I turn now to Moore's analysis of perception. As we have seen in Chapter III, in any situation in which one perceives a material object, *e.g.*, a chair or a hand or a table, he distinguishes between the material object which one may be correctly said to perceive on the one hand, and an object which he calls the presented object or, alternately, a sense-datum on the other. This distinction on the side of the object corresponds to a distinction which he make on the side of consciousness. He expresses this latter distinction in "The Status of Sense-data" as follows:

We must distinguish that sense of the word "see" in which we can be said to "see" a physical object, from that sense of the word in which "see" means merely to directly apprehend a visual sensible. In a proposition of the form "I see A" where A is a name or description of some physical object, though, if this proposition is to be true, there must be some visual sensible, B which I am directly apprehending, yet the proposition "I see A" is certainly not always, and probably never, identical in meaning with the proposition "I directly apprehend B." [17]

Moore expresses this distinction again in "A Reply to My Critics" by distinguishing between seeing (perceiving) a material object on the one hand and directly seeing (directly perceiving) something else on the other.[18] The distinction is implicit in the passage from "A Defence of Common Sense" discussed in detail in Chapter III.

Moore's analysis of an act of direct apprehension has been already discussed. Now I must say what can be said about his analysis of an act of perceiving. The strongest claim he makes – the one of which he is most sure – is that whenever a person perceives a material object part of what occurs in his mind is a direct apprehension of some object. The claim is made in several papers; the clearest statement is perhaps in "A Reply to My Critics."

... whenever a person is seeing his right hand *as well as* something else (*e.g.*, a black background), he *must* be *directly seeing* at least two objects. ... And when I say *must*, I mean, of course, that it is not a mere empirical fact, ... I mean that the propositional function "*x* is seeing at least two objects" *entails* the propositional function ... "*x* is *seeing directly* at least two objects." One can say that [this] is *part of the very meaning* of the assertion that a person is seeing his own right hand. ...[19]

The introduction of the second object, the black background, can be safely ignored. The point Moore makes is that when one perceives one's own right hand what occurs in one's mind is an act of direct apprehension and something else; one's state of consciousness consists of these two elements. Using the phrase 'act of perceiving' to refer to this complex one can say that for Moore an act of perceiving includes as a constituent an act of directly apprehending some object. An act of

[17] "The Status of Sense-data," *op. cit.*, pp. 187–188.

[18] "A Reply to My Critics," *The Philosophy of G. E. Moore, op. cit.*, pp. 628–631. The difference between seeing and perceiving, whether "direct" or not, is that seeing is perception by sight, or, perhaps, perception of visual objects. Hearing is perception of auditory objects, touching perception of tactual objects, and so on. Seeing, hearing, smelling, touching are not different acts; to hear a sound is to have a perceptual awareness of an object exemplifying a pitch, rather than a color, or a tactual quality. Whether any given perception is visual or auditory or tactual or a combination of some or all of these depends upon the physical processes (including the physical conditions of our sense organs)which "cause" our perception. This is part of the scientific account of perception with which I am not concerned. I am concerned only with the state of consciousness which one is in when one perceives.

[19] "A Reply to My Critics," *op. cit.*, pp.630–631.

perceiving *is* an act of directly apprehending and something else. Using 'act of perceiving' in this way will, I think, be seen to be justified by what follows. The substantive question is, what is this "something else" that occurs when one perceives a material object?

Moore maintains that the "something else" which is a constituent of an act of perceiving is not the constituent characteristic of acts of judging. When someone perceives a material object he is not, insofar as he is perceiving, making a judgment about the object.

> I do not know what conditions must be fulfilled in order that I may be truly said to be *perceiving*, by sight or touch, such things as that that is a door, this is a finger, and not *merely* inferring them. . . . it seems to me that we do, in ordinary life, constantly talk of *seeing* such things, and that, when we do so, we are neither using language incorrectly, nor making any mistake about the facts – supposing something to occur which never does in fact occur. The truth seems to me to be that we are using the term "perceive" in a way which is both perfectly correct and expresses a kind of thing which constantly does occur. . . . [20]

When saying such things as "I am perceiving a door," or, the somewhat different statement, "I am perceiving that that is a door," one is, of course, using language correctly. In other words, there is a use of the word 'perceive' such that one can, without linguistic impropriety, say of human beings that they perceive material objects. But Moore maintains that in such cases we are *also* not "making any mistakes about the facts." That is to say, when one perceives a material object one is in a state of mind different from the state one would be in if one were making a judgment about a material object. Nevertheless, though distinguishing between perceiving and judging, he maintains that the "something else" in an act of perceiving has a certain "judgmental feature."

> It would be very rash to assert that "perception," in this sense of the word, entirely excludes inference. All that seems to me certain is that there is an important and useful sense of the word "perception," which is such that the amount and kind of inference, if inference there be, which is involved in my present perception that that is a door, is no bar to the truth of the assertion that I do perceive that it is one.[21]

Phenomenologically, the threefold distinction among directly apprehending, perceiving and judging is correct. There is a clear phenomenological difference between any two of these three. But there are two structural reasons why Moore makes these distinctions which play a crucial role in his analysis of perception. The first is justifiable;

[20] "Some Judgments of Perception," *op. cit.*, p. 226.
[21] *Ibid.*, p. 227.

the second rests on a mistake. (1) Were Moore to assimilate perceiving to direct apprehension he could not maintain that one can perceive material objects, for one certainly does not directly apprehend them. There is always more to a material object than what one is immediately or directly presented with when perceiving it. The object presented (*i.e.*, directly apprehended) in a perceptual situation is not itself a material object. (This point was discussed in Chapter III.) (2) Were Moore to assimilate perceiving to judging he could not possibly believe himself capable of giving an adequate analysis of perception. A judgment, like a belief or an imagination, can be mistaken; one can make a judgment when what is judged is not the case. Moore, we saw, gives up the attempt to analyze these kinds of acts for which this is true because he cannot account for the cases in which the intention of the act does not exist. In the case of perception, however, he maintains that no such mistake is possible. In other words, he claims that one cannot be correctly said to perceive something if there is no such object as that which is claimed to be perceived. Perception, that is, is always veridical.

I may, for instance, judge, with regard to an animal which I see at a distance, that it is a sheep, when in fact it is a pig. And here my judgment is certainly not due to the fact that I see it to be a sheep; since I cannot possibly see a thing to be a sheep, unless it is one. [22]

This claim of Moore's is mistaken. I shall first show what I mean by calling it mistaken, then explain why Moore made the mistake. Consider a situation in which someone, call him A, perceives a rat running along a wall. Assume that there is actually a rat running along the wall, that is, that the sentence 'A rat is running along that wall', uttered by A is true. Assume also that A is perceiving this state of affairs and not, for example, wondering whether what he perceives is a rat, or doubting that there is really a rat there. There is, then, a constituent of the state of consciousness of A which accounts for the fact that he is perceiving this state of affairs, and not wondering about it or doubting that it is the case. With this Moore agrees. Consider next a situation in which someone, call him B, is, as we should say speaking from the outside, not *actually* perceiving but having an hallucination of a rat running along a wall. (I choose my words deliberately). The sentence 'A rat is running along that wall', uttered by B, is false. Nevertheless, the state of consciousness of B is precisely

---

[22] *Ibid.*, p. 226.

the same as that of A. A and B are both perceiving a rat running along a wall. With this Moore disagrees.

Moore analyzes an hallucination as an instance of direct apprehension. In "The Status of Sense-data" hallucination is listed as one of the five kinds of sensory experiences. According to his analysis an hallucination of a rat running along a wall consists of an act of directly apprehending a rat-like figure (and other sense-data). It is of course the case that when one has an hallucination one directly apprehends some object. But such an hallucination does not consist merely of directly apprehending a rat-like figure; it *also* includes perceiving a rat. Looked at from the outside one may say (and this is a commonsensical way of speaking) that whereas A is *actually* perceiving B is merely having an hallucination. What justifies this claim is the difference between the two situations of which the onlooker is aware, namely, that in the first situation there is a rat running along a wall whereas in the second there is none. But looked at from the point of view of the percipients there is no difference at all. If A and B were each to describe his own state of consciousness, each would reply that he is perceiving a rat running along a wall.

Moore's assimilation of hallucinations, as well as all other cases of perceptual error, to sensory experience or direct apprehension is supported by that use of 'perceive' in which one is said to perceive only in those cases in which one's perception is veridical. In the preceding two paragraphs this use of 'perceive' is signaled by the word 'actually.' But though this commonsensical use supports Moore's claim, there is still another reason for his making it. According to him, there are two conditions which must be satisfied for it to be the case that someone is perceiving a material object. (a) One must be directly apprehending some sense-datum, and (b) this sense-datum must be representative of a material object. I have already discussed the connection between the sense-datum (presented object) and the material object which Moore expresses by saying that the one is representative of the other (Chapter III, section I). Moore does not know what this connection is. But there is one thing he knows for certain about it, namely, that a sense-datum cannot be representative of a material object unless there is a material object for it to be representative of. The connection between a sense-datum and a material object is not, in other words, intentional in character. Both entities must be there in order for the one to be representative of the other. It follows, then, that if there is no material object in a particular situation, none of the sense-data which are directly apprehended in that situation can be representative of it, *i.e.*, (b) is false. But if (b) is false, then one cannot be perceiving. In other words, one can only perceive when *what* is perceived exists.

Moore is not maintaining that an act of perceiving a material object consists merely of an act of directly apprehending a sense-datum which is *as a matter of fact* representative of a material object. Such an analysis would be patently inadequate. On such an analysis there would be no constituent in one's mind to account for the difference between perceiving and directly apprehending. Indeed, one could not be said to perceive a material object at all; one could only directly apprehend sense-data. What he is maintaining, or should consistently maintain, is, rather, that in perception, when the directly apprehended sense-datum *is* representative of a material object, one is aware that it is. An act of perceiving a material object consists of an act of directly apprehending a sense-datum and an awareness of the sense-datum's being representative of a material object.

It must already be clear why I consider Moore's analysis of perception to be inadequate. It is inadequate because it insists on an "intrinsic" criterion by which to determine whether or not our perceivings are veridical and because there is in fact no such criterion. According to this analysis one need merely be aware that one's act is one of perceiving, either while perceiving or upon reflection, in order to know that one's perceptions are veridical. But as I have already pointed out this is simply not the case. One cannot, merely by reflecting upon one's own state of consciousness, know that one is *actually* perceiving, *i.e.*, that one's perceptions are veridical, and not, for example, hallucinatory. The motive behind Moore's analysis of perception is his desire to guarantee ontologically that in perception we not only reach the non-mental world of non-acts but also the real non-mental world of ordinary material objects. The cue for this analysis he takes from that ordinary use of 'perceive' in which to "perceive" is to "actually perceive" – to perceive what is the case. Moore fails to realize that this use of 'perceive' has nothing to do with one's conscious state at all, but is always used from the outside to describe which non-mental states of affairs are and which are not the case.

The constituent in one's conscious state when one perceives something which Moore fails to take account of is the intentional character. What an intentional character is has already been explained.

It remains to show how intentional characters enter into the analysis of perception.

Consider a situation in which someone perceives a chair. He is presented with an individual (or individuals) exemplifying a character (or characters) characteristic of chairs, *e.g.*, a certain shape, size, color, if he is perceiving by sight, tactual qualities, if he is perceiving by touch, and so on. The state of affairs which consists of this individual or these individuals exemplifying this character or these characters is the intention of an act of direct apprehension which is *a* constituent of the perceiver's state of consciousness. But his state of consciousness does not consist merely of this act of direct apprehension. He is not directly apprehending presented objects; he is perceiving a chair. There is, then, in the conscious state also an act of perceiving. ('Act of perceiving' here is so used that an act of this kind does not include an act of direct apprehension as a constituent.) The act of perceiving consists of an awareness; of perceiving which is a character of this awareness; and of an intentional character. A likely candidate for the intentional character in this situation would seem to be the character, (being) of-a-chair. But this will not do. When one perceives a chair one does not have "before one's mind" the entire pattern of entities which constitute a chair. One has before one's mind an individual (or individuals) exemplifying the material object character, chair. The intention of one's act of perceiving is the state of affairs referred to by the sentence 'This is a chair.' The intentional character which is the constituent in one's act of perceiving which accounts for the fact that the awareness in this act is of this state of affairs is the character, (being) of-this-being-a-chair.

On this analysis of perception one cannot know that what one perceives exists merely by being aware of one's act of perceiving. One learns that one's perceptions are veridical by experience. Moore would consider this feature of this analysis a fatal weakness; it is in fact its strength. For this is exactly how it is that we do know that there are chairs and tables – that our perceptions are veridical. Moore's desire to ground our knowledge of the existence of material objects in a single act of perceiving is a desire for the wrong kind of certainty; wrong because this is a kind of certainty which in fact we do not have.

V. PROOF OF AN EXTERNAL WORLD

In "The Refutation of Idealism" Moore refutes idealism; he does not secure realism. The latter involves (1) giving an adequate analysis of acts such that the independence of the objects (intentions) of acts from the acts themselves can be accounted for, (2) giving an adequate analysis of material objects which are, commonsensically, sometimes the intentions of acts, and (3) distinguishing material objects from other entities which are the intentions of acts, but which are not themselves acts, for example, after-images, pains, hallucinations, or what Moore calls generally, sense-data.

Moore's analysis of acts was discussed in Chapter IV. He proposes an analysis of acts of direct apprehension in which the intentions of such acts are independent of them. An object A is directly apprehended when A and an awareness jointly exemplify the relation called direct apprehension. Such an object is independent of acts in the sense that it is ontologically of a kind which can exist when not the intention of any act; hence the possibility of unsensed-sense-data which Moore insists upon in his early writing. Yet he does not propose an adequate analysis of acts of perceiving. The perceiving of a material object does not consist of a material object and an awareness jointly exemplifying a relation. The fact of perceptual error protrudes. The consistent way out, for Moore, is to maintain that perceptual error is not error in perception at all, but the direct apprehension of sense-data with a mistaken judgment as to what material object, if any, the sense-data are representative of. The inadequacy of this move has been discussed.

Moore's analysis of material objects was discussed in Chapters II and III. He adopts a substance analysis of material objects. Having adopted this analysis he finds himself incapable of characterizing the connection between the sense-data presented in a perceptual situation and the material object, if any, of which they are representative. This difficulty can only be overcome by denying that material objects are substances.

In "Proof of an External World" [1] Moore attempts to distinguish material objects from pains, after-images, hallucinations, and so on. In "The Refutation of Idealism" no such distinction is attempted.

---

[1] G. E. Moore, "Proof of an External World," *Proceedings of the British Academy*, XXV (1939); reprinted in *Philosophical Papers, op. cit.*, pp. 127–150. All page references are to the latter.

In that early paper he merely distinguishes act and object; after-images, hallucinations, and material objects all fall alike on the side of the object. This is part of what is meant by saying that in that paper he does not secure realism. In the later paper he attempts such a distinction. It fails. This failure is the subject of this chapter.

Moore attempts to provide an ontological characterization of the difference between things like hands, on the one hand, and after-images and hallucinations, on the other, which accounts for the fact, or perhaps justifies it, that in certain contexts we are absolutely certain of the existence of such things as hands, tables, chairs, and so on. Considering Moore's "proof" of an external world makes clear that he takes this criterion to be essential.

> I can prove now, for instance, that two human hands exist. How? By holding up my two hands, and saying, as I make a certain gesture with the right hand, 'Here is one hand', and adding, as I make a certain gesture with the left, 'and here is another'. . . . by doing this, I have proved *ipso facto* the existence of external things. . . .[2]

This "proof" involves two assumptions. (a) A hand is a paradigmatic example of an external thing. Hands are the kinds of things we mean when we use the phrase 'external things'. (b) Holding up a hand, making a certain gesture, and saying 'Here is one hand' is the kind of evidence which substantiates a claim such as that this is a hand. 'This is a hand,' uttered in such a context, makes a claim the truth of which is beyond all reasonable doubt. Both (a) and (b), if taken commonsensically, are truisms, Indeed, if taken commonsensically, Moore's "proof" is a mere restatement of such truisms. But this is not what he intends. Rather, he intends his proof to be of some philosophical significance. Indeed, he believes that it is a philosophical task of some importance to determine what *sort* of proof of the existence of external things can be given, and, also, that he himself is giving a proof of this sort.

The sort of proof of the existence of external things he gives is one which "gets us to" the external world "immediately" in such contexts as that described in (b). Perceiving one's own right hand while it is two feet in front of one's nose is an instance of an awareness of an external object. The difference, then, between such things as hands and after-images must be such that in some contexts, at least, one can know "immediately" that what one is aware of is an external thing. In other words, the difference between hands and after-images

---

[2] *Ibid.*, pp. 145–146.

must be intrinsic to them. Moore attempts to characterize this difference in a manner that makes it so.

> ... we can say that the felt difference between bodily pains which I feel and
> after-images which I see, on the one hand, and my body on the other, ... is just
> this, that whereas there is a contradiction in supposing a pain which I feel or
> an after-image which I see to exist at a time when I am having no experience,
> there is no contradiction in supposing my body to exist at a time when I am
> having no experience. ...[3]

An after-image differs from a hand or my body in that the former
cannot exist when there is no experience of it whereas the latter can
so exist. An after-image is the kind of entity which can only exist
while in the intention of an act; a hand is not of this kind. In other
words, after-images and hands are different *in kind*. After-images are
ontologically (Moore uses the word 'logically') dependent upon the
awareness of them; hands are ontologically independent of such
awarenesses. If one's conscious state ever consists of an awareness of,
say, a hand, then one is *ipso facto* aware of an independent existent,
that is, an external thing. And if one is aware of an external thing,
then it follows that there is at least one external thing. One cannot
be aware, in perception, of what does not exist. Commonsensically,
there are contexts in which we are aware of external things. The
existence of an external world is thus guaranteed.

In "Proof of an External World" Moore has come full circle from
the position he held in "The Refutation of Idealism." In "The
Refutation of Idealism" he maintained that to have a sensation of blue,
for example, is to be aware of an entity, namely, blue, which is

> ... as much an object, and as little a mere content, of my experience, when I
> experience it, as the most exalted and independent real thing of which I am
> ever aware. There is, therefore, no question of how we are to "get outside the
> circle of our own ideas and sensations." Merely to have a *sensation* [italics
> added] is already, to *be* outside that circle. It is to know something which is as
> truly and really *not* a part of *my* experience, as anything which I can ever know.[4]

In "Proof of an External World" he categorically denies this claim,
Having a sensation of blue is being aware of an entity, blue, which
is *in some sense* a part of the experience of it. In the sensation of blue,
blue is the kind of entity which depends for its existence upon the
awareness of it. Having a perception of a material object, on the other
hand, is being aware of an entity, an external thing, which is in *this*
sense *not* a part of the experience of it. In the perception of a material

---

[3] *Ibid.*, p. 143.
[4] "The Refutation of Idealism," *op. cit.*, p. 27.

object, the material object is the kind of entity which does not depend for its existence upon the awareness of it. To turn Moore's own words against him, there is no question of how we are to get outside the circle of our own ideas and sensations. Merely to have a *perception* (of a hand) is already to be outside that circle.

Neither of these two positions suffices to secure realism. If anything, the former is nearer to the truth than the latter. At least, it is perfectly clear in what sense an intention of an act is not dependent for its existence upon the act; an intention is in no case a quality or content of an act. On the latter the clarity of this distinction is blurred. Sense-data are *in some sense* dependent upon the awareness of them. What this sense of 'dependent' is is by no means clear. Indeed, it is doubtful that any plausible explication of it can be given. Nor shall I attempt to propose one. Specifically, I shall not attempt to explain what Moore could possibly mean when he says "there is a contradiction in supposing a pain which I feel or an after-image which I see to exist at a time when I am having no experience." Rather, I shall describe what *in fact* the difference between an after-image and a hand is, and show how, and perhaps why, Moore mistakes this difference for another which he thinks supports his ontological claim. In the first three-fourths of the paper he provides a commonsensical description of what he takes the difference to be. The trouble is that, under the pressure of providing a "proof" which secures the certainty we have of the existence of external things in contexts such as that described in (b), Moore describes the difference incorrectly. Once one has seen, first, what in fact the difference between, say, an after-image and a hand is, and, second, that Moore's description of it is incorrect, one also sees that his proof of the existence of an external world is of no philosophical significance whatsoever.

By 'external things', or, synonymously, 'things outside of us', 'things external to our minds', Moore means, roughly, material objects. At one point in his paper we are given a list of examples.

My body, the bodies of other men, the bodies of animals, ... mountains, the sun, the moon, ... houses and other buildings, manufactured articles of all sorts – chairs, ... etc., ...[5]

The roughness results from the fact that there are things which are outside of us and which fall under the category of external things which yet cannot be called material objects, according to the ordinary

---

[5] "Proof of an External World," *op. cit.*, p. 130.

use of 'material object.' Shadows are Moore's only example. Rainbows and mirages, as contrasted with hallucinations, would seem to be others. All things of both of these two sorts are subsumed under the general heading 'things to be met with in space.' These entities are contrasted with others which, though not "to be met with in space," *i.e.*, not external things, are nevertheless "presented in space." Pains, visual and auditory hallucinations, dream images, and after-images are examples of this latter kind. Moore gives the following description of a situation in which one can see an after-image:

> ... I took the trouble to cut out of a piece of white paper a four-pointed star, to place it on a black ground, to 'look steadfastly' at it, and then to turn my eyes to a white sheet of paper: and I did find that I saw a grey patch for some little time – I not only saw a grey patch, but I saw it *on* the white ground. ... [Such a gray patch is] what is called an 'after-image' or 'after-sensation'. ... [6]

All instances of both of these two kinds of entities are alike in that they are *in* space. This means that each instance of both of these two kinds of entities stands in at least one spatial relation to some other entity which is either of the same or of the other kind. Mountains stand in spatial relations to the sun and the moon, houses to other buildings, chairs to human bodies, and so on. The various figures in hallucination stand in spatial relations to each other, and, as in Moore's example, an after-image stands in a spatial relation to a white sheet of paper. This feature, namely, of being in space, which both of these two kinds of entities have in common, sets them apart from other entities mentioned but not discussed in this paper. These are what Moore calls the *"mental* occurrences" of, for example, seeing, hearing, having a bodily pain, remembering, thinking, imagining, and so on. Having a bodily pain as contrasted with the bodily pain itself, seeing a chair as contrasted with the chair, are not in space. They do not stand in spatial relations to anything. My remembering a grey after-image which I previously saw does not stand in any spatial relation to the grey after-image, though the after-image stands in a spatial relation to the white sheet of paper on which it was seen.

Moore, then, is attempting to distinguish between two kinds of entities the instances of both kinds of which are in space. But the instances of these two kinds are in space in different ways. They are either "to be met with in space" or "presented in space." How do the two ways in which these entities are in space illuminate the difference between these two kinds of entities? To answer this question one must

---

[6] *Ibid.*, p. 131.

understand the difference between these two ways of being in space. The two kinds of entities are mutually exclusive, though the two ways in which their instances are in space are not. Entities which are "to be met with in space" can be, and often are, *also* "presented in space." A hand, for example, which is being perceived is "presented in space." That is, on this occasion it is a constituent of an intention of an act of perceiving other constituents of which stand in spatial relations to it. But not all these entities "to be met with in space" are presented in it. Some of them stand in spatial relations to other entities on occasions in which none of them are constituents of an intention of an act. On the other hand, after-images and hallucinations, entities which are presented in space, are *merely* presented in space. They are not to be met with in space at all. In other words, they stand in spatial relations to other entities only while, or on those occasions in which, they are constituents of the intention of an act.

The difference between these two ways of being in space can be, illustrated by an example. Consider two situations, call them A and B, respectively. A consists of a pencil on a white sheet of paper; B of a grey after-image on a white sheet of paper. Both A and B contain two objects; A a pencil and a white sheet of paper, B an after-image and a white sheet of paper. Each contains the spatial relation of contiguity. All subtleties apart, A and B each consists of two objects standing in a spatial relation. Assume that at some time both of these two situations are being perceived. The pencil, the after-image and the two sheets of paper are, therefore, presented in space. But the pencil, and not the after-image, is *also* to be met with in space. This means that there is, or at least that there may be, a situation, call it A', which consists of this *same* pencil on, let us say, another white sheet of paper, and that A' may, at some time at which it obtains, be perceived. There is, in other words, a sense of 'same' such that it can meaningfully, and of the pencil in A' truly, be said, "This is the same pencil as was seen just now (in A)." [7] On the other hand, there is no situation, B', which corresponds to B as A' does to A'. In other words, there is no after-image of which one can truly say, "This is the same after-image as was seen just now." To put the same point differently, pencils can be re-identified; after-images cannot. There are criteria, though they are not always conclusive, by means of which one can identify a given material object as the same object as that previously observed, or as a different one. There are no such criteria

[7] This sense of 'same' was explicated in Chapter III. See pages 147–148.

for after-images. That material objects can, and after-images cannot, be re-identified is, of course, a matter of fact which depends upon the difference between these two kinds of entities and not upon our knowledge about them. It is the difference that is commonly expressed by saying that material objects are continuants, in the non-ontological sense of that word, while after-images are momentary entities.

Moore expresses the difference between these two kinds of entities quite differently. Consider the following passage:

> To say that so and so was at a given time 'to be met with in space' naturally suggests that there are conditions such that *any one* who fulfilled them might, conceivably, have 'perceived' the 'thing' in question – might have seen it, if it was a visible object, have felt it, if it was a tangible one. ... But, in the case of those grey after-images which I saw, it is not conceivable that anyone besides myself should have seen any one of them.

Further on he says:

> One reason, then, why we should say that none of the grey after-images which I saw was 'to be met with in space', ... is simply that none of them could conceivably have been seen by anyone else. It is natural so to understand the phrase 'to be met with in space', that to say of anything which a man perceived that it was to be met with in space is to say that it might have been perceived by *others* as well as by the man in question.[8]

According to Moore the difference between material objects and after-images is that, whereas the former are "public," the latter are "private" objects. Hands are such that several persons can perceive the same hand; after-images are such that only one person can perceive an after-image. The difference which Moore finds between hands and after-images is thus quite different from the one described. The latter is merely that while hands are continuants, after-images are momentary entities. (As I have analyzed material objects in Chapter III, that means that a material object is a pattern of momentary entites and an after-image is not such a pattern.) The one is no more "private" to the perceiver than the other.

A perfectly intelligible sense can be given to the claim that after-images are not private. Essentially, it involves stating those conditions which must obtain for it to be the case that two persons, at a given time, are perceiving the same after-image. Or, to put the point differently, one must specify what 'same' means in this context. Likewise, certain conditions must obtain for it to be the case that two persons, at a given time, are perceiving the same material object. The criteria

---

[8] "Proof of an External World," *op. cit.*, p. 132.

for sameness in both these cases are alike in one respect, and different in another. In both cases there are certain "external," or environmental, conditions which must be satisfied. For two persons to perceive the same after-image there must be some designated spot on a given white sheet of paper at which both are looking from roughly the same position, and so on. On the other hand, certain "internal" conditions must be satisfied in the former case though not in the latter. To perceive the same after-image two persons must both "look steadfastly" at, say, a four-pointed white star, then turn their eyes to a white sheet of paper, and so on. The state of the body, at least the sense organs, of the perceiver is crucial for perceiving an after-image in a way in which it is not for perceiving a material object. There is a certain "special" conditioning required in the former case that is not required in the latter. Perhaps this provides, at least in part, an explication of what philosophers have meant by saying that after-images are mind-dependent. To perceive an after-image the perceiver must be in a "special state of mind." An after-image can only be perceived when the perceiver is in such a state. To perceive a material object there is no such requirement. Moore mistakenly shifts from 'mind-dependent' in the sense just specified to 'mind-dependent' in the sense of private. Having made this shift Moore gains support for his conclusion that after-images are mind-dependent in some ontological sense.

To summarize: There are two commonsense senses in which after-images are, and material objects are not, mind-dependent. (1) After-images exist only while in the intentions of acts; material objects exist on other occasions as well. This means there are criteria for re-identifying the latter, but not the former. Perhaps this point might be more accurately stated thus: The question whether after-images exist other than in the intentions of acts does not arise. There are no criteria in terms if which an answer to this question can be given. (2) There is an obvious sense in which the *perceiving* of after-images does, while that of material objects does not, depend upon the state or condition of the perceiver. It follows from this that not merely the perceiving of after-images, but the after-images themselves are mind-dependent, since it is a fact about after-images that they themselves can only be perceived when the perceiver is in these special conditions. Neither of these two essentially causal senses of 'mind-dependent', nor both together, entail any ontological claim about the relation of after-images to acts. It does not follow, nor even is the supposition warranted, that an after-image is more intimately related to the awareness of it than material objects are to the awarenesses of them. Moore's ontological claim is wholly unjustified.

The following three steps help to explain why he nevertheless makes the claim he does. First, he *confuses* the two senses in which after-images are *in fact* mind-dependent with privacy, *i.e.*, that no two perceivers can, at a given time, perceive the same after-image, Second, he strongly *desires* to secure the certainty we have of the existence of external objects, *e.g.*, material objects, under certain conditions, *e.g.*, those stated in (b). He *believes*, third, that this certainty can be secured only if there is an ontological, or intrinsic, difference between, for example, after-images and hands. The belief accounts for his making the confusion as the first step toward satisfying the desire.[9]

Since the commonsensical difference between hands and after-images is that while the former are continuants, the latter momentary entities, rather than that the former are public and the latter private, Moore's proof falls to the ground. To determine that one is aware of an external thing, it is not sufficient merely to have an act of perceiving, say, a hand. To determine that one is "actually" perceiving a hand, and not merely having an hallucination, that is, that one's perception is veridical, one must check whether the entities presented fall in the relevant pattern with others presented on other occasions. The "proof" of an external world is, in other words, coherence. It does not follow, however, that one is not *certain* in such situations as that described in (b) that there is an external thing. (b) mentions the kind of situation in which the checking has been done. One knows, from experience, that in such a situation one is not deceived; one is *as certain* of the existence of an external world as one can ever be.

Moore himself realizes that checking is relevant to determining whether in *some* situations one is "actually" perceiving a hand. He says in reply to an objection which he himself believes may be raised against his proof:

If one of you suspected that one of my hands was artificial he might be said to get a proof of my proposition 'Here's one hand, and here's another', by coming up and examining the suspected hand close up, perhaps touching and pressing it, and so establishing that it really was a human hand.[10]

---

[9] I say "first step" because it would not follow, even if no two perceivers could perceive the same after-image, that after-images were mind-dependent in some ontological sense. Or, to turn the point around, it would not follow from the fact that after-images are "part of the experience of them" that they are private.

[10] "Proof of an External World," *op. cit.*, p. 149.

Yet he denies that "any [such] proof is possible in nearly all cases." [11] He mistakenly believes that, because in some contexts the reality of a hand cannot be reasonably suspected, some "more fundamental" distinction between after-images and hands is required than merely that the latter are patterns of the kind of entities which constitute the former. This desire for certainty, though wholly unjustified, is in large measure responsible for Moore's failure to achieve the adequate realistic position he strove so hard to reach.

BIBLIOGRAPHY

All of Moore's works on perception are included in this bibliography. Those which are not specifically mentioned in the text or footnotes are starred (*). A complete bibliography of Moore's works up to 1952 can be found in *The Philosophy of G. E. Moore* (ed. Schilpp).

Allaire, Edwin B., et. al., *Essays in Ontology*, Martinus Nijhoff. The Hague, 1963.
Bergmann, Gustav, *Logic and Reality*, University of Wisconsin Press, 1964.
— *Meaning and Existence*, University of Wisconsin Press, 1960.
— *The Metaphysics of Logical Positivism*, Longmans, Green and Co., New York 1954.
Berkeley, George, *The Works of George Berkeley*, ed. A. A. Luce and T. E. Jessop, 6 vols. Nelson and Sons Ltd., London, 1949.
Locke, John, *An Essay Concerning Human Understanding*, ed. A. C. Fraser, 2 vols. Oxford, 1894.
*Moore, G. E., *Commonplace Book 1919–1953*, ed. C. Lewy, George Allen and Unwin Ltd., London, 1962.
— *Philosophical Papers*, George Allen and Unwin Ltd., London, 1959.
— *Philosophical Studies*, Routledge and Kegan Paul, Ltd., London, 1922.
— *Some Main Problems of Philosophy*, George Allen and Unwin Ltd., London, 1953.
*— "Are the Materials of Sense Affections of the Mind?", *Proceedings of the Aristotelian Society*, Vol. XVII, Harrison and Sons, Ltd., 1917.
*— "The Character of Cognitive Acts," *Proceedings of the Aristotelian Society*, Vol. XXI, Harrison and Sons, Ltd., 1921.
*— "The Nature of Sensible Appearances," *Methods of Analysis*, Aristotelian Society, Suppl. Vol. VI, Harrison and Sons, Ltd., 1926.
*— "Visual Sense-Data," *British Philosophy in the Mid-Century*, ed. C. A. Mace, George Allen and Unwin, Ltd., London, 1957.
White, Alan R., *G. E. Moore A Critical Exposition*, Basil Blackwell Ouford, 1958.

[11] *Ibid.*, p. 149.